THE MARKET
IS ALWAYS
RIGHT

THE MARKET IS ALWAYS RIGHT

The 10 Principles of Trading Any Market

Thomas A. McCafferty

McGraw-Hill

New York   Chicago   San Francisco   Lisbon   London   Madrid
Mexico City   Milan   New Delhi   San Juan   Seoul
Singapore   Sydney   Toronto

Library of Congress Cataloging-in-Publication Data

McCafferty, A. Thomas
    The market is always right : the 10 principles of trading any market
/ by Thomas A. McCafferty.
        p. cm.
ISBN 0-07-139698-5 (acid-free)
1. Stocks. 2. Futures. 3. Securities. 4. Speculation. I. Title.
HG4661.M35 2002
332.64—dc21

                                                                    2002005905

1 2 3 4 5 6 7 8 9 0   DOC/DOC   0 9 8 7 6 5 4 3 2

ISBN 0-07-139698-5

All figures in the book are courtesy of Stan Yan, Squid Works Comics
(www.squidworks.com).

RealTick is a registered trademark of Townsend Analytics, Ltd.

McGraw-Hill books are available at special quantity discounts to use as premiums and
sales promotions, or for use in corporate training programs. For more information,
please write to the Director of Special Sales, Professional Publishing, McGraw-Hill,
Two Penn Plaza, New York, NY 10121-2298. Or contact your local bookstore.

This publication is designed to provide accurate and authoritative information in regard
to the subject matter covered. It is sold with the understanding that neither the author
nor the publisher is engaged in rendering legal, accounting, or other professional service. If legal advice or other expert assistance is required, the services of a competent
professional person should be sought.
—*From a Declaration of Principles jointly adopted by a Committee of the American
Bar Association and a Committee of Publishers.*

 This book is printed on recycled, acid-free paper containing a minimum of
50% recycled, de-inked fiber.

To MarrGwen and Stuart Townsend

For their contribution to leveling the playing field for the average investor-trader through the development of direct access computerized trading platforms, ECNs, and a direct access exchange. We have never seen the markets so clearly.

But most importantly, for the support and devotion they provide their employees.

Contents

Acknowledgments   ix

Introduction: The Wisdom of the Ages   xi

1 The Market Is Always Right   1

2 It's All in Your Head   15

3 You Can't Prepare Enough   27

4 Supply and Demand Rule the Markets   49

5 Commit Your Thoughts to Paper   61

6 Developing and Perfecting Your Trading Shtick   81

7 Enhancing Your Shtick   103

8 Dealing with One of the Toughest Parts of the Game: Discipline   123

9 Staying the Course   143

10 On Becoming the Ideal Trader   163

Appendix A: Types of Orders   185

Appendix B: Know the Market Makers on Level 2   189

Appendix C: Sources for More Information   191

Glossary   199

Index   225

Acknowledgments

I would like to acknowledge the help of the staff and students of the Market Wise Trading School, especially the founder, David Nasser, in Broomfield, Colorado, for providing many of the insights I hope you, the reader, will find meaningful. Trading for a living is not the easiest profession one could choose. Nevertheless, it has a certain amount of glamour and excitement about it. Many are drawn to trading like moths to the flame of a lighted candle, only to experience the unpleasant demise of those who fly too close. But others circle the blaze—absorbing light, heat, and energy—then soar to new heights of freedom and success. The purpose of the school and this book is to shield you from the fire long enough for you to learn to take more than your fair share of what the markets of the world are willing to give you.

In the preparation of this book, I received some excellent advice and input from Sam Krischbaum. In another life, Sam was (and still is) a licensed professional counselor. He introduced me to the use of the enneagram, which put a structure around the classification of trading personalities. This is a valuable tool to help traders realize why they are not reaching their trading goals. More importantly, it can help them prepare in advance to withstand the inevitable stress of trading. Thanks, Sam.

I would also like to thank Brian Shannon. He is a professional trader and the technical analysis instructor at the Market Wise Trading School. He freely shares his experiences and insights as a trader and technician with me and the students. For that, we are all appreciative.

As with several of my other books, Stan Yan was kind enough to help with the illustrations. Stan is one of the rare breed of brokers who puts their clients' interests ahead of their own. Additionally, he is a gifted cartoonist.

As always, Stephen Isaacs of McGraw-Hill is a pleasure to work with. He gets the job done, encourages his writers, and is always available for consultation.

I would also like to thank all the traders, writers, and industry professionals who were kind enough to share their insights into trading over the years. It is from them that I attempted to gather together the good ideas that have been printed and have been taught at seminars. Much of this wisdom has been handed down so often from one trader to the next, it has ended up in the realm of the cliché. Nevertheless, these words of wisdom are valuable, particularly to the next generation of traders. The hope is that they will learn and enhance this body of information as our generation of traders attempted to do.

A WORD OF CAUTION

Becoming a professional trader is a journey, not a destination. It takes years of hard work, study, experimentation, and even some luck. Along that journey you will encounter many obstacles that must be overcome. One of the toughest is losing your trading equity. All traders lose at some point in their career, most commonly in the beginning. Many never recover from this setback. It affects them personally, spiritually, and financially. It is for this reason that you must have an in-depth understanding of yourself and how the losses you will sustain will impact yourself and your loved ones. Sound mental health is a prerequisite to becoming an active trader.

You do not have to trade stocks, futures, or options. Please do not if you suspect you are not psychologically and financially prepared. It could be hazardous to the rest of your life.

Introduction: The Wisdom of the Ages

Much of the collective wisdom of the human race is contained in the philosophical concept known as law, meaning patterns of behavior that govern, or should govern, certain activities of humans and the universe. The great philosopher and theologian, Thomas Aquinas, distinguished four categories of law: eternal law, natural law, human law, and divine law.

Eternal law comprises all the scientific laws that have been discovered over the centuries—astrophysics, chemistry, medicine, psychology, etc. These are the laws that attempt to explain how the universe and everything within it works. Natural law governs the behavior of beings possessing reason and free will; it is hoped that this includes traders. How do and how should we behave? Human law refers to the rule of law societies create for themselves. This can be anything from which side of the road we drive on to capital punishment. For a law to be classified as divine, there must be some type of divine intervention. These laws deal with how humans can achieve eternal salvation.

There is also a broad body of laws involving trading, which is every bit as old as any of the rest. Unfortunately these rules definitely lack any divine intervention, even though a few friends of mine have tried to convince me otherwise. Brethren, whose skills in trading have become the grist of legends, have supported many of the writers of the most ancient portions of the Old Testament. I have even heard a trader from the Chicago Merc suggest that a gene or two evolved during the sojourn of his people in the desert. You just can't wander aimlessly for 40 years without the ability to trade.

As civilization became more organized, trading was raised to the fine art it is today. Like any other popular and profit-generating endeavor, it is constantly changing and evolving. As you read this book, a great meta-morphosis is taking place before your eyes. The open-outcry trading pits of the stock, options, and futures markets of the world are becoming virtual markets. More and more trading is being done electronically via telecommunications lines each day, week, and month. Today, much of the trades are executed on ECNs (electronic communications networks) directly between the buyers and sellers, circumventing the traditional intermediaries on the floors of the exchanges. Even the exchanges, such as the Nasdaq and the International Securities Exchange (options), trade in a virtual reality, while an ECN like Archipelago has metamorphosed into an electronic exchange of its own, ARCHEX.

This new stage of direct access trading, linking buyers to sellers and sellers to buyers, has given increasing authority to the individual traders. Average investors have opened tens of thousands of stock, options, and futures accounts in which they make their own trading decisions and telecommunicate their orders directly to the real or virtual exchanges. Orders can be filled in nanoseconds when high trade volume and volatility exist. Simultaneously, the advent of the Internet information age has unleashed a deluge of web sites catering to these individual traders, as the professional analysts of the old school self-destruct due to one scandal after another.

The long-neglected individual trader, all of a sudden, is presented with the means and the opportunity to directly guide his or her very own financial future. All the tools—reasonably priced but powerful computers, broadband Internet access with high-speed connections, and tons of information and advice—can now be downloaded to any trader, any place in the world, any time of the day or night. And it all happened in less than a decade. There is even a plethora of schools teaching trading and/ or investing, complete with fully equipped, state-of-the-art trading floors.

Individual traders now can even function as their very own order desk, a role shrouded in secrecy in this country for almost 200 years by the security industry professionals. The lone trader or investor sees all the bids and offers made by market makers on the Nasdaq and by specialists on the listed exchanges, as well as observes the order flow from the futures and option pits. A click or two on a mouse enters or cancels an order at the speed of light, calls up sophisticated technical studies, alerts the trader to news, or provides in-depth fundamental information about the entities being bought or sold. Well-equipped individuals, sitting before their computer connected to the Internet, are virtually on a level playing field with professional traders at the major trading firms.

Despite all this state-of-the-art magic, the computer jockey of today and the camel jockey of Old Testament days have much in common. The computer age may have tossed us into a brave new world of instant access and gratification, but we dragged our human nature right along with us into the twenty-first century.

The key to enjoying a successful and rewarding life is living in such a way that our conscience does not plague us with regrets. Following the laws of God, as we perceive the concept, or the natural law is one way to achieve this goal in our personal lives. We can sleep at night knowing that we have not transgressed our beliefs of what governs the universe. And we would not feel responsible for the misery of others due to the commission of any cardinal sins. Living a moral life is its own reward.

If part of your successful life involves trading, following the rules of trading contained in this text can help you achieve the rewards and peace of mind you desire. The insights herein described are no more original to me than the ones of the ancient philosophers were to the persons who revived them in the Renaissance. What I attempted to do in this book is to gather in one place the best advice and insights about trading that I have read, heard, and been taught over the last 30 years.

Much of what you read may be familiar; some, I hope, will be completely fresh. With luck, all of it will bring new meaning into your life as a trader. Since so much of living and trading centers on dealing with greed and fear or pleasure and pain in our lives, is it little wonder that these laws reflect so much of what has been learned over the centuries humans have walked upright?

Traders must deal with human nature as they trade, both their own and their counterparts', as they collectively react to the markets they trade. The purpose of this book is to give you an insight into what hundreds of other traders have found that works when it comes to harnessing and directing human nature most productively.

This book is for traders new to the markets, with the aspiration of getting them off to a sound start. If you follow these guidelines, you can avoid many of the pitfalls experienced by those who have gone before.

This book will also help those who have been trading for a while without experiencing the level of success desired; you may well find the help you need within this text. This is the type of book that the professional or semiprofessional trader should peruse periodically. Read it to refresh your mind and reinforce your trading discipline regarding what has worked in the past and will work again—or to find and repair bad habits that you have acquired since you last gave serious thought to your trading.

So much of trading depends on good habits. There is a body of truths that have been shared and recorded over the centuries about what makes good traders better, just as there are truths about what makes good people better. I have attempted to assemble as many of those insights as I could find into this text. I hope just one of them improves your trading because there is such a fine line between just surviving as a trader and being recognized as one of Jack Schwager's "market wizards."

THE MARKET
IS ALWAYS
RIGHT

C H A P T E R

1

THE MARKET IS ALWAYS RIGHT

A trader must bend his will to the market, as a sailor to the sea. The saltiest captain, with years of training, mentoring, and command experience and with the latest in technology, risks losing his ship whenever he sails from port. The dangers at sea range from being engulfed by a typhoon to hitting an iceberg. If caught in a perfect storm with waves geometrically growing in size from 1 foot to 4 to 16 to 64, does the captain steer directly into harm's way or try to run before the wind? The correct decision must be made without hesitation or all hands can be lost. The characteristics of the vessel must be matched with the sea and wind conditions—it is not a simple decision or an exact science.

TRADE WITH YOUR EYES, NOT YOUR HEART

Traders often face similar circumstances, and the market can be as unforgiving as any body of water. Market conditions can change abruptly— perhaps a limit down-up day will occur in the futures market, or volatility in the stock market will be violent enough to bring the trading curb rules into play. If you attempt to fight or to impose your will on the market, you court disaster. The biggest losses I've seen traders and short-term

1

investors experience occur when they hold long positions and wait for the market to turn losers into winners. Sad to say, even very experienced and knowledgeable traders are seduced by this faulty thinking from time to time.

Ego overrules reality. "I've done my research. I know I'm right and the market has got to turn, if I just hold on for a little while longer." By not respecting the power of the market, these traders violate one of the most basic rules of trading. If you see the market moving against your position, get out of its way. If your analysis tells you the reversal has strength, jump on the bandwagon or stand aside.

BECOME AS HUMBLE AS A LAB MOUSE

The market will teach you to pull lever 1 for food and lever 2 for water. If you pull lever 3, you'll get an electric shock. Over a period of time if you successfully pull levers 1 and 2, you think yourself a genius. "I've mastered the market!" But are you the genius, or is it the market you are trading? Never mistake a bull market for brains. Learn and follow the rules of the market to avoid shocking results.

This does not mean you cannot take some heat in a trade. But it does mean you should have a predetermined amount of money you are willing to risk on any one trade. This can be set in dollars and cents or as a percentage figure. Professional traders often determine the amount of loss they will endure depending on the current volatility of what they are trading, where the next support or resistance level is, as a percentage of the price of the entity, or as a flat dollar amount. The method is not anywhere near as important as the discipline it imparts.

NO EQUITY, NO ACTIVITY

For example, on a very volatile stock or futures contract with a history of making very wide price swings, you might use a tight stop loss. The reason is that if the price moves against you, it may very well be a massive move. In their heyday, some tech stocks moved over 25 points in a single trading session. Live hog futures have limited down over 5 consecutive days. The risk of trading these types of stocks or futures contracts is that your stop order becomes a market order when your stop price is hit. At that point, you have no control over the price you get filled at. It could result in a loss that would cripple your ability to trade. If you use a stop-limit order, you may never get filled or out of the position if the stock or futures never trades at or better than your limit price.

NIP YOUR LOSERS IN THE BID

Cut your losers as soon as you see they are not working. Do not miss the opportunity to get into future winning trades by having capital tied up in losers or by wiping out your risk capital. You can always buy the stock, futures, or option back at a later time—more often than not at a better price if you are still convinced it is worth owning. The public markets are always right because, in these days of instant communications and real-time quotes, they are the only markets available worldwide, no matter what you are trading. All the buyers and sellers are together at one time determining the value of what you wish to own or sell. As a buyer or seller, there is no place to hide. If you try to fight the tape, you will have the same fate as the sea captain who attempts to bully a storm.

This advice may seem trivial, just plain common sense, or too obvious to waste your time on. Believe me, it is not! If you do not totally accept what the markets are doing and what they are telling you they are going to do, the way a sailor must accept—without reservation—what his barometer, radar, senses, and intuition are telling him, you'll join the unhappy crews in Davy Jones's locker. Even very experienced traders and sailors occasionally let their emotions and ego cloud their judgment—do not become one of them.

Respecting the market also means thoroughly mastering it on a variety of levels. You need to know everything—from how to calculate the risk-reward ratios of trades, to what the tax implications are of different types of trading activity, to how to read your account statements. You have to understand the mechanics of electronic order routing and the Internet. Most importantly, you must know yourself. Ignorance is anything but bliss when it comes to your trading account.

The first thing to do is forget everything you ever learned about investing, if you want to be a successful trader. I am not telling you to discontinue investing. You should always maintain a solid, long-term core investment portfolio, life insurance, and an emergency nest egg. What I am saying is that far too many very intelligent individuals confuse trading and investing or attempt to do both at the same time. The mindset of the trader must be short term in nature, whereas the investor is interested in the long term. When you think investing, you think about holding positions. The traders' thoughts must be on flipping stocks, futures contracts, and options for fast profits.

Another way of looking at this dichotomy is that investors should not receive margin calls. If they are buying for the long haul, their account should be financed for long-term holds even if it is a margin account. Their objective is wealth, whereas the traders' is income. Traders are different. Their time horizon is shorter. They hold larger positions because of their short-term perspective. Using margin, which can enhance risk and reward, is right for traders since they are expected to keep a vigilant eye on the market and adjust positions frequently. They are not buying and holding as investors do. When the investors trade on margin, they are attempting to enhance their return through leveraging. This means they borrow money from their brokerage firm and pay interest to be able to buy a larger number of shares than they otherwise could. The cost of this borrowed money must be deducted from the return generated by the investor. Pure day traders, utilizing margin, are not assessed interest on day trades, and interest is not a big concern for swing traders with short holding periods lasting only a few days or a week at the most.

Traders should be prepared for the stress of meeting margin calls and, conceivably, having to explain major drawdowns in trading funds to their spouses. If they do not dump their losers promptly, they risk being taken out of the game. For example, I know one short-term trader whose trading success rate is over 80 percent, but he is a net loser and a legend around our back office when it comes to making margin calls. He just hangs onto losers until they become winners, most often small winners or breakeven trades. This person periodically loses his ability to trade, or put on new positions, because he uses all available funds to make margin calls. Additionally, the stress of the call destroys his concentration. He is not positioned to select his next trade, nor does he have the capital to take any heat on a trade when it may be called for.

The way traders manage their mistakes and capital tells a lot about how much respect they have for the market. How much money do you think you need to trade? Should you open a cash or margin account? How much do you risk on any one trade?

For example, a cash account shows a certain amount of respect because it only allows you to buy up to the amount of "free" equity, or maintenance margin excess, in your account. Free equity is generally defined as one-half of fully paid-for securities, excluding options, plus any cash not being used to margin other securities in a stock account. Trading a cash account is a way of forcing some monetary discipline, but not the most efficient way. This is often a good way for novice traders to begin. With a margin account, you can borrow money from your broker by leveraging the market value of the stock or other securities being held in your account. The current federal rule, called Reg T (T as in Treasury Department), governing the stock market is a two-for-one margin for non-day trading accounts. The leveraging effect of futures and options is considerably higher.

For example, if you trade stocks priced at $100 per share and you plan to trade a 1000-share lot, you would need $50,000 free equity, plus enough to cover interest, fees, and commissions. The other $50,000 is borrowed from your brokerage firm. With a cash account, you would only be able to trade half as much, or 500 shares.

Leverage can work for or against you. It can double your profit in the case described above, or you can lose twice as much or more because your account is leveraged. With futures, leveraging is much more of a concern since it is much higher. It can be 20:1 or even 30:1 or more.

Does the acceptance of the use of leverage, particularly a large amount of leverage, mean a trader does not respect the market he or she is trading? What about fear of the market? The concepts of respect and fear are closely allied. When does respect for the market become fear? And if it does, how do you deal with it?

Before I get into that, let's talk a little about the stocks, futures, or options you select to trade, because that choice, and the size of your proposed trades, also reflects how much you respect (or fear) the market. For example, do you trade stocks priced at $10, $20, $30 . . . $90, $100, or more? How many shares will you trade at a time? 100, 200, 500, or 1000+? The same goes for futures and options. Do you plan to trade 1, 5, 10, or 100 lots? What percentage of your trading account would be tied up in any given trade? And what percentage of your net worth and liquid net worth is represented by your trading account? If you lose your entire trading account, would it change your style of living?

Additionally, there is a world of difference in trading very volatile Nasdaq stocks compared with the more well-behaved blue-chip stocks. With the OTC (over-the-counter) stock traded on Nasdaq, market makers and ECNs are the kingpins. Specialists manage the listed stocks on the trading floor based–exchanges. The key word is *managed.* The specialists have the power to postpone the opening or halt trading in midstream if the supply-demand equation for the stock they are responsible for gets substantially out of balance.

This doesn't happen on the video screen–based Nasdaq or OTC markets. Thus the Nasdaq is historically more volatile because all the players are competing against one another. There are no referees, like the specialists, to call time-out when a brouhaha breaks out. If a serious imbalance in demand occurs before the open due to some overnight news, the stock price gaps up on the open on the Nasdaq. If that same situation occurred for a listed security, the specialist, who is responsible for that issue, would request a delayed opening and take steps to get supply and demand in line before the opening. The specialist does this by negotiating with the crowd of buyers and sellers around his or her booth. The specialist also can infuse more shares into the market from his or her inventory to increase supply or reduce demand by buying shares from the crowd. It is this ability to pause trading or adjust imbalances that can calm down a disorderly market. Plus the floor traders know that the specialist is not going to let the market run roughshod over him or her. These smoothing measures are not available on the Nasdaq, ECNs, or futures markets. Keep in mind, it is not a fail-safe system. In very turbulent times, all markets can run out of control. For this reason, all the major markets have curb rules to stop the trading and let the activity cool down. Again, nothing is guaranteed.

Over in the futures or options pits, the trader must make the same decision about what to trade. There is a world of difference between trading corn and trading the S&P 500 futures contracts. Both can be very volatile and risky, but the amount of money on the table varies widely. For example, if corn is priced at $2.50 per bushel, each 5000-bushel contract amounts to $12,500. If the initial margin requirement is $500, the contract is leveraged 25:1. If the S&P 500 futures contract is trading at 1400, the futures contract is worth $350,000 (1400 × $250) and the leverage is 17:1 ($350,000/$20,500). Technically, the corn is more highly leveraged, but the total dollars involved, combined with historically higher volatility in the S&P 500 futures contract, can strike fear into the hearts of more traders than the corn contract.

Or do you trade the very volatile options that are in-the-money and close to expiration, as opposed to out-of-the-money contracts with months to expiration? What about selling naked calls versus buying calls? There are substantial risk-reward differences in these choices, which reflect the amount of respect, or fear, a trader must deal with.

Your trading strategy also reflects your respect or fear of the markets. Short-term traders generally trade heavy, meaning buying and selling a large number of shares. They control risk by holding positions for relatively short periods of time, i.e., minutes and hours. One of the keys is not holding positions overnight. The introduction of trading in decimals has had a sobering impact on this strategy, since penny moves—the minimum incremental moves now—are not as conducive to scalping SIPs (small incremental profits) as sixteenths ($0.0625) or eighths ($0.125) were when they were the common incremental moves back in the good old days of trading in fractions.

Traders who hold positions longer compensate for the risk factor by reducing the number of shares in each position. Where a day trader might buy 1000-share lots, a longer-term trader or swing trader might wheel and deal with 300- or 500-share lots.

Intraday trading negates the risk associated with breaking news hitting overnight since the trader offsets or goes flat at the end of each trading session. If you hold positions, particularly leveraged positions, overnight or for days, weeks, months, etc., you face the risk that negative news stories—stories that can move the market against you—will be reported when you cannot trade or, by the time you become aware of what is happening, it is too late to react. Additionally, you must pay your broker interest if you trade on margin.

On the other hand, the news could be very positive and substantially increase the value of your holdings. You could wake up a millionaire. The big difference is that you are leaving your fate to chance when you hold positions long term. To do this you need faith in the future and the willingness to accept the consequences. Historically, this has worked, particularly over very long periods of time, but there are always periods of recession and retraction that must be weathered.

The more active traders prefer to take their own fate in their hands and maintain total control. But to do this, they must be able to spend the time it takes to become competent and to monitor the market whenever trading. This requires more of a commitment than most traders are willing to make, as you will see as you get deeper and deeper into this book.

KNOWING WHAT, HOW, AND SIZE DEFINES YOUR ACCOUNT TYPE

Most brokerage firms have a minimum account size. It is less for online trading accounts, like an E*Trade, than a firm specifically devoted to direct active trading, such as a Terra Nova Trading, L.L.C., for example. The reason is the online accounts tend to be less active and therefore less risky for the brokerage firm. Remember, within the industry, the brokerage firm guarantees the financial integrity of your account. Some day trading firms seek only the most active traders, and their minimums are high, as much as $100,000 or more. Other firms seek the active trader who possesses discipline and control—therefore they require less of an initial deposit in the account. The requirements of online firms range from an amount sufficient to cover each trade to $2500. All margin accounts, by federal regulation, must have at least $2000, and all day trading accounts must maintain $25,000.

For the record, day traders, or pattern day traders as characterized by the NASD, are traders who make four or more day trades in 5 business days. But if the day trading activity in an account is less than 6 percent of the total trading activity, you would not be considered a day trader. Stock day traders are permitted 4:1 margin, while non-day traders are allowed only 2:1.

Let's discuss margin calls for a minute. A margin call is a demand from your brokerage firm for you to add additional funds to your account. There are three types of margin calls: (1) the basic Reg T (as in Treasury Regulations), (2) the intraday call, and (3) the maintenance call. These can be warning signals that you are overtrading, taking too much risk, or that your account is underfunded.

A margin call can even occur in a cash account. For example, you have $5500 free equity in your account. You place an order to buy 100 shares of a stock priced at $50 per share using a market order. What happens if you get filled at $60? You are short $500 plus commissions and fees. You would get a Reg T call from your broker to cover the shortfall. If you do not meet the call, your brokerage firm has the right, specified in the account papers you signed when opening the account, to sell as much of your stock as necessary to satisfy the debit in your account. Additionally, the firm might close your account and only allow you to trade whatever stock is in the account for liquidation only. Or you could transfer to another brokerage firm once the debit was satisfied, not before.

For day traders, the Reg T call is often referred to as an overnight call because it occurs when a day trader holds a position overnight without sufficient funds. That is to distinguish between an intraday margin call. This later type of call is triggered when a day trader exceeds his or her daily buying power, the maximum free equity, during a trading session. This figure appears at the beginning of each trading session in a window of the trading software platform used by day traders. The software is programmed to prevent this from happening, but it still occurs occasionally.

A trader's margin amount is calculated by doubling the cash plus half the value of any other securities being held in the account, except for options, which are not marginable. For day traders, this quantity is quadrupled. For non-day trading accounts, it is doubled. For example, if you are a day trader with $50,000 in cash and $50,000 in marginable securities, you would have $300,000 in buying power. Remember, only half the stock value is allowed because it will fluctuate, and the day trader gets a 4:1 margin. A non-day trader would have only $150,000 in buying power.

So how could a day trader get an intraday margin call if the software prevents that from happening? There are at least two possible scenarios. First, it could just be timing. For example, the day trader has buying power of $300,000 and sends an order to buy 1000 shares of a stock priced at $100 per share. The stock gains 50 cents, which is the trader's profit objective. He then sends a limit order to sell those shares at the asking price of the inside bid-ask and a second order to buy 2000 shares of a stock trading a $150 per share. He gets partial fills on both orders, rather than getting filled complete in the sequence he fired them into the market. In the process he ends up holding more than $300,000 in stock for a fraction of a second.

Another possibility is the trader who is anxious to buy one stock and sell another. He must get the job done quickly because his account is not properly funded. He decides to multipreference the sell order. Multipreferencing is the practice of sending the same order to the market via multiple routes. In this situation, he sends his sell order to the market on the Island ECN and the Archipelago ECN simultaneously. The idea is to cancel one of these orders as soon the other is executed. But both ECNs are very liquid in the stock being traded, and the both are filled simultaneously. Now, instead of being flat the stock, the trader is short. At the same time, the order to buy the stock to replace the one he is selling is filled. Since he does not have the margin money to be short one stock and long another, an intraday margin call is triggered. If the stock he oversold was not done on an uptick, he would have violated the uptick rule and be in even more trouble. Multipreferencing is a tactic used by very aggressive day traders and it can get them in hot water with their brokerage firm and the federal regulators.

A maintenance margin call is the type of margin call that occurs when you have been holding a position in your account and it loses value. You must maintain enough equity in your account to satisfy the maintenance margin, which is lower than the Reg T margin. It is 25 percent for long positions and 30 percent for shorts. A higher percentage is required for short positions because they are considered to be of higher risk by the federal regulators. If your equity falls below these levels, you will be required to bring them up to Reg T levels. You usually have 3 days to meet margin calls, and it is common to get a 2-day extension if your account is in good standing.

The money used to meet margin calls does not have to stay in the account once the account meets and exceeds Reg T requirements. Excess funds can be withdrawn. Brokerage firms usually require a 10-day waiting period to assure checks clear. Also keep in mind that some types of accounts are not marginable. These are qualified retirement accounts, such as IRAs, 401(k)s, or accounts held for the benefit of minors.

Futures and options have their own margin rules. A margin committee at each futures exchange sets the amount of margin for futures contracts daily. The size of the margins varies depending on price volatility: The higher the volatility, the higher the margin. With options, the margin depends on whether you are buying or selling and if the underlying entity is a futures contract, shares of stock, or indexes. Long options are not marginable; you paid 100 percent of the premium. Margins on short options depend on the underlying entity and basically equal an amount the exchanges and the clearing firms are comfortable with. If you are combining buying and selling, at the same time (a spread), you are credited with the amount the positions are in-the-money.

Let's turn our attention to risk versus reward. First I need to remind you which risks you can control as a trader, i.e., time in the market, the entities selected for trading, the size of your position, the side of the market you are on (long versus short). The longer, the more volatile, and the larger any of these characteristics is, the more reward you should anticipate from a trade. Conversely, the more risk you will be accepting.

REWARD MUST BE PROPORTIONATE TO RISK

On very short-term trades, characterized as scalping, you can be success-ful with a 1:2 or even a 1:1 ratio. This means if your loss limit is a nickel, you can accept a reward of a dime or even a nickel per the species the underlying entity trades in, e.g., shares, bushels, barrels, bales, pounds, etc. With swing trades, you will be in the market longer (several days to a week or more) and should be looking for ratios of from 1:4 to 1:10. With the former, you are trading heavy and the latter light. Never violate this rule. Long-term investors can look for 100 percent, 200 percent, and more for holding positions for months, quarters, and years.

BEARS WIN! BULLS WIN! HOGS GO TO SLAUGHTER!

One of the keys to trading is being in tune with the market. You get out when you want to, not when you are forced to, and with a reward com-mensurate with the risk assumed. This means setting realistic risk-reward objectives and taking what the market gives you. Many traders have re-tired very wealthy by exiting trades too soon.

PROACTIVELY MANAGE YOUR ACCOUNT

Your brokerage firm should provide you with a convenient method for reviewing all the activity in your account before you receive daily trade confirmations and monthly statements in the mail. The firm clearing your trades should have a web site, and it should post the activity in your account daily. Learn how to use and read these reports. They are not always as straightforward as they could be. Your broker or customer service representative can help—bug him or her until you fully understand the reports. Whenever there is the slightest discrepancy, get it resolved promptly.

One of the handiest features I found on some of these customer ser-vice sites is a profit-and-loss report. You can request, via email, a P&L statement on your account over a given time period, usually going back at least 3 months. You input the beginning and the ending date. Then the company generates the statement during off-peak hours on its computers and emails you the report. You open it and print it. For active traders, I recommend you request one each week, say Saturday or Sunday.

On the report, each buy and sell is matched. The report also shows the profits and losses by trade. Any open positions are listed at the bottom of the report. Your responsibility is to verify all this information against your trading log or journal. Once you are satisfied it is correct, write a one-sentence summary of the trade to reinforce your thinking. Be brutally frank with yourself.

LEARN FROM THE GOOD, THE BAD, AND THE UGLY

For example:

> "I entered this trade too late because I hesitated, afraid to pull the trigger."
> "I did not buy in anticipation—must learn to be proactive, not reactive."
> "Good trade! I exited with a 2-cent loss the instant it turned against me."
> "Great trade—got out with 2 sticks (dollars) just before it hit a resistance level."

Displaying your respect for the market can take the form of knowing how to make the best of what the market gives you. In most cases, trading is feast or famine. When you are in sync with the market, you can make phenomenal amounts of money. When you are not, you bleed until you turn anemic. It is the "7 years" of plenty, offset by the 7 lean years referred to in the Bible, but compressed into days, weeks, and months.

WHEN AFRAID, DON'T TRADE

One last key issue: When does respect for the market become fear of the market, and how can it impact your trading?

Thousands of professional sailors and fishermen drown each year. My guess is that even a greater number of traders lose all or a substantial portion of their risk capital annually. Going broke for a trader is the virtual equivalent of drowning for a seaman. But at least a trader is alive and can recover. On the other hand, if the market has ever crushed you, you feel just as low as whale droppings, which are on the seafloor. And believe me, losing money is a major part of trading.

You must be prepared to deal with losses, particularly large, unexpected losses. If you take a hit and your respect for the market turns to fear of the market, you must quit trading or do some serious reprogramming of your psyche. Be aware also that it is equally difficult to adjust when the market acts totally irrationally and rewards you after you've broken every rule in the book.

Fear and respect must also be conquered. They are developed within us using both our intellect and our emotions—our left- and right-brain hemispheres. The difference is which side dominates. The left side is our investor side. It deals with reason, logic, math, analysis, order, reality, and, most importantly, safety. On the other hand, our right side is our trader side—characterized by emotion, fantasy, impetuousness, and, most importantly, risk taking. Fear is rooted in the left side and can spill over to stimulate the right. When this happens, an active trader can become paralyzed.

Respect emerges from the left hemisphere. It must play a major role in the trader's makeup, but it must be tempered with a lot of right-brain risk taking for an individual to become an active trader. Left-brain people make great mid-term and long-term investors.

Determining which side of the brain is dominant is not as clear-cut as one might think, especially for very active traders. For example, if you are (or plan to be) a momentum trader executing a hundred or so trades each trading session, you will find yourself acting and reacting so quickly to the ebb and flow of volume and volatility, you must rely on your right brain. But if you are too right-brain-dominated, you will eventually get yourself into a predicament where you overstep your risk limits and blow out of the market. At this point, any respect you have for the market is replaced by cold fear and panic. You become the weakest link in the pits, and you are done!

Respect for the market monitors your risk-taking inclinations. It tells you when you are overstepping your boundaries. It makes you do your homework before trading. It alerts you to take profits. It warns you when greed is turning you green. Without it, you are a lost soul. That is why accepting the fact that the market is always right is the primal law of trading.

2

IT'S ALL IN
YOUR HEAD

If it is all in your head, why do you hear so little about the psychological side of trading when you are at seminars or when you are talking to other traders? First, teaching specific trading techniques is much easier because you can show concrete examples, demonstrate how to use software, and provide case histories. Second, it is what most traders ask for, especially in the beginning. "How do I start trading? When can I put on a trade? I can't wait to begin making money!"

Another part of the answer is that, in reality, you must teach yourself to trade. The only way to learn to trade is to actually trade. You must obtain a good deal of background information and develop some skills, all of which I will discuss shortly. But when it comes down to putting on trades, nursing them, and closing out positions, you are on your own. Trading is not a team sport, like investing can be. You are not interacting with a financial planner, studying research reports, looking for long-term trends, and building a bulletproof portfolio, if such a thing exists. Good investors are good managers of resources. They pay and supervise a team of experts to develop an investment strategy.

Traders are entrepreneurs, not managers. Think of trading as running a one-person business. Traders do their own research, make each stock selection, execute their own orders, and evaluate—most importantly live with—their results. Trading enterprises either flourish or perish. You must think of trading as a business because it is. Businesses either make money or fail. Unfortunately, it is as simple as that.

YOU MUST BE PASSIONATE TO SUCCEED

Because trading is so personal—your money is on the line every time you put a trade in the market—it is very difficult for anyone to tell you or show you how to do it. As I will discuss in greater detail later, you must develop your own, personal approach to trading. To do that takes dedication and patience. To persevere, you must have a passion for the market. And through passion comes understanding—such as the deep, quiet realization that a point on a price chart or the inside bid on a Level 2 window represents the emotional state of the majority of investors and traders in the world at that given moment.

It is for this reason I put so much emphasis on understanding the ebb and flow of the supply and demand of the float. It tells you the emotional state of the market as a whole. Is the market upbeat? Depressed? Undecided? You can see how confident the body of the market is, or how fearful. An orderly trending market shows consensus, while a wildly sporadic price pattern signals conflict. Uptrends are naturally optimistic; downtrends pessimistic.

As you become attuned to the market, you begin to develop a trading system. Some would call it a trading style that puts you in sync with the market you are trading. The approach you take to the market must be very personal. No one can teach it to you. That is why a mentor is important. The mentor draws out and formalizes your relationship to the market. We are often too close to what we are doing to be able to sort out the really brilliant moves from the meaningless and stupid trades we make. Finding the pearls in the ugly oysters and putting them together into a beautiful necklace is the secret to becoming a market wizard.

The term *market wizard* became popular in trading circles with the publication of Jack Schwager's three excellent books on trading and traders, *The Market Wizards, The New Market Wizards*, and *Stock Market Wizards*. All three should be on the top of your reading list. Mr. Schwager interviewed the most successful traders he could find. Naturally, he sought the Holy Grail of Trading. Accepting his conclusion is critical to your success: "The secret to success in the markets lies not in discovering some incredible indicator or elaborate theory; rather, it lies within each individual."*

That is all good and well—but how do you bring out the wizard within you? Unfortunately, there is only one answer: *Combine your passion for the markets with action!*

Passion for the markets means commitment: Hard work. Devotion. Discipline. Sacrifice. All the pesky virtues most of us lack in abundance. You know you have a passion for the market if you can answer yes to all the following questions:

1. Do you read at least one book a month on trading, the psychology of trading, or trading strategies? (And are 99 percent of the books you read each month on trading?) Is the market your only serious interest?

2. Do you set your morning radio alarm to *The Bloomberg Morning Show*?

3. Is the first paper you grab each day *Investor's Business Daily* or the *Wall Street Journal*?

4. Do you turn on the television first thing in the morning to watch CNBC to follow the premarket activity of the financial futures to get a feel for how the markets will open?

5. Do you jump on your computer each morning and search the top financial news web sites for clues to how the markets will trade and for trading opportunities?

6. Does your spouse ask you repeatedly to talk about something other than your last or next trade? Does he or she keep pitching market newsletters and magazines left in the bathroom? Do you hear complaints that you spend money more on subscriptions to Internet market reports than on your kid's education fund?

7. Do your friends tell you to get a life when you try to tell them about an upcoming trading opportunity? Would you prefer to update your charts on Saturday than play golf?

8. In the evening, do you watch the *Daily Business Hour* and/or *Wall Street Week*?

9. Is your brokerage statement the first thing you look for in the mail?

*Jack D. Schwager, *The New Market Wizards: Conversations with America's Top Traders*, HarperBusiness, 1992.

10.   Are you the one at work everyone comes to for a trading tip? Or
       the one everybody comes to with a question about the stock mar-
       ket? Or the one always trying to start a trading club?

11.   Are you haunted by the Phantom of the Market? Is there anything
       more important in your life than the market?

12.   Is your lifelong goal to trade for a living?

Once your passion is raised to a fever pitch, you must act. That means
trading. Again, you must learn to do that in a manner that suits your
psyche. **Find your own game or recipe for success!** As we mentioned
earlier, a sound financial and educational base is imperative.

You must also be *emotionally* comfortable with the level at which
you enter the trading arena. On day one, you should be as bad as you are
ever going to be. Therefore, carefully select the time, the market, and the
trades. Use the rules in this book to guide you—then develop your own
rules. Where is the best place for you to begin to compete—home, a
professional trading floor, a trading school? How large a share size are
you comfortable trading on day one? Should you trade a thin or a thick
market? Should you trade at the open, close, or somewhere in between?
My hope is that I will have done my job well enough for you to answer
these questions by the end of this book.

One of the truly difficult psychological barriers to breach is learning
to lose. But you do not have to be graceful about it, nor do you have to
learn to love to lose, as some pundits suggest. I hate losing money. It
makes me mad! Nevertheless, you need to take the attitude that every
loss must have a lesson in it somewhere. It is particularly important to
analyze your emotions on entering and exiting losing trades, as well as
dissect your technique and market activity. You must record your feelings
in your trader's journal.

For example, I often sit with traders and watch them trade. After they
get into or out of a loser, I ask what happened. Their answer all too often
is something like, "I just pulled the trigger too late. The move was over
by the time I got in." Lacking the confidence in one's judgment, which
equates to waiting for confirmation of a move before acting, is a critical
flaw that must be overcome. You can work at overcoming this problem
by reducing the size of your trades so the amount at risk is lower. Also
put the cost of trading, i.e., commissions, out of the profit-loss equation
for this period of time. Strictly concentrate on anticipating moves in ad-

vance of them actually occurring. I will discuss the signals to look for in Chapter 6 on entering trades. Right now let's concentrate on your state of mind.

You must have the mindset that learning to trade, like just about any other educational experience, is going to be costly in time and money. You must be able to think of the money spent on commissions and losses as tuition. If you can't think of it as an investment in a business or your future, you will have a serious problem as your risk capital evaporates. But isn't it somewhat unreasonable to think that you could open a retail business or start up a manufacturing facility without investment capital or risk of loss. Learning to trade is no different. The beauty of becoming a professional trader, one who does nothing else for a living but trading 6½ hours a day, requires low overhead in the traditional sense of the word. All you need is a place to trade (at home or in an office), a computer wired to the Internet, trading software, and enough money to fund a trading account. You don't have to buy a building, invest in machinery, or hire staff.

That's the good news. Here is the bad news. You need an education. A good trading school runs $3000 to $5000 and lasts about a week, plus you may need some advanced courses in technical analysis, options, or unique trading strategies. Another couple of thousand is needed for a robust computer that can support multiple screens. You will have to support yourself and your family for approximately 6 months while sustaining trading losses, which could easily run as high as $25,000. If you trade on a professional trading floor, you may have a monthly seat charge in the range of $500, which covers the use of a desk, computer, Internet connection, and trading software. If you trade at home, you still must pay a monthly fee for the software-trading platform, which includes the fees paid to the various exchanges for real-time price quotations. This could run up to $300 per month, but it can be offset through trading activity. For example, you are not charged for the trading software if you do 25 to 50 trades a month, depending on which brokerage firm you are trading through. Of course, the brokerage firm makes its money on commissions. These run from $10 to $15 per month based on your trading volume. If you trade enough to get the software free, you will be paying several hundred dollars a month in commissions.

My point is that learning to trade is not necessarily cheap. You could easily invest $50,000 or more if you jumped right into full-time trading. The stories you hear, or worse yet the commercials some brokerage firms

air, about youngsters riding in helicopters to school or truck drivers buying islands with money earned from trading a few times, are just that:
stories. More correctly, they are advertising daydreams of agencies trying
to sell brokerage services. Learning to trade is arduous, time-consuming,
and difficult. More importantly, it is as risky as any dot bomb ever funded
by a venture capitalist.

All this may be running through your head as you are attempting pull
the trigger on your next trade. Is that why you are looking for confirmation the move has started before clicking the mouse to initiate an order
or why you are hesitating? What is holding you back? You saw the trade
develop. The momentum was building at the 20-interval moving average
and support was holding. The trade was ready to pop. It was time to act.
You know you must respond before the move actually starts—action, not
reaction!

If you didn't fire the trade off, was it lack of confidence or fear due
to the financial pressures bearing down on you? You need to talk to
yourself (or your mentor) and find out what is going on. Develop a plan
or an exercise to increase your confidence. Work on your skill at reading
technical signals or market sentiment. You might go back to using sim-
ulation software to remove the pressure of live trading or, better yet,
reduce the number of shares you are trading until a small loss is not
significant to you. Trade hundred lots, rather than thousand lots. This
gives you more freedom to act and dispels some of the negative influences
that can hold you back from realizing your full potential.

If you have ever played a contact sport, such as football or soccer,
you may have been in a situation where you are coming back from an
injury. If you hold back because you are afraid you will get reinjured,
you are almost sure to get hurt again. You must overcome this fear. You
must play with a certain amount of abandonment. Trading is the same
way. Scared money never wins. If you can't afford to lose what you put
at risk, you should not be trading.

You will have to make hundreds of trades before you become competent as a day trader. For many people, that may seem like an insur-
mountable mountain to climb. In reality, it only takes a few weeks. The
number is less for swing and midterm traders. The reason for the difference is that short-term, momentum trading is very instinctual. These
instincts must be honed to a razor's edge. Swing and midterm trading
are more cerebral and involve a greater degree of analysis and planning. The trades often develop more slowly and are held for longer periods of time. I do not mean to insinuate that day trading does not re-

quire a lot of research and preparation. It does, but of a different nature, as you will learn in Chapter 5 on doing your homework before making trade one.

Which trading style fits your personality? Would you be more comfortable as a fighter or an airline pilot? Are you the type of person who enjoys hair-raising action or the type who methodically wants to take more than his or her fair share out of the market? Can you comfortably afford the cost of learning how to trade? There is only one right answer to these questions, and it is what suits your personality best. Which matches your lifestyle? Which do you have the time and inclination for? Either one can be a vocation or an avocation. Only you can decide. Once you do, go after it.

But along the way there will be many psychological detours. The rules in the remainder of this chapter should help—for example: **Never let your attitude suffer.** Trading is not a profession for the depressed or moody. Active traders lose on more trades than they make money on, but they make it up by having big winners. It is simply a fact of trading. Put yourself in the cleats of a baseball player hoping to get in the Baseball Hall of Fame. He would be a shoe-in if he could only get a hit every other time at bat. Maybe he could do it if his batting average was 300, or even 250. Any way you swing at it, this player is on the bench more than he is in the batter's box whenever his team is at bat. You can make a nice living hitting 300 in the market.

TIPS ARE FOR WAITERS, NOT TRADERS

One of the most important keys to psychological health and trading success is that you must always take responsibility for your own trading decisions. Ignore tipsters. Do not listen to anyone but your mentor or your teacher. Even then, you must make up your own mind. Play singles or not at all. Every entry and exit decision is yours alone, and you must accept that responsibility.

Once you begin to pass the blame onto another trader or associate, you have a serious decision to make. Should you continue trading or give it up? Are you tough enough to take the pounding the market gives us all from time to time? Unfortunately, it seems most severe when we are first starting. That is what is meant by **Knowing your "uncle" point!** Occasionally, we all get to the point when we have taken enough punishment or are under so much stress that we just yell "uncle!" Time to take a break. Just walk away and rest until you really want to come back trading. Vacations are for everyone.

Good times can be just as dangerous. For example, there will be times when every trade you put on works. Your account multiplies like an amoeba at Club Med. Slow down; you do not have the Midas touch. The risk is overtrading. **Learn to pace yourself.** If you don't, you will find yourself jumping into higher-risk trades because you are doing so well. You need to take a virtual cold shower and review every trade based on the rules you have developed for yourself. If you find yourself cutting corners on the rules, you will eventually pay the price. That is one of the big reasons you must put your daily plans on paper—so you can go back and make sure you are doing what you are supposed to be doing.

Overtrading often occurs during a sustained bull market. Good markets can cover up a multitude of sins. It's like horseshoes or hand grenades, where being near the target can count. The key to long-term success as a trader always goes back to accepting that the market is always right. You must be humble and take what the market gives. Then adjust as it changes. All this became painfully true to many day traders, who believed they had totally mastered the market when the bull of the late 1990s was slaughtered by the bear of the 2000s. All too many could not adjust and perished with the bull.

Self-analysis is more critical during winning streaks. You must be able to distinguish if it is your trading system that is really working or if the market is just temporarily cooperative. If it changes, will your system continue to generate profits? How will you recognize when the change comes and make corrections fast enough? What adjustments will you make to your system to take advantage of the new market? Think of the market as you do the weather. Every day is hot or cold, sunny or cloudy, windy or still, or some other combination. Some days look like others and yet each is distinct.

The stock market is the same. It is either up or down, volatile or quiet, exciting or dull—but each day, each trade even in the same security, is unique. How does this fit your personality? Are you secure facing a new challenge each time you trade, or are you more at home dealing with something that is very dependable? The answer does not matter. What is important is that you are not anxious when you make trading decisions. Always remember that you do not have to trade. Only trade when and if you really want to and when you see a profit opportunity. Trading out of boredom is like a kiss from the spider woman.

TRADE LIKE AN ACTUARY

That means cold, rational, and calculating. Know your entry and exit points. Visualize how the trade will unfold. Pick your stop-loss price. Be prepared to take profits as you sell into strength. But be just as prepared to exit a trade when it is not working or you do not know what is happening. Never let your discipline waver.

Discipline often means never doing anything when there is nothing to do. If you find yourself tinkering with a trade, say making adjustments in the entry or exit price without a sound reason, that is your wake-up call that you are in a bad trade. Get out of the trade, analyze what you should be doing, and reenter the trade if it is still available. Never hesitate to walk away from a trade or to exit one just because, all of a sudden, it does not make sense to you. The market is trying to tell you on a subliminal level that a change has taken place and your trade no longer fits.

FOLLOW YOUR INSTINCTS

When trading, you are attempting to foretell the future. This is obviously impossible. And this is what makes your instincts such an important tool; harness your sixth sense. Find out early on if you have good instincts for the market or not. That is important because your instincts are often all you have to rely on when chaos strikes. Having good trading instincts is not unlike having a good sense of direction. When you come to a crossroad in a strange location, is your guess on which direction to take generally reliable? As you trade, you will find yourself in the same type of situation. Do you buy now or wait? You must become sensitive to your instinctual ability. If you determine it is unreliable, you must adjust and exit any trade when it comes to a crossroads.

Learn to be totally honest with yourself. For example, when you follow your instincts and it works to your favor, imprint those feelings. It's like making a perfect swing with a golf club. When you feel the groove, you must imprint it in your mind so you can repeat it. On the other hand, if you take a profit totally by accident, be able to separate this feeling from the feeling you had when you honestly followed your instincts. Accidental wins are not repeatable, but instinctual trades are. Big difference!

You must be prepared for the way the market irrationally rewards and punishes traders. For example, you execute the perfect trade—and lose 2 sticks (dollars in trading parlance) in the process. Another time, you are bored and put on a trade just for something to do—it's up 5 sticks and climbing. Let's face it—the market is not rational, it is not predictable, and none of us can foresee the future. You must be able to function in a very unfair and uncertain world.

By now, you should have a good idea of the personality type that brokerage firms are looking for when they place help-wanted classified ads for traders. Would you apply?

Some have described the trader as a puzzle master attempting to complete a puzzle in which the pieces are continuously changing shape. The task sounds impossible, but the puzzle master can often get pieces in place before the shapes change. That is called a winning trade. If it is a large piece, the puzzle master will be particularly pleased.

Besides puzzle masters, there are puzzle journeymen and journey-women, perhaps journey-persons nowadays. These are traders who have the passion, but not the time, confidence, or means, to trade full time. As with most professions, journey-persons can do very well, but it is still not easy. Hours must be spent studying the markets, practicing trading, and learning new skills.

The constant learning is one of the aspects of trading I enjoy the most. It never stops. Best of all, traders are constantly learning about themselves. Handled properly, this learning carries over into their private lives. Good traders are often good people. They are humble (the market sees to that). They are sensitive (to feel the subtle moves the market makes to warn of dangers or alert to opportunities). They are giving (often back to the market). And obviously, they have enough of a sense of humor to laugh at themselves, as the market often laughs at them.

If you wish to join this journey of discovery, you are most welcome. But first think hard about it. Do you want to trade? If so, how and how much?

Then look at your primary motive. Is it your passion for the market, or is it your desire to make a lot of money fast? Are you in it for the self-discovery, or are you an action junky? If you answered yes to either of the latter parts of these questions, try Las Vegas. My experience has been that trading is too much hard work for fortune hunters and excitement junkies.

The hard, often frustrating, work comes in as you try, and try, and try again, to develop a trading system that matches your personality and still gives you an edge on the market. Without an edge—an ever so slight statistical advantage—you are in for a long, cold winter of discontent. That edge is usually doing your homework. It means finding trades, like earnings plays, splits, and others that are reliable. And then you have to have a well-thought-out plan and the discipline to execute it.

You know, by the ease of execution, when you have reached the point of becoming a professional trader. All the hard work and practice pays off. You look at the market and can just know what it is going to do. Now this does not occur all the time or even most of the time. But even when you are out of sync with the market, you know that as well, plus you have the discipline to stand aside.

One last thought: Never lose your fear of or love for the market. Just like Captain Ahab did not want anybody in his whaleboat who was not afraid of old Moby Dick, I do not want any clients who do not have a healthy respect for the power of the market. You must learn to take the fish and the whales the market offers without thoughts of blaming, taming, or changing it, because **the market is always right!**

I'll get back to how you can best prepare yourself psychologically for the market in the last chapter, after you have a more in-depth understanding of what will be expected of you.

C H A P T E R

3

YOU CAN'T
PREPARE
ENOUGH

$\mathbf{A}$ 19-year old lance corporal enters the G-3 tent for a briefing. The captain in charge of the intelligence unit goes over a plan with the young Marine. It is a 3-day mission. He will hook up with a patrol from Bravo Company, which will escort him and his spotter to the drop-off point. From there, the two will proceed to Hill 507, which provides an excellent field of fire into Elephant Valley and the trailheads leading in and out of it—a target-rich environment for a Marine sniper.

Put yourself in this sniper's jungle boots for a few minutes. Imagine how prepared he must be for the work he has been asked to do. It is dangerous. It requires precision and a great deal of preparation. It is totally independent duty once behind enemy lines and out of the range of any protective cover available from the nearest fire base camp. Every detail must be thoroughly thought out and planned in advance. Amateurs need not apply.

The briefing begins with the captain reviewing all the intelligence gathered regarding Hill 507 and the valley. How active are the Vietcong? What units have been spotted over the last few days and weeks? Are the indigenous inhabitants actively supporting the VC? What targets are of the highest priority? The corporal is supplied with the most accurate map available. It is a contour map showing the elevations of the valley floor and the surrounding hills. A trained map reader can visualize all the prominent features of the valley and its surrounding terrain. Marked on the map are the locations and capabilities of supporting artillery that can be called upon to provide cover fire in an emergency. The call signs and radio frequencies are memorized. As little as possible, including personal property, is to be taken into "Indian" country.

Once the briefing is finished, the sniper begins his ritual of preparation. He becomes as solemn as a cardinal performing a requiem mass for a deceased bishop. Those who have seen a veteran sniper perform this ceremony say it reminds them of a matador preparing for the bullfight of his life. The purpose of this rite is to clear the mind of everything other than the mission and to prepare to kill or be killed.

It usually begins with the sniper returning to his hooch. He pours over the map with his spotter. They select locations, known as "hides," which provide deep cover but also have wide fields of fire. Each hide must also include several avenues of escape. Once the sniper opens fire, he must be able to move undetected to the next hide. Additionally, safe locations must be found to spend the nights, plus there must be access to the rendezvous point where they will meet up with another patrol, which will escort them back to the base camp. Also, additional alternative assembly points must be designated, just in case the VC are in hot pursuit at the time of extraction. The rest of the day and evening is devoted to personal preparations. The sniper:

- Gives his weapon, a Winchester model 70, caliber .30–06, a final cleaning.

- Carefully mounts the Redfield 3 × 9-power scope.

- Waterproofs his boots one more time.

- Selects and packs rations; takes the minimum because trash leaves a trail the VC can follow.

- Inspects all 782 gear—web belt, canteens, light marching pack, etc.—and loads enough supplies for the 3 days.

- Sorts ammo to suit the anticipated range of 300, 800, or 1000+ yards and the anticipated heat and humidity conditions.

- Writes a letter to his wife, just in case—to be mailed if he does not return.

- Spends a period of time in prayer or meditation.

The sniper's spotter has a similar ritual. Neither talk much. Both concentrate on the task before them. They have no one to rely on but each another. Anything overlooked could mean the difference between life and death. Soon after separating from the patrol, they apply black and green grease paint to all exposed portions of their bodies and add camouflage to disguise their human profiles. It is at that point they experience an earthmoving high—the hunt is on!

SURVIVE BEFORE YOU THRIVE

I have used the analogy of a sniper for a very important reason. I want to impress on anyone considering becoming a professional or active semi-professional trader just how serious a business it is. Granted, you will not become a POW if you fail as a trader, but you must nevertheless possess a very strong desire to survive. Trading is one of the ultimate survival-of-the-fittest professions.

You must be prepared for the reality that the majority of individuals, who feel they have been mystically called to this vocation, receive a dishonorable discharge. Anyone who does not take trading as seriously as the sniper takes his work will be drummed out of the service. These are tough words—and I mean them. Successful traders, contrary to popular fiction, tend to be conservative risk takers. This may sound like an oxymoron, but it isn't. The true art of trading is discovering how to get an edge on the market you trade. How can you put the odds, even if ever so slightly, in your favor? The trader who does not do this is a gambler. That is the difference between trading and gaming. Casinos, for example, add a "0" and "00" to their roulette wheels so the house has the edge over the gambler.

How can a trader get an edge on the markets? There are several ways. One is to develop and follow a ritual. The purpose is to drive everything from the mind except trading, when trading. A full-time stock trader's daily ritual might be as follows. The trader:

- Wakes up to Bloomberg radio to catch up on the overseas and overnight markets.

- Goes to the gym to alleviate tension from the body.

- Watches CNBC while pumping iron to catch the day's news stories. Wants to get an idea of what stocks may be in play that day due to earnings reports or other news, and to get more insight into the overnight trading worldwide and the direction of futures contracts of the stock indexes, as a harbinger of the direction of the opening of the stock markets.

- Arrives at trading station at least an hour before the market opens, to search key news web sites and run programs that filter for stocks to watch for the day.

- Reviews and updates key leading indicators.

- Compares technical signals on all the stocks on his or her watch list with key indicators.

- Analyzes new stock symbols and adds to the watch list.

- Prepares a trading plan for the day—stocks to watch or trade, entry and exit points, risk-to-reward ratios, stop-loss levels, key indicators to track, trade size, etc.

- Blocks out everything, especially all human contact, to concentrate solely on making good trades!

Over the years of working with traders, I have seen a close similarity between snipers and traders. For instance, their rituals extend beyond hunting or trading hours. For example, the first thing a sniper does upon returning from the bush is to clean his weapon, then his equipment, and finally himself—that's the priority. Quality traders unwind in a similar fashion—they update their trading log or journal, charts, and technical indicators; review all trades; and run a profit-loss tally. Then, and only then, are they ready to return to the world.

There are other similarities as well. First, the sniper has his spotter, and the trader should have a mentor. The spotter's job in the bush is to watch the sniper's back so the sniper can concentrate on his prey, to provide extra firepower by carrying an M16, and to watch for targets when the sniper rests. The trader's equivalent of a spotter is a mentor.

The spotter does not shoot for the sniper any more than the mentor trades for the trader. Both have supporting roles. And just as a good mentor knows how to trade, a good spotter sports expert marksmanship badges below his ribbons on dress uniforms.

A quality trader takes his trading every bit as seriously as the sniper does his job. Trading may not entail life-and-death decisions, but the concentration, the focus, the passion a trader has for trading needs to be on the same level of intensity. If it isn't, the market will waste the trader.

Trading is more about being mentally prepared than it is about the markets themselves. Lose concentration in an active market and you will lose capital. Lose enough capital and you are dead as a trader. The sloppy trader has a life expectancy of a sloppy sniper. I don't mean to be overly blunt, but if you are contemplating a career as a full-time, professional or active trader, you need to know what to expect and how to prepare. I don't want you coming into my office some day crying about losing your child's college tuition.

READY, AIM, FIRE!

The primary weapon of the sniper can be an old fashioned Winchester model 70 or a modern Kevlar barreled M40 with a nightscope. Either will work. The trader's weapon of choice is technical analysis. It is the only type of analysis that works for trading. You may be wondering where fundamental analysis fits into the picture. It doesn't. Fundamental analysis is the province of investors, not traders. If you are salting away a stock in your long-term portfolio, by all means learn all you can about the company behind the stock. You must project earnings for the next 5 or 10 years, study the strength of the markets for the company's products or services, find out what competitive advantage the company may have, and learn about the people who run the company and what their philosophy is. All this is key to making long-term decisions. But none of it is of importance to the trader, particularly the short-term trader.

Let me clarify what I am talking about when I use the term *trader* and specifically *short-term trader*. A security trader is someone who acquires an entity (stock, futures contract, option, bond, currency, etc.) with the intention of disposing of it at a profit as soon as possible. The trader's intention is to buy low and sell high or sell low and buy back high (shorting). The trader is not concerned about the long-term prospects for the entity, only the immediate price activity. Many stock traders know only the stock's symbol and not even the company's name, let alone what the company produces or provides. A good investor, on the other hand, knows the company he or she is investing in right down to what the CEO breakfasts on each day.

If you come from an investing background, the fact that you may be expected to trade an entity you have no knowledge of, or don't even know its corporate name or where it is grown, can be very unnerving. You may find yourself going to web sites, like Company Stealth, to learn the fundamentals of some of the stocks on your watch list. This can be a dangerous mistake. It would be akin to the sniper meeting the wife and children of his targets. It is the fundamentals of a stock or a commodity that make us fall in love with the entity. And as we all know, love is blind. It is emotional. It clouds our judgment and causes us to miss the target. Keep love, and even familiarity, out of trading. You must be as cold-blooded as the sniper.

Please don't be put off by the previous statements. You are being asked to be totally indifferent to stock or futures symbols—not the human beings behind them. Traders are not cold-hearted creatures of the dark. It is just that if you think about what you are trading as nothing more than a symbol, it becomes much easier to act totally rationally. I know from my own experience that if I trade a stock in my long-term portfolio, I have emotional problems cutting a loss promptly. I end up thinking about all the good, fundamental factors, e.g., how the earnings are increasing, sales are up, new killer products are about to be launched, etc. I know too much about the stock and why it makes sense to hold it to avoid taking a loss.

This is wrong thinking. It confuses you. Confusion begets hesitation, which can be very expensive for a trader. When a trade begins to go against you and it reaches your stop-loss levels, you must be prepared to drop that stock as fast as you would if you picked up a pit viper, mistaking it for kindling wood, in the boondocks. A good trader never lets anything emotional prevent him or her from pulling the trigger to get into or out of a trade.

Now I am talking about preparing yourself to be a disciplined trader. Without discipline, you cannot survive as a trader. One of the best ways to instill discipline is to trade using technical analysis. If you become a strict technician for your short-term trading, you can get an edge on the market and survive until you really learn how to trade. Survival is always the first order of business. Never let it out of your mind. If you do, you will get overconfident and sloppy—two sins you will pay for dearly.

It is at this point that many trading mentors or instructors start talking about learning to love your losses. I hate each and every one of mine. But I do attempt to learn from them and try not to repeat them. Always keep in mind that there are only five possible outcomes to every trade. You can make a large profit, make a small profit, break even, take a small loss or take a large loss. If you can just eliminate the last one, the large loss, you may be able to survive until you really get the hang of trading, which usually takes 3 to 6 months or as many as a thousand trades. Most importantly, there is only one way to learn to trade—and that is to trade. It is important to get a sound background in trading by attending a trading school, practicing diligently on the software platform you will use to trade, hooking up with a competent mentor, and reading all you can. But until you begin executing trades using real money, your education has not actually begun. Paper trading or trading on a computer simulator is helpful. It teaches you something about market movement and how to physically execute trades.

Unfortunately, it is nothing like putting your hard-earned money on the line. Think of how the sniper learns his trade. It is one thing for the sniper to spend hours on the rifle range target-practicing. It is quite another for him to draw a bead on another human being who is totally unaware of his presence and pull the trigger. Add to this the pressure of knowing that once the report of the rifle is heard, every enemy soldier within earshot will be on his trail. There are a lot of excellent marksmen in the Marine Corps, but few have what it takes to become snipers. The same goes for a trader; practice is never like being in the game.

When you compare fundamental and technical analysis from the standpoint of preventing a large loss, you begin to see why traders rely on technical analysis. For example, if fundamental analysis calls a stock trading at $40 a share or a commodity at $2 per unit a good buying opportunity, it stands to reason that when the stock drops to $20 per share and the commodity to $1 per unit, they must be twice as attractive. This of course is false because the entities have lost half their value, indicating something is probably wrong with the analysis. If the same thing happens to a technical trader, as soon as the trendline is broken she would exit her position and halt losses or take a profit. Or she could even reverse her position and take advantage of a profitable short. My point is that technical analysis has a self-correcting mechanism built into it, something that fundamental analysis lacks.

The value of technical analysis is that it gives you immediate feedback. It is more self-correcting than fundamental analysis. Granted the fundamental trader could have used stop-loss orders to prevent large losses, but repositioning takes time. With fundamental analysis, the facts usually seep slowly into the market or they don't become common knowledge until all the market impact has occurred. Even if the fundamental information is readily available, e.g., Brazil or the Ivory Coast announces a moratorium on coffee or cocoa sales, respectively, or GM issues an earnings warning, it often takes time to determine the impact. All the supply-demand numbers must be reworked. Estimates must be made regarding how long the sales moratorium is expected to last and how processors and consumers will react. In other words, the fundamental trader knows the analysis has changed, but does not know exactly what to do next. As she continues to do the analysis, the market overreacts.

As anyone who trades knows, the market is famous for acting, reacting, and overreacting. When news hits the floor, no one really knows if the news is constructive or destructive for the market or if it is even true. Yet people are holding positions and must react. When in doubt, they get out. Once they digest the information, they may change their minds and reenter the market. This causes volatility, the trader's best friend, because it equates to opportunity. A good example is unemployment numbers. When they are first released, there is an immediate price move that could be up or down. Within a half hour, the floor digests the numbers and looks at how last month's numbers have been adjusted up or down. At this point, there is another jolt to the market, often in the opposite direction of the first one.

Charts help traders using technical analysis to get a fix on volatile markets because the charts reflect all the public and private information known at any given moment of a trading session—because the ticks on the charts represent actual trading activity. This is especially true of the futures markets since there is no concept of insider trading, as there is in the stock market. But even in the stock market, some people and entities know more than others do. For example, a large institution knows it must sell 5 million shares of IBM over the next few weeks to meet a commitment. This sale has the potential to impact the stock's price negatively. The institution may be in a position to take some protective measures, but no one else is. Another example would be a market maker showing a bid for 1000 shares of INTC. But how many shares does it need to fill the order it has in house? 10,000? 20,000? 50,000? More? The size of that order impacts price, but only the market maker knows.

The fundamental trader is at a loss because some of the information influencing the price activity is usually unknown. The technical trader works from the market action only. She doesn't have any more of a clue about what is driving the market lower, higher, or sideways, but by using technical analysis she can still trade it. The strict fundamental trader must stand pat or exit the market for a period of time until the picture becomes clearer. This delay can be costly in lost opportunities.

All this is not to say that either trader will outperform the other. Where the fundamental trader may catch long moves and make large profits on these moves, the technical trader gets stopped out on normal price retracements just as the stock or commodity begins a long-term move. It always falls back to the skill of the individual trader and the quality of the tools being used. But a trader, particularly a short-term trader, cannot stand aside while the dust clears. The active, short-term trader relies on technical trading because it continually provides trading signals. The accuracy and reliability of them is another story, which I'll discuss shortly.

Again, all technical trading systems provide signals to prevent the trader from taking a large loss. Plus they provide immediate and continuous trading signals throughout every trading session. Fundamental systems do not necessarily provide adequate loss protection, nor do they provide continuous trading signals. There is just a world of difference between the two. One is for traders, the other for investors.

When I use this argument with new traders, they often become very discouraged because their impression of technical analysis is that it is extremely complex, requiring years and years of study before one can become competent. For example, www.echarts.com lists over 100 technical studies that can be used by technicians to predict the direction of prices and price trends. This web site is worth studying to get an overview of the subject. Technical analysis also smacks of black magic and fortune-telling. How can someone look at a price chart and foretell in what direction a stock or commodity will go?

Fundamental analysis is much more understandable. When supply increases and demand stays the same, prices go lower. If demand increases and supply remains constant, prices go higher. The reverse of these two laws is equally dependable. As demand lowers, so does price. Decreasing supply drives prices up. When both supply and demand change at the same time, prices move even faster. If demand decreases as supply increases, prices plummet. Or if supply is reduced when demand is roaring ahead, prices skyrocket. If supply is adequate for the demand, the price stabilizes. What could be simpler than that? The catch-22 is that you get all the facts needed to build an accurate supply-demand model but the key elements of the model can change without notice or warning. Then the model must be rebuilt, which can take time the active trader does not have.

Therefore, in my opinion, the true trader must use technical analysis. On the other hand, it does not have to be as esoteric, or as complicated, as many gurus try to make it. A careful study will show you that technical analysis is just as simple to understand as fundamental analysis. The price movement graphically portrayed on a price chart or expressed as an index, band, ratio, oscillator, angle, trendline, or some technical analytic study is nothing more than the reflection of the psychology of the majority of everyone who has or had a position in the market during the life of the entity being traded. Some entities, stocks for example, are technically eternal, meaning they continue to exist or trade for an indefinite period of time. Others, such as futures and options, have specific, predetermined life expectancies.

The whole concept of technical analysis becomes even simpler when you consider the fact that prices can only move in one of three directions at any one time. They can go up, down, or sideways. Tying this thought to the fact that the underlying factor moving the price up, down, or sideways is the sentiment of all those who are trading, you come to the conclusion that those trading are positive (uptrend), negative (downtrend), or uncertain (sideways).

ASCERTAIN THE MOOD OR SENTIMENT OF THE MARKET. THEN SUCCESSFULLY TRADE IT

The basic building block of technical analysis is the price chart. It is a graphical representation of the price history of any entity that trades. There are a variety of types of charts (bar, line, percentage, candlestick), which can depict the trading activity of the entity being traded over virtually any time frame. The long-term investor studies charts that entail years or even decades of trading, whereas the day trader watches 1-minute charts from the opening bell to the close.

This book is about trading. Therefore, I am going to take time to provide you with enough background on technical analysis that, if you master just what I teach here, you will actually be able to trade. *Caveat:* As I mentioned previously, you can only learn to trade by trading. Expect to lose money. It is an intrinsic part of the game. Expect to make dumb mistakes. Expect to get into tight spots. Just thank the powers that be that you are a trader and not a sniper. Nevertheless, be just as paranoid as the sniper and just as survival-oriented.

Let's make today day one for you as an active short-term trader utilizing technical analysis to:

- Evaluate the overall mood of the market
- Find and select stocks to trade
- Calculate risk-reward ratios (money management)
- Enter and exit trades
- Evaluate your performance

Before we dive into how to use technical analysis, I just want to remind you that long before you actually begin to trade, you must develop a trading plan, preferably in writing. This will be discussed in a later chapter.

This chapter deals with your preparation to trade, and without knowing how to use technical analysis, you will never be ready. If you take nothing from this book but the following, you will be well on your way to becoming a successful trader.

TRADE ONLY WHAT YOU OBSERVE ON THE CHARTS

Think about how you would trade the following market. The Dow and the Nasdaq have been showing weakness. Then some really bad news hits the market. Both indexes plunge. After a couple of days of trending lower, these indexes show signs of leveling off and trading in what is often referred to as a congestion phase. Basically, they are trading sideways within a range—a 100-point range for the Nasdaq.

While the market trades sideways, it is deluged with negative news and financial reports. The MSNBC Layoff Report shows more than 100,000 people laid off, bringing the total for the year to well over 1 million. The airline industry begs Congress for financial support as air travel comes to a near halt. In a domino effect, this leads to the closing of some major resorts and some big players file for bankruptcy within weeks. Las Vegas looks like a ghost town. Just as the first batch of bad news is being digested, a biological attack is launched on the headquarters of the major television networks and Congress. The outbreak of this deadly disease spreads to the postal system, and tons of mail are held in quarantine.

The great engine of our economy, the retail customer, is dumbstruck. Retail sales drop by 2.4 percent and the Christmas shopping season appears to be in jeopardy. If this isn't enough, the President declares war, the United States begins bombing a third world country, and the fears of another Vietnam War spread. The cost in dollars alone is in the millions per day.

INVESTORS HAVE OPINIONS; TRADERS HAVE OBSERVATIONS

What do you do as a trader? Are you prepared to enter the market on a daily basis? The general opinion would be to short the world, right! Of course that's wrong, as the Nasdaq and the Dow marched north for the next couple of weeks. I have a friend who called me every day during this period. He kept asking: "Why is the market going up? It shouldn't be. The Fed just made the ninth rate cut in a row. Business never looked worse. Unemployment is climbing. Earnings reports keep getting lower? Why up? Why? Why?"

The analysts naturally generated some creative answers to these questions—for example, the hedge funds were short for the last 2 months and were unloading positions. Or the mutual fund managers, since most can't short and they had piles of money lying around their offices for the last month or so, had to do something with that money. The truth is no one really knew for sure, but the market did move higher—and it is always right.

My point is that if you plan to be a trader, you must take your cue from the market and only the market. In literature it is often referred to as a willing suspension of disbelief. For example in a play, something happens that you know just couldn't happen in real life, but it works in the play. You overlook it because the play is so convincing. You must be prepared to take that same attitude to the market. In this case the market was totally defying gravity. The incident in question was naturally the horrible terrorist attack on the World Trade Center on September 11, 2001—after which stock markets were closed for 4 days. Markets all over the world reacted negatively and dropped precipitously. When the New York Stock Exchange reopened on September 17, the DJIA free-fell 684.81 points. It continued lower and began to climb higher against all odds.

My point is, and I cannot emphasize this single concept enough, *only trade what you see on your price charts*. As an active trader, you can only trade when you have access to live prices. You cannot open positions and walk away from a market and call yourself a trader. You are a long-term investor, a gambler, or a fool, but not a trader. A trader can hold positions overnight, as a swing trader, or even for days or weeks. But your head must be "in the market" to consider yourself an active trader whenever you have a position on.

Most active traders do a lot of day trading. They enter a position and exit that position during a single trading session. Some entities, bond futures for example, may have a day and an evening session, which are treated as two distinctly separate sessions. Or with stocks, you can trade before or after normal trading hours. If you enter before the market opens and you close your positions during regular trading hours, it would be a day trade. If you open a position during regular hours and close it after hours, it may or may not be a day trade depending on the cutoff time of the clearing firm your broker uses. All this can impact your buying power for the next day, and so you need to monitor it closely.

If a trade is working, the trader often holds on to it for more than one session. But he or she must be watching the position through each session as intently as our sniper friend stalks his prey. The moment the position reaches the profit target or its stop-loss price, offsetting orders are fired into the market if they aren't already in place.

There is only one way you can logically track your trading positions, and that is through technical analysis. The key word is *logically*. I mean rationally, impersonally, unemotionally, even coldheartedly if you will. Only technical analysis shows you all the facts in a simple, black-and-white decision-making format. It tells you exactly when to enter a trade and exactly when to exit.

Is it always right? Of course it isn't. What is? Trading must be a precise activity; that's why I compare it with sniping. You must have a method of jumping on a trade, abandoning it just as fast, protecting yourself from large losses, and taking profits unemotionally. Fundamental analysis, while I love it dearly as an investor, is useless to the active trader. The trader is generating income; the investor is building wealth—two distinctly different pursuits in life. Confusing the two is like our sniper friend single-handedly rushing a whole platoon of the enemy. The sniper's methodology is to stalk and pick off one enemy soldier at a time. The sniper melts into the background, only to strike again at a different location when it is least expected. The trader enters and exits the market in a similar stealth fashion when, and only when, she has a definable edge and target.

Technical analysis gives you that edge. But just as the sniper will not hit his target every time, the trader may well have more losing trades than winners. But if the stop-loss positions provided by technical analysis are utilized, the trader will not get killed either.

At this point, I am often asked if there is any rational explanation of why technical analysis works. I like to answer that question two ways. First yes, I think there is. And second, if you are asking, you may not have truly grasped the whole concept.

Being human, I personally like things that are reasonable, cause and effect, that I can understand, etc. Therefore, technical analysis works because it is the only way to exactly measure the sentiment of any market. If 10 shares of a stock are bought and 15 shares of the same stock are sold, more stock is sold than is bought and the price goes down. If more shares are bought than sold, the price goes up. In the first case, supply—or the number of shares to be sold entering the market—increased. The increase of supply caused prices to decrease, everything else being unchanged. In the second situation, demand rose, forcing prices higher—again all things being equal.

These rules of supply and demand work well for a stock issue, because the float, or the number of shares in the market at any one time, tends to remain the same. The exceptions to increases in supply are new or secondary issues, the release of treasury stock, and stock option plans, and the decrease in supply when a company buys its own stock, taking it out of circulation. But these are generally rare circumstances and well publicized due to SEC regulations. With some other tradable entities, such as commodities, the supply-demand equation becomes much more difficult to assemble, calculate, and evaluate. Supply can be unexpectedly increased or decreased as a result of changes in weather. Demand patterns often change when new products and technology appear. Even changes in fashion can impact demand. Futures and options contracts, as well as stocks, are heavily influenced by politics and breaking news.

My point is that there are so many fundamental things that can start or reverse a bull or bear move, it behooves you to adopt a system that takes all these things into consideration. My answer is technical analysis. The impact of every entity or individual that has a strong enough opinion to make a trade in any market can be precisely measured by technical analysis.

Opponents of technical analysis will say at this point that by the time you see the impact in the market, it is history. Their answer is to use some method of fundamental analysis to develop a way to quantify supply and demand. This would allow them to predict what price will be at some time in the future. I accept this to some extent. Analysis of certain long-term trends seems to be possible, such as trends in population. Using this premise, an investor might select individual companies that will benefit from these long-term trends, as long as these companies are well managed and well financed and buy their stock for long-term holds. But on any short-term, tradable time horizon, I disagree. Again, avoid confusing investing with trading.

As far as technical analysis being historical data, whether that is over seconds, minutes, days, weeks, months, etc., I still like it. History is real. Predictions are imaginary. I can act on historical data. I can only dream about the future.

If you happened to be one of the few who just accepted my statement that technical analysis works and did not need an explanation, you may have the makings of a super trader. That is what I meant when I said if you are asking, you may not get it. Some of the most competent traders just learn and follow the rules without question or explanation. If a trend is broken, they exit or reverse the trade they are in, depending on the circumstances. Obeying rules is second nature to them. The time for thinking and analyzing is before or after market hours. For a trader, the execution of orders that are dictated by market action is the only proper activity when trading. It is this single-minded focus on extracting what the market lets you take from it, while protecting yourself when the market tells you that you are wrong, that distinguishes the master trader from the journeyman.

To make the trail of history created by the price movement of a stock work for you, you need some tools. The most basic and valuable technical analysis tool is the price chart. It is to the trader what the contour map is to the sniper. As I mentioned earlier, I cannot provide an in-depth study of technical analysis. But I will discuss what I believe to be the most important trading tools. Master these by actually trading, and you will have an edge on the market.

Four types of charts are in common use today. They are the line, percentage, bar, and candlestick charts. The simplest is the line chart. It connects various price points, most commonly the close for each trading session, with a line. A variation of this is the percentage chart. Again it is a line chart, but the points connected represent the percentage of change in price from a baseline date. For example, on a monthly percentage chart, the first trading day would be the baseline or zero. Each point after that would be the percentage, up or down, from the base point.

FIGURE 3-1.   Basic Stock or Futures Price Bar Chart

Bar charts are the most basic tool of most technicians. The vertical axis represents price; the horizontal axis represents time. Volume is located below the bar portion of the chart. Charts can be for any length of time, from minutes to decades. It is common to overlay technical studies, such as moving averages, over charts.

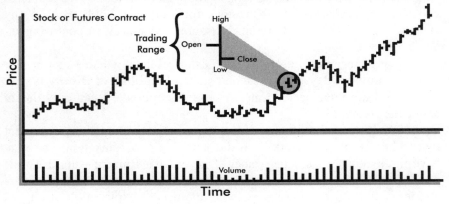

The most common types of charts used by active traders are the bar and the candlestick charts. The bar chart marks each interval of trading with a vertical line (Figure 3-1). The top of the line is the highest price reached for that interval, and the bottom is the low. Therefore, the length of the line indicates the trading range for that interval. A small horizontal line extending to the right of the vertical line and perpendicular to it indicates the last price registered for that interval, or the closing price. The term *interval*, rather than a specific measure, is used because the time frame could be anywhere from a minute to a month. The trader sets the interval, using a computer program, depending on the market view desired. For example, a day trader would be interested in viewing a weekly chart showing hourly intervals and would compare that with the current daily chart that has 1-minute bar lines. An investor might study the monthly chart over a year or so.

Candlestick, or Japanese candlestick, charts were invented in Japan. The Japanese had a very active rice exchange, the Yodoya Rice Exchange, in Osaka in the mid-seventh century. The first I can remember seeing any widespread use of these charts in the United States was the early 1970s by futures traders. Since then, these charts have become very popular. Like bar charts, candlesticks have vertical lines indicating the high and the low for the interval of trading set. It is how the high and the low for the period are marked that sets candlestick charts apart from bar charts. The distances between the open and the close are marked by a rectangle, which resembles a candle. The wick of the candle extends out of the top of the body of the candle, designating the high for the day and below it for the day's low. This is the day's trading range. To distinguish a day that closed higher than it opened, the body of the candle is colored or shaded. On a computer screen if the close is above the open, the candle is usually colored green. If the close is below the open, the candle is red. In the case of charts printed in black and white, the positive or uptick candles with the close above the open are blank, and the negative candles are shaded.

Many traders prefer candlesticks because they can see the relationship between the open and the close, interval by interval. Plus the positive and negative intervals pop out at you. Classic western technical analysis looks at the close from one trading session to the next to determine positive or negative momentum. The eastern school of thought evaluates the opening and closing of each trading session. If it is red, the momentum is down. If green, up. Over the centuries, analysts have assigned a specific interpretation or trading signal to each candlestick formation.

TRUTH IS WHAT WORKS

Which traders are right? Those who follow the western school or those who follow the eastern? The answer is neither or both, and this is one of the tough axioms of trading you must be prepared to accept. Nothing having to do with predicting the future is foolproof. No matter how much humans have attempted to quantify trading, they have been unsuccessful. This is true for fundamental analysts as well as technicians. For example, econometric models that would accurately predict supply and demand for physical commodities, such as corn, wheat, soybeans, etc., were once the rage among institutional traders. Even the CIA got involved predicting the strengths and weakness of our cold war friends and enemies based on their ability to produce enough food for their citizens. All the thousands of factors affecting supply (weather, historical yields, supplies in storage, etc.) were compared with all the demand factors (usage trends, population patterns of consumers, etc.). The old-fashioned mainframes crunched the numbers for days on end. Out popped projected yields and prices, year by year, for the next decade. In most cases the results were little more than rough estimates, which became more unreliable the farther they went into the future. Too many of the variables were either unstable, like weather conditions, or undependable, like the information competing nations made available.

The same goes for technical analysis. The buck stops with the person looking at the inkblots. At some point in the analysis, science stops and art takes over. Anyone looking at a chart can see an uptrend, especially if it is one that has continued over a considerable period of time. The trick is determining when it will reverse. That is where experience, intuition, and discipline separate the winners from the losers.

Of these three characteristics—experience, intuition, and discipline— the last is the most important. The greatest strength of technical analysis is that it can usually prevent you from taking a major loss that will take you out of the game. But this same characteristic of technical analysis may get you out of a trade prematurely. You can be whipsawed. This can occur when you have your stop loss set too close to the market. On a long position, prices retrace just far enough to pick off your stop. Then they skyrocket higher. You miss a big move and profit.

Be prepared for this. Accept it. Do not let it modify or weaken your discipline because of it. Continue to use stops. Place them close to the market if that is the right place for them. Remember that the market could have just as easily plunged lower. Futures traders must be especially careful because futures markets can lock limit up or down. If you do not use stops, you leave yourself open to suffer a mortal loss. Survival must always be on your mind. If you miss an opportunity, be patient, because another one is right around the corner.

The question of using bar or candlestick charts is a personal one. Most of the time it relates to who teaches you to trade and what that person uses or the preferences of the school you attend, if you do spend some time at a trading school. A good school is a good way to prepare. It can substantially reduce the learning curve, which can save you money in trading losses. But again, you cannot learn to trade without trading. Nor can you develop the intuition successful trades possess without putting your cash on the barrelhead.

Now let's get back to charting. What can you learn by studying a chart? Think of it as a tug-of-war between buyers and sellers, greed and fear, or demand and supply. The buyers greedily demand more and more stock, futures, or option contracts, driving prices higher and higher. The best cure for high prices is higher prices. Higher prices cause supplies to increase. Greater availability of supply brings fear of lower prices to the trading pits, and the buyers cannot become sellers fast enough. The rare occasions when demand equals supply will result in stable prices.

The chartist pours over the charts looking for clues to determine if the current trend—up, down, or sideways—will continue. If so, for how long? If not, when will it change direction? At this time, the trader needs some additional data, just as the sniper requires input on wind conditions. How much windage must be accounted for in a 500-yard shot when the wind is moving at 5 miles per hour across the target? The equivalent of windage in trading is volume.

Volume measures the number of transactions executed during the interval under review. Across the bottom of most bar or candlestick charts, below each bar or candlestick a vertical line represents the volume for the interval of the chart. On a 10-minute chart, it would indicate the number of transactions during a specific 10-minute period. The higher the volume, the more important and reliable the signal given at that point on the chart. The low volume also provides insights, but it must be read differently.

For example, a stock makes a new high for the day, in its history or after recovering from a downturn. If that high is accompanied by high volume, this reinforces the analysis that the stock is going even higher. By higher volume, think of 20 percent higher than the average volume. If the volume is 100 percent higher, something very positive has happened to attract so many buyers. But, and here is where the art of charting comes into play, excess volume could also be a sign of a blow-off top signaling lower prices—all the longs are headed to the exit at the same time. If a stock retraces on low volume, that is not as scary to the longs as the stock price losing value on high volume. Low volume in this case may denote some profit taking, rather than a total reversal of a trend.

To this mix, I would like to add just one additional element—moving averages. Moving averages have been around for a while. The first managed futures account, traded by Richard Donchian, began in 1930 and used moving averages as its primary decision-making mechanism. Donchian's fund was very successful. He became known as the Father of the Managed Futures Industry and the Father of Trend-Following Trading Systems. Ironically, he developed the system trading stocks for a Wall Street firm.

The beauty of using a trend-following system is that can be learned—and learned easily. It is not an esoteric, black-box system. If the system is followed with strict discipline, it can be very rewarding. Nevertheless, some skill and intuition are involved. For example, there is much debate among professional traders about which moving averages to use and if you should vary the ones used based on market conditions. In very fast

moving, volatile markets or entities (tech stocks, bond futures, etc.) or
thin markets versus thick (meaning lightly traded, low-volume stock or
commodities compared with heavily trade ones), do some moving averages work better than others? Questions like this one can only be answered by experience. You can never learn to trade without trading.

The construction of a simple moving average is easy. Here is how a
10-day moving average is calculated:

1. Pick a start date and select the first 10 days' prices.
2. Total them.
3. Divide the sum by 10.
4. Subtract the first day and add the eleventh.
5. Divide the new sum by 10.
6. Then subtract the second day and add the twelfth.
7. Divide new sum by 10.
8. Simply continue doing this for each consecutive day.

The price used in the calculation is usually the day's closing price.
But for some analyses, one could conceivably use the open, high, or low.
Day traders use intraday prices, and the moving averages are intervals of
less than a day. Common moving averages are 10-, 20-, 50-, 100-, and
200-day periods. Futures traders will often see 4-, 9-, or 18-day moving
averages plotted. Long-term investors put particular strength in the holding power (support or resistance depending on where the price of the
stock is) of the 200-day moving average.

There is also what is known as a weighted or exponential moving
average. It is one in which the analyst decides that all the prices should
not get equal representation. The analyst may decide that the most current
price is more representative of the trend than older prices. Therefore in a
5-interval (meaning minute, day, week, month, etc.) moving average, the
analysts would give the most current price a weight of 5, the previous
day a weight of 4, the next day a 3, then 2, and then 1. The idea is that
a weighted moving average alerts the analyst to trend changes sooner.

Traders of all time horizons use moving averages. The long-term traders or investors often rely very heavily on the 200-day moving average,
which represents almost a year's trading activity and is considered a
strong area of support. If a stock or an index trades down to its 200-day
average, analysts look for buyers to come into the market and support the

price of that entity. If prices cannot hold above it, analysts will take a dim view of the prospects for that stock.

As a trader, you may use moving averages to show you the trend of the stock or futures contract you are trading. Earlier I mentioned that one of the criticisms of technical analysis by fundamental analysts is that fundamental analysis is not self-correcting. This is what technicals meant. But technical analysis is self-correcting—this happens when a trend is broken or a moving average changes direction. I will get more specific in a later chapter, but let's end this chapter with one more rule.

NEVER POP A WATER BUFFALO

When Recon Marines, scouts, and snipers get together to tell sea stories, one sea lie invariably gets told about a sniper who kills a water buffalo at 1000 yards. The person telling the story—first liar never has a chance in these bull sessions—attempts to impress on his associates just how great a shot his friend is. But the message you must take from this story is that the sniper most likely took that shot out of boredom. The sniper lay in the jungle for hours and hours waiting for a target. Strange creatures, some that bite and others that sting, pester him relentlessly, yet he has nothing to shoot at. Then a poor old water buffalo lumbers into his field of fire, but at a distance that would normally be out of range. The sniper stimulates his mind by thinking about how he would take the shot. How much windage? Elevation? Could he even hit it at this distance? What the hell, he takes the shot. But he has compromised his position for nothing of strategic value. How smart is that?

Traders get bored too. Trading out of boredom, of course, is just as stupid. Learn to just walk away from the market when you cannot see a profit opportunity.

SUPPLY AND DEMAND RULE THE MARKETS

One of the most basic and most important concepts a trader must fully comprehend is supply and demand. Even though supply and demand is the providence of fundamental analysis, you, as a trader, must have a solid understanding of it and its impact on price trends and support-resistance levels. So far I have just touched on supply and demand. Since the concept of supply and demand differs drastically among stocks, futures, and options, each area will be discussed separately.

First let me deal with a few generalities so we are all on the same playing field. When trading, think of supply and demand in terms of buyers and sellers. If you visit a farmers' market and the streets are lined with booths teeming with tomatoes, what would you think? Tomatoes are everywhere. Even as you approach town, there are stalls along the road offering tomatoes at discounted prices. When you reach Main Street, tomato vendors constantly accost you. The farther you walk, the cheaper the prices get. You look around and notice you are one of the few people in the village interested in buying tomatoes.

After you buy all the tomatoes you need, you mosey on to the next village to buy some potatoes. Only this time there is a shortage of potatoes and the farmers aren't as aggressively eager to sell. The streets are crowded with buyers. You must elbow your way into the crowd of buyers and outbid them to fill your potato needs—if you can.

From these two scenarios, it is easy to deduct the basic rules of supply and demand:

1.   When the number of sellers increases, prices decrease.
2.   When the number of buyers increases, prices increase.
3.   When the number of sellers decreases, prices increase.
4.   When the number of buyers decreases, prices decrease.

I just substituted *buyers* for *demand* and *sellers* for *supply* since that is the way we usually view the markets as traders. In most cases, we trade stocks in street name and futures contracts, rather than the actual entity, with the true commodity hedger as the exception. Trading contracts back and forth is more impersonal, which is important.

These rules have physical and emotional limits. For example, there is the concept of elasticity and inelasticity. A commodity is said to be elastic in demand when a price change creates an increase or decrease in buying or demand for that entity. Traders determine the entity being traded is too cheap or too expensive. The supply is said to be elastic when a change in price creates a change in demand or the number of buyers. Inelasticity of supply or demand exists when either supply or demand, or the number of sellers or buyers, is relatively unresponsive to changes in price.

The grains—i.e. corn, soybeans, wheat—are classic examples of commodities that are classified as elastic. The overabundance of these grains drives prices lower and increases usage by cattle feeders, who often expand their herds in response to excess supply. Cocoa reacts the opposite when prices skyrocket. Chocolate addicts will pay whatever it takes to get a fix. Coffee is another in this general category, where prices fall when supplies are plentiful and increase rapidly if supplies are limited. Most of the time stocks are elastic. If the price-earnings ratios get too rich or too lean, traders will buy or sell, respectively. But this is not always the case. A sector will get hot, and prices can soar no matter the financial logic. We all saw this in the heyday of the dot-coms. Stocks without any earnings, or even the prospects of earnings, reached phenomenal price levels. Did you buy Amazon.com at $200, $300, or $400 a share? The same can happen to commodities. Were you a buyer or seller of silver when it hit $50 an ounce, gold at $800 per ounce, or soybeans at $14 per bushel? Somebody did. Eventually the market comes to its collective senses and prices return to normal, often violently.

Now let's get to specifics and begin with the stock markets. When we are discussing the supply of a stock trading on the secondary market, we are talking about the float. The float, of course, is the total number of shares of any company being traded publicly. It does not mean the number of shares the board of directors has authorized, nor does it include the stock certificates the company may have in its treasury. As a trader, you are only interested in the number in the market when you are trading.

As an investor holding a stock for an extended period of time, you are interested in any plans the company may have to issue more shares, like options given to employees that will be converted to new shares. As a trader, if there are any rumors or news that a stock you are trading is about to issue more shares, buy back shares, or split its shares, you must be prepared to deal with any of these changes in supply or use them as a trading strategy.

The issuance of new stock certificates or the release of treasury stock by a company increases the float, meaning supply. As a general rule, this decreases the price per share. If a company decreases supply by buying its own stock to meet obligations, for example to fulfill demand by employees to redeem stock options, the price per share normally rises. When supply and demand are in equilibrium, the price of a stock is stable and trades in a narrow price range. These are rare situations, and the impact on the market is usually short-lived.

The stock split may appear to be an exception to this rule, but it really isn't. When a stock splits, the price is adjusted accordingly. The capitalization of the firm stays the same. For example, a two for one split of a $50-per-share stock creates twice as many shares at $25 per share without changing the net capitalization. Prices tend to increase because the trading public sees this as very positive news. The company normally has good earnings and is trending higher at the time of the split. The pop in price is due to the momentum of the stock's price, rather that the split itself, which leaves supply fundamentally unchanged since the price is adjusted.

Keep in mind that so far we have been only looking at one factor, i.e., supply or demand, in isolation. This is not how it works in real life. The more common situation is when there is conflicting information or news regarding either supply or demand, or even both. The trader must be able to decipher which factor or factors are dominant and then determine if prices are headed up or down. If you are a short-term trader, you may only have seconds or minutes to make decisions that could generate a large profit or loss.

Because of the lack of time to do an analysis, when news hits the pits that has positive or negative market-moving potential, the market heads south by reflex. "When in doubt, get out!" This explains the reaction to common, but unexpected, news. For example, retail sales figures are released but don't hit the Street's expectation. The market dips. Once all the figures are out and analyzed, traders have a chance to digest them. Then they decide the numbers are positive, and the DJIA and Nasdaq head higher again. This is just business as usual, but if you are not prepared, you could be whipsawed.

There are rules to help you no matter what your time horizon of trading is. For example, the long-term investor will look at a 1- to 5-year price chart to see what happened to the price of a stock when changes in number of buyers and sellers occurred. The most common practice is to draw some long-term trendlines. What did it take in the past for the stock to break a long-term trendline and move in the opposite direction creating a new trend? You must additionally compare the price action of the individual issue under study with that of the major market index it is a part of and its sector subindex. A stock in the Exxon-Mobil class is compared with the Dow Jones Industrial Average and the index of the oil sector since it is part of both of these, for example. A Cisco would be evaluated against the Nasdaq and the tech-sector index.

THE TREND IS YOUR FRIEND

This ancient rule of investing guides the long-term investor. As long as the trend continues to head north (after being adjusted for splits), the investor sits pat. But what if the long-term trend is penetrated? What does the investor (not the trader) do? This is where I find all too many investors have a serious problem. They do not have a plan of action thought out in advance, and it often costs them dearly. Investors, like traders, must have a plan and the discipline to follow it. Do they just hold the stock? If it penetrates the long-term uptrend by 10 or 20 percent, do they liquidate, reevaluate the fundamentals, and buy in again when the uptrend is reestablished? Or do they just hold on for dear life? Do they buy puts or sell calls to hedge? These are questions for another book and another time.

My concern here is for active, short-term traders. How can they gauge supply and demand? How can short-term trends be discovered and tracked? The very short-term or day traders and the swing traders, who hold stocks for a few hours or days, have a different set of rules than long-term investors have.

A key element in determining the trend of the stock being traded is learning how to recognize what phase the stock is in. (See Chapter 6, Figure 6-1.) Four distinct phases reflect the three possible directions the price of a stock can move. The price can be increasing, which is called a bullish move (phase 3). If the trend is up, you see higher highs and higher lows. The opposite direction is also a possibility. The price of a stock can be trending lower, meaning lower highs and lower lows (phase 1). This is described as bearish. If the price of a stock is not going up or down, it is going sideways, usually in a tight channel. If the entity is moving sideways at the bottom of its trading range, it is said to be building a base (phase 2). If it is at the apex of a move, it is topping (phase 4). If the trend appears stalled in the middle of a move, the term *area of congestion* is often used. If this area of congestion prevents the entity from going lower, it is support. If it halts an upward thrust, it is referred to as resistance.

When the stock is in the base-building phase, investors are accumulating shares without driving prices higher. This is the area of equilibrium in the supply-demand equation when the number of sellers (measured in share volume) approximately equals the number of buyers. A base-building formation follows a downtrend in price. At some price point, buyers enter the market saying, "At this price that stock is a good buy." Or:

- The price-earnings ratio becomes attractive.

- The dividend alone makes the stock a good buy.

- Some good news about the stock seeps into the market.

- The bad news or information about a stock changes or is determined to be false.

In other words, the market changes its opinion about a stock and stops the price bleeding. The folks selling are the ones who held the stock too long and have finally given up. The buyers are long-term investors who are building positions for the next rally. The Street characterizes them as value investors. Short-term traders watch this action but do not participate yet.

During this base-building phase, or phase 2, moving averages and volume are little help in determining the trend. The reason, of course, is that there is not a prolonged uptrend or downtrend. The longer moving averages, the 50- and 200-day ones, are the key. They flatten out. The shorter-term moving averages snake up and down as prices fluctuate in a sideways pattern, within a closely defined price range. The market is trying to make up its mind about whether it is bullish or bearish. One of your key indicators is volume, which holds steady with occasional flare-ups. If you study some long-term charts, it is easy to recognize these long flat price formations. It is not uncommon for them to last months or longer. They are often referred to as saucer or rounded bottoms. This is the province of value investors, such as mutual funds, who build large positions over long periods of time, living on the dividend returns. When the market finally moves up, they enjoy spectacular returns. Until then, the return is lackluster.

The move out of the base-building phase into the uptrending phase, or phase 3, is usually confirmed by the longer-term moving averages. The 50-day moving average crosses the 200-day moving average. If this is accompanied by a sustained increase in volume, it may be a breakout move. I emphasize the conditionality of these indicators. You will always be looking for additional confirmation from other key indicators.

The patterns are easy to spot on historical, long-term charts. But active traders must be able to do the same analysis using short-term time frames, which I will discuss in greater detail in Chapter 6. Where long-term traders are studying a weekly or monthly chart covering several months or more, short-term traders are viewing daily charts displaying 35 to 45 days of hourly price activity. The same price patterns show up, but they are compressed, making them harder for beginners to see. Nevertheless, the patterns are there, and with a little training and experience you will learn to spot them. But the short-term traders are not interested in building large positions over time. The art of short-term trading is to get in and out fast. The major risk of trading for short-term traders is staying too long in the market. Where long-term traders control risk by limiting the number of shares they own of any one stock or by dollar-cost-averaging, short-term traders limit risk by not being in the market for long periods of time.

Therefore when short-term traders spot a stock in phase 3, it may be there for only a day or two (compare this to the long-term phase 3 pattern that can continue for weeks, months, or longer). The more experienced that short-term traders become, the easier it is for these traders to spot the different phases and do it over shorter and shorter time frames. Eventually, you will learn to see all four phases repeating themselves in very short time frames. This is a critical skill that can best be taught by working with an experienced trader and having that person point out each phase as it occurs throughout the trading session or over a series of trading sessions.

Phase 3 is the most opportune one for traders of all time frames who plan on being long the stock. It is the most bullish phase. All the old owners of a stock who rode it down to the point of price equilibrium are out and have been replaced by investors and traders who plan to sell only if the stock goes higher. The bulls rule the arena for the time being. As a technical trader, you do not worry about the reason for the upward momentum. You see all the moving averages moving higher, accompanied by volume and other indicators you rely on, which could be stock index futures, the overall market, the subindex of the sector of the stock being traded, etc. The fundamental reason for the move is of no consequence to you. Oddly enough, the fundamental situation is often unclear at this point. All markets move up or down on the anticipation of what is going to happen, not on what is happening. If you wait for proof a move has begun, you will miss the opportunity.

When phase 3 kicks in, the investor or trader watches the appropriate moving averages. The value investor begins aggressive buying when the 50-day moving average crosses the 200-day one on the daily chart. In a more compressed view of the market, the swing trader acts when the 20-period crosses the 50-period on an hourly chart, and the day trader acts when the 20-period crosses the 50-period on the 10-minute chart. All three are simply reacting to the basic rules of supply and demand as stated in the opening of this chapter and revealed by the moving averages. They become classified as aggressive buyers when there are more buyers than sellers, which explains why volume is such an important part of any trader's decision-making process.

SELL INTO STRENGTH

Once all the serious buyers are satiated, the stock slips into the fourth phase. This phase mirrors phase 2. Where phase 2 represented congestion or a sideways trading pattern on the bottom, phase 4 is the same thing but at the top of the trading cycle. Again, we look at volume to see what is happening. Prices are still inching higher, but volume is tapering off sharply and the moving averages are flattening out. Some traders are asking how much higher this stock can go, while others are beginning to take profits. You should be among the profit takers at the very beginning of this phase.

Nonetheless, the mood is still bullish. The reason is that the fundamental news is usually the most bullish at this point. As they say on the exchange floors, "All the good news comes out at the top." The analysts are touting the stock like there is no tomorrow. If one says the stock will hit $100 per share, the next pegs the high at $200. If you are a cynic, you would swear that the analysts are trying to lure the public into the market to bail out their firms' institutional clients—but that's probably just my jaded view of life in the pits.

The key moving average to watch is the 50-period one. If it does not act as support, you can expect a correction. Again, you should be out by this point. You never go broke taking profits. If you wait too long or try to pick tops, you will live to regret it. On the other hand, if the stock's price bounces off the 50-period moving average and volume increases, it may be going higher and you might want to reopen a long position. Again, your decision would be made using other reliable indicators to determine that another leg up is occurring, rather than a blow-off top.

If the 50-period moving average does not hold, look for the beginning of phase 1. As you have already guessed, it corresponds to phase 3, but it is bearish rather than bullish. The sellers rule the arena. This phase usually is of shorter duration than phase 3. Markets fall faster than they rise. One of the key reasons is the difference between strong and weak holders. Strong holders have deep pockets. These are the institutions, i.e., mutual and pension funds, banks, investment houses of all sorts. Weak holders are individuals. At the top of a move, particularly a long-term move, the institutions sell to the individuals at the blow-off top. Once phase 1 begins, too much stock is held by weak hands and must be dumped. Short selling, particularly by market makers who are not bound by the uptick rule, accelerates the downward movement of bear markets. The uptick rule requires individual traders to wait for an uptick in the price of a stock before they can initiate a short position.

Some traders, known as contrarians, attempt to trade against the trend. They buy when everyone else is selling and sell when the crowd is buying. This is a legitimate strategy, but one that should not be attempted by anyone new to the markets. In the beginning, I strongly recommend keeping the wind at your back. In time, you may learn to tack upwind.

COMMODITIES, FUTURES CONTRACTS, AND OPTIONS

First, you need to make a distinction between physical commodities and financial futures contracts. The reason is that physical commodities must be produced, whereas financial futures are intellectual creations. Physical commodities must be grown, bred, dug, stored, shipped, and assayed. They have a physical presence in our lives. We eat, wear, and heat our homes with them. Financial futures reside in the minds of the financial players and computer storage devices.

The supply of physical commodities is complex and dependent on a wide variety of factors. Futures and options contracts are created at will whenever traders or investors wish to buy or short them. For these financial contracts, only the demand side of the supply-demand equation is important. Demand creates supply.

To understand the supply side of physical commodities, I separate the commodities into categories based on how supply is created. Also, I can't cover all the commodities traded on futures exchanges worldwide. I will just provide a quick overview of the ones most actively traded on the U.S. exchanges—i.e., the Chicago Board of Trade, Chicago Mercantile Exchange, New York Mercantile, New York Commodity Exchange, New York Cotton Exchange, MidAmerica Exchange, and Coffee, Sugar, Cocoa Exchange—to give you an insight into the complexity of determining supply.

Let's start with agricultural commodities, specifically the grain complex. It includes corn, wheat, soybeans, soybean oil, soybean meal, oats, and rice. The basic supply-demand equation is

Beginning stocks + production + imports = total supplies
Feed, seed, residual + food + export = total usage or demand
Total supplies − total demand = ending stocks or carryover

Sounds easy, doesn't it? Beginning stocks is the carryover from the previous crop year, which is October 1 to September 30 for most grains. At best this is an educated guess. Keep in mind that grains are grown and used worldwide. Therefore all the estimates made to determine supply or demand encompass world production and usage.

One problem is that many countries will not supply reliable information. Many will not even cooperate at all—they won't supply any information. Others outright provide disinformation. The most prominent example of this occurred during the cold war. Mother Russia had agents in Switzerland building enormous long positions in futures contracts while hiding from the world that the Russian grain crop was having severe problems. When the news finally came out about the grain problems, futures soared, and so did Russian profits. Russia used these profits to buy grain to feed its people and cattle and to fill Swiss bank accounts. This became known as the Great Grain Robbery.

In the futures market, there is no such thing as insider information as we know it in the U.S securities business. The world's largest grain companies, for example, are privately held, and all but one is domiciled outside the United States and not subject to any of our self-regulatory agencies. They are free to do as they please. Plus they are very wealthy, owning or handling almost all the free stocks of the grains in the world. Furthermore they aggressively compete with one another and are active futures players.

The next totally uncontrollable factor that grain traders must contend with is weather on a global basis. Excellent weather in the major growing areas sends grain prices tumbling, and drought sends them skyrocketing. Even minor disturbances, such as rainy planting or harvesting seasons, can provoke limit-up or -down trading days and super trading opportunities or gigantic losses.

The futures price prognosticators, using supply and demand as their primary analytic tool, must contend with unprincipled governments, greedy multinational corporations with substantial insider information, and unpredictable weather. If that weren't enough, even the American farmer shaves the truth at times. Farmers are asked to complete surveys for the U.S. Department of Agriculture (USDA). When it comes time to complete the Planting Intentions Survey and the farmer is sitting on 100,000 bushels of corn in on-farm storage bins, does he tell the USDA that he is planting the maximum acreage of corn or that he is switching a good percentage of his fields to soybeans? If enough farmers switch but he doesn't, he'll see a rally in corn and be able to sell a good amount from his storage bins. Then he can plant all the corn he wants. What does he do?

These stumbling blocks are found not only in the grains sector. In the meat complex, meaning feeder and live cattle, boxed beef, lean hogs and pork bellies, similar problems occur. How do you factor in mad cow disease? If a disaster occurs in the grain complex, prices for feed will skyrocket and cattlemen will liquidate their herds, creating a short-term bear market followed by a long-term bull market. Or look at the food and fiber group—i.e., coffee, cocoa, sugar, orange juice (FCOJ, frozen concentrated orange juice), and lumber. One major factor, not surprisingly, is the weather. Another is that foreign governments control the export of several of these commodities and will manipulate prices to their advantage if they can. Brazil and the Ivory Coast, for example, will hold coffee and cocoa, respectively off the market if prices drop too low. The same thing can happen in the crude oil and byproducts complex (crude oil, heating oil, gasoline, natural gas, and propane) if OPEC can get cooperation from non-OPEC members. Then there are the metals, which are silver, gold, platinum, palladium, aluminum, and copper. With several of these, silver and gold for example, the forecaster is faced with a supply increase based on the mining of base metals such as lead or copper since the precious metals are often by-products. When demand is down, supply can still be growing.

If all this did not cause fundamental analysts to pull their hair out, the amount of information available will. The USDA issues approximately 300 reports a month on every conceivable aspect of the grain and meat complexes. In addition, there are dozens of private services and even more commodity brokerage firms offering their take on supply and demand. Despite all this, or because of it, I feel the average trader cannot do justice to fundamental analysis.

My recommendation is to consider using technical analysis, which is discussed in later chapters. This suggestion is particularly relevant for active traders, who are in the market most trading days. As for day traders, it is really your only option.

In my opinion, even long-term traders or investors, who dote over earnings ratios, personnel changes, product development, marketing gains, and other fundamental factors, should still utilize a combination of fundamental and technical analysis. Technical analysis strictly uses price activity. By understanding it, the fundamental analysts can spot important changes in the price of their stocks or futures contracts before the fundamental reason for the change is known publicly. If nothing else, fundamental traders would do well to use technical patterns as a first alert system even if they are not convinced or comfortable using it as their main forecasting tool.

C H A P T E R

COMMIT YOUR THOUGHTS TO PAPER

Before we go too much further, you need to begin developing a plan. A good plan has a beginning, a middle, and an end. The first part is the most important, yet the most neglected, by the majority of traders. It entails developing your trading philosophy. The middle section requires you to write an action plan. This is the backbone of your day-to-day trading plan. The last part has to do with how you enforce parts one and two.

Obviously from the title of this chapter, you know I expect you to put your plan in writing. Here's where all too many traders balk. The common response heard is often, "I know what I'm going to do—trade and make money. Preparing a written plan is a waste of time. Time I could be trading. End of story!" In other words, it is not unusual to see the majority of new traders start off half-cocked. Then they wonder why most lose their risk capital in less than 3 months!

Dear Bunkie Buddy, there are literally thousands of reasons to write down your thoughts of how you plan to trade. Those thousands of reasons all have dollar signs on them. Over the decades I have been intimately involved with traders of all stripes, and the most common reason so many of these traders have left the market broke is that they lost track of their primary objective and trading strategy. They never spent any time seriously thinking about what they were getting into and how well they must be prepared to accomplish their goals. Clearly defining exactly how, when, where, what, and why you plan to trade goes a long way toward building a trading philosophy that will sustain you during the first 3 months of trading. Additionally you must clarify your thinking behind your decisions.

If you think you can just work all this out in your mind over a week-end or while you are trading, stop reading right now. Give up the idea of being a professional or semiprofessional trader. Go back to dabbling on an online brokerage site or whatever you were doing. Save yourself the stress and financial loss awaiting you. Or take the time to think this whole idea out and put it on paper, which is one of the keys to being prepared for the unexpected.

The reason I insist that you put your thoughts on paper is that there is no better way of totally exploring and fully understanding the challenges ahead of you. This process is not just for trading or investing in high-risk ventures. It works for every major, life-altering event. I wish more people would adopt this concept when considering marriage. It would cut the divorce rate in half, in my opinion.

The development of a written trading plan will substantially improve your chances of surviving the first 3 months of trading and guide you through your entire career as a trader because it prepares you for the obstacles you will encounter. A well-thought-out plan is to the trader what the ocean charts are to the sea captain. It gives you insights into what you will probably encounter as you enter this new phase of your life and how you will have to adjust. By answering the questions asked in this book and providing the information requested, you solve problems that could otherwise stall or destroy your chances of success—problems you may not consider without going through these exercises.

You cannot hold in your head all the information you need to trade successfully. You must have some written document to refer to when you encounter one of the many obstacles you will face. The most debilitating of them will be your own personality. The most valuable function of the exercises in this book may well be to do some serious soul-searching to determine if you are psychologically prepared and suitable to be an active trader. Your emotions will try to tell you the market is not always right. This will often result in a drawdown of your risk capital. It is at these times that you will need a written document to refer to and to help you get back on track.

Trading is a business. You buy and sell valuables with the objective of making a profit. It is no different from buying and selling boats, cars, homes, or any other tangible objects. Traders often overlook this simple fact because they never take possession of the stock certificates, physical commodities, or option contracts. All are held in street name by your brokerage or clearing firm. If you had to provide for the safekeeping of these entities or, as in the case of trading precious metals, obtain assaying reports before you could transfer the entities to another buyer, you might think differently. Then it would seem more like a business. Don't let these conveniences get you off track. Active trading is a business, and every business needs a plan.

Another very important reason for writing a plan is that writing evokes thought. Once you begin putting your ideas on paper, your mind kicks into a higher gear. Thought number 1 spawns thoughts 2 through 10. Your mind races, and you are thinking about things you never considered previously. The more you write, the more clearly defined your ideas become. Writing is like planting acorns. It helps your ideas grow to mighty oaks, strong enough to weather the tempests you will endure as a trader.

"I SEE," SAID THE BLIND MAN WHEN HE NEVER SAW AT ALL

Writing helps you see what the blind man sees. It provides a much deeper insight into what you plan to do by eliminating the distracting activities that surround you. If you are thinking, for example, of getting into trading because there is a raging bull market going on and all your friends are trading their collective brains out, your decision-making process is faulty. This happened at the tail end of the 1990s. Day trading was all the rage. Millionaires populated the trading floors as we moved to the 2000s. Then the market took back what it had given and a goodly number of those invincible traders left the trading floors bleeding and naked.

A wild bull market forgives arrogance and ignorance. Some traders have been known to mistake one for their own skill and expertise. During these major bull moves, they picked the wrong stock and made a handsome profit based on the momentum of the entire market. These traders got rich by being lucky. They began to trade at the best of times. They also made money because they could get by being nearly right, rather than being absolutely right. And they gave all or much of it back because they never really understood, when the market turned against them, why they were so successful in the first place. Another big reason so many gave so much back was that they had not thought out what they were doing. They did not develop a plan. No thought was given to mapping out avenues of escape, protecting profits, or knowing when to step aside. Nor did they do any soul-searching. They just charged blindly into the market.

I know many of those traders now, and they are having big problems adjusting. Not long ago, they considered themselves wealthy and brilliant. They were totally independent, working solely for themselves as professional traders. This allowed them to set their own hours, work whenever they felt like it, and vacation at will. The dream lifestyle was theirs while they were still in their twenties. Then the market turned on them. It was right. They were not invincible. The easy money of the 1900s became the blood bath of the 2000s. The easy-rider lifestyle vanished. It reminds one of how it must be for a star athlete who gets permanently injured in his rookie year in the NFL and then is never heard from again.

If these traders had prepared themselves better with a written business plan and some serious soul-searching, more could have survived. That's what writing a business plan for trading is all about. That's what realizing what the market is and accepting it for what it is, is all about. That's what surviving and being paranoid is all about. That's what this book is all about.

Writing is also about commitment. When you put your thoughts in writing it somehow makes them more real. You are more responsible for them and must live up to them. To really put the pressure on yourself, give your plan to your mentor to read. Or you can share it with a fellow trader or a trading instructor you may have met. Better yet, give it to your spouse. This act alone demonstrates your commitment and your confidence that you have developed a good plan. If for some reason you are reluctant to share your plan, perhaps because you think it is too personal or you are ashamed of it for some reason, that is a sure sign you are not ready to trade.

Ask these mentors to second-guess you. Let them pick your plan apart. It's like presenting your master's thesis to the review committee of your professors. You need their blessing before you launch into your new profession. If you have been dishonest with yourself, they should tell you. If you have held back key information, especially about yourself and your weaknesses that may impede your success, they should tell you. If you have overlooked some key area, they will send you back to the drawing board.

Find your weakness before the market does. If the market discovers you cannot control your greed, it will wipe you out. If it learns you cannot control your temper, it will aggravate you until you are out of control. If it sees any weakness in you, it will exploit it. Before I go too far, please understand that I do not think the market is a conscious being of any sort. But all the individuals who pour their emotions into it are out only for themselves. Therefore when you trade, you respond to the emotions of others, and this brings out the best or the worst in you. Facing the market is not any different from facing any other challenge that can have a profound impact on your life—you either rise to the challenge or succumb.

A written plan defines what you do once you take the plunge. For example, what will be the time frame of your trades? Will you be a day trader? A swing trader? Or will you be holding positions for longer than a few days or a week? What style of trading will you specialize in? Momentum? Trend following? Do you expect to adapt any special strategy? Trading stock splits? Specializing in playing earnings reports? IPOs? If you trade commodities, will you be a day or position trader? A scale or contrarian trader? What about options? Do you plan to be a buyer or seller? Or do you plan to combine more than one trading vehicle? Or to use trade combinations, like spreads and strangles, or use one entity to hedge the risk of the other? My point is simply that stating you will be a trader is not enough.

Preparing a written plan is also the first step of visualization. This is a technique borrowed from sports psychology but used by many professional traders. Just as athletes picture in their minds the perfect golf swing or pole vault before attempting one, traders run through their minds how a trade will play out. On a broader scale, your plan should describe exactly how you want your new profession to roll out. Granted, the odds of being right on the money with your predictions are probably slim to none, but the visualization of what you think can or may happen becomes your benchmark. When you review your progress on a daily, weekly, monthly, quarterly, and annual basis, you will know where you stand. By knowing that, you can adjust your trading and your plan.

Further analysis provides insights about what areas of your trading need extra help, where you can get that help, and in what areas you are excelling. In a later chapter you will see how you can precisely measure your progress. Naturally, you want to eliminate the negative and accentuate the positive. This will come into greater focus when we discuss making individual trades and evaluating your performance.

A big part of developing any plan is setting goals. Far too many traders never take this step, or they shortcut it by stating a dollar amount they want to generate daily, weekly, or whatever. Being profitable certainly is important, but it is premature to set it as your first and only goal. I tell the traders I mentor to begin by thinking about just making good trades. For the first week of trading, set a goal of making four good trades, for example.

WHAT IS A GOOD TRADE?

A good trade is simply one you are satisfied with, meaning one in which you maintain total control. You begin by doing your research, selecting a stock to trade, and visualizing the trade. For example, you do your homework and become proficient enough in technical analysis to spot a stock that is in an uptrend. It has moved up a few points and encounters some resistance. Then it trades sideways and drifts back. Checking volume tells you that buying has dried up. The price has stabilized, and you believe it is again heading higher. The only area of resistance above it is $3.50 away. It is currently sitting on its previous resistance, which is now support. The 10- and 20-day moving averages are heading higher on the 60-minute chart. You enter a limit order after the first 20 minutes of trading a few pennies higher than the offer. You are immediately filled.

Once in the trade, you watch it like a sniper stalking prey. Your price objective is 1 stick (dollar) of profit. Your stop-loss order is placed a quarter lower, which is just below the first level of downside support. If the stock plods higher on weak or mediocre volume, you will exit promptly with whatever profit you can get or exit on any sign of weakness. If the price moves higher on medium-to-strong volume, you will hold your position and move your stop up appropriately. Your stop-loss order becomes a trailing spot and will follow prices higher. It will be kept below the upward-moving price around areas that will become support if the price falls. Areas of resistance or support tend to have more trading activity and thus give you a better chance of getting your stop-loss orders filled. Your trailing stop follows the price higher as your position gains in value. As the position approaches the next area of resistance, you close the position at a profit.

That's a good trade. Not necessarily because you made a profit, but because you maintained control. If the trade had drifted aimlessly sideways, you would have exited with a small loss or would have broken even, particularly if volume waned. If the price moved south, your stop-loss order would have taken you out of the trade.

Goal one for new traders is to only make good trades. Too much emphasis on making money, especially from day one, is unrealistic. No one starts out at the top of his or her profession. It is usually a slow, steep climb to the top. A newbie day trader might set the goal of not being down more than 20 percent over the first quarter of trading.

Also remember, you must pay commissions on each transaction (a buy or a sell, two commissions per round turn, or a complete trade). Commissions draw down your equity the same as losses. Nevertheless, you must learn to accept them just as you would any other overhead in a business. No one wants to pay salaries or office rent or insurance, or buy expensive equipment, or hold inventory, etc. But one must if one is going to run a business. Trading is a business, and it has its overhead. I'll go into the expenses shortly in more detail because every business also needs budgets. You must know how to calculate your breakeven to plan how you transition to become a full-or part-time trader.

An initial goal of just making good trades is more realistic than setting a gross dollar amount. Keep in mind you must set goals that harness your psyche and emotional energies. Do this first and then go back to the monetary side later. The reason I say this is that your emotional side often colors how you set all other goals. For example, I like to exceed my financial goals. It means more to me to double my set goals, rather than get halfway to what is an unreachable goal. The end result can be the same, but it is what you are comfortable with and helps your trading that counts.

Let's say we had two traders expecting to make $200,000 a year in net trading profits. One performs better being under constant pressure; the other doesn't. Trader one sets a profit goal of $400,000. The other prefers to set modest goals and exceed them. So trader two sets a goal of $100,000. Both make $200,000 and are satisfied. When trader two reaches the goal of $100,000, he or she becomes more relaxed and trades better. Trader one, on the other hand, knows that not being under pressure will lead him or her to become careless and inattentive.

It is just a matter of creating the goals and routines that address your personality, especially your emotional makeup. A key issue is always discipline. I know one trader who does substantially better when he is being observed. He knows the rules of trading and will follow them if someone is there to police him. If he trades alone, he tries to bully the market by overpowering it with volume. For example, he'll try to create a mini bear market by showing large sell orders, so the other traders key off his orders and short with him. This can sometimes drive the market lower, and if he is trading large volume, he can take a small profit, a few pennies, and get out with a few hundred dollars' profit. But if he attempts this when the market is not just right, he takes large losses. Believe me, risking $5000 to make $500 is not the way to get rich in this business. When this trader is wrong, he gives back all he has won and more. Therefore, this trader should make it part of his plan never to trade alone.

Let me tell you another little tale of woe. I worked with another trader, let's call him Jackie, who traded great in the morning. Most days the markets open with a shot of volatility as overnight and early morning orders are fed into the systems. Volume continues to stay strong until just before noon in New York (EST). Then there is a slowdown until the traders set up for the close. Now Jackie did very well from the open until the morning lull, which begins anywhere from 10:30 to 11:00 a.m. He would be regularly up anywhere from a thousand to several thousand dollars. Then he gave it all back—up big by 10:00 but then break even or worse by 2:00 p.m.

I would tell Jackie, "Go home before noon. Find something to do. Lift weights (he was a body builder). Play golf. Pick your kids up from school. Study trading. Anything but trade!" Now those are strange words to hear from someone who works for your brokerage firm since it makes its money on trading volume. Nevertheless, I wanted him to succeed and trade for years, rather than months. Jackie wouldn't listen. Eventually, he got tired of hearing me harp on leaving early and began trading from home. Within a few months, he had lost all his risk capital and was back to his day job. If he had only written a rule prohibiting trading after noon in his plan and followed it, I believe he would be still trading and would be much wealthier than he is today.

That is only my opinion, and I have not followed his career since he closed his account. But my point is that we all have certain shortcomings that we must plan to control if we are going to succeed at trading. I, for example, have a propensity to hold on to trades too long. Then I find myself fighting to get out of a trade. If I would only sacrifice a few cents profit when a trade is heading into resistance, I'd be better off. To deal with this personality quirk, I force myself to always trade with a stop-loss order in place. Another trader I know does great analysis but does not always follow his own advice. My sin is overconfidence, and his is lack of confidence. If you are aware of your shortcomings, you have an opportunity to deal with them.

Before I leave this discussion of goal setting, let me outline some basic rules to follow that will make your goals more meaningful. Goals that are about improving performance, rather than static goals like making $1000 per day, seem to work better and have longer-lasting results. Therefore, set goals around the performance statistics you are going to maintain, which I'll discuss in detail in Chapter 9. For example, a goal might be to increase your win-to-loss trade ratio or reduce the average size of your losing trades. It is my understanding that performance-based goals are superior because they reinforce positive emotions, which have a stronger impact on future performance. You just feel better, have more pride in your trading, and have fewer negative feelings, such as anxiety, fear, lack of confidence, etc. All this will become clearer by the end of this book.

What are your deep secrets that will impair your trading? You may say that since you have not traded yet, you don't know. I don't buy that. You, like everyone else on the face of the earth, have characteristics that are part of your personality and that will become magnified when you begin to trade. You must be brutally honest with yourself from the very beginning and put your strongest characteristics on paper. By writing them down, you admit to them, which is the first step in dealing with them. If you do not deal with them now, it will be too late when you are in the heat of battle. Here are some questions you should consider:

- How greedy are you?

- Is your greed controllable?

- Do you become jealous when you see others succeed?

- Do you cheat on yourself or others?

- Are you overly aggressive?

- Can you control your temper?

- Do you believe you are always correct?

- Can you take advice from others?

- Must you always learn on your own?

- Is your self-image strong? Too strong?

- Do you believe deep down that trading is easy?

- How strong is your passion for the markets you trade?

- If someone in authority told you that you were not cut out to be a trader, would you listen to that person?

- How well do you handle unexpected emergencies?

- What would cause you to panic?

- Would losing a great deal of money break your spirits or your bank?

- What do you feel when you hear the words, "You have a big margin call, and it must be met by tomorrow"? Or someone calls to say your account is in debit!

- Do you think becoming a successful trader will make others love or appreciate you more?

I strongly recommend that before you open an active trading account, you ask yourself these types of questions and write down the answers. Then read them aloud. When you are completely satisfied with your answers, read them aloud to your spouse and mentor. Most importantly, heed the advice and reactions that you get from them.

The above questions deal with some of the worst things that might happen. If you prepare for the worst, you are seldom disappointed. I know from experience that delivering good news—"Hey, that trade you held overnight long gapped up 10 bucks on the open!"—is never very traumatic. It is the margin calls that I have had to make to my customers that were stressful for my clients and myself. It is easy to tell which ones never planned on anything adverse ever happening. Assuming you will begin to trade and live happily ever after is a bit unrealistic, to say the least.

Some of the questions above were trick questions. How would you answer the one about taking advice from others? This is one of the two-sided questions. First, there are two kinds of information you need. You need to learn an enormous amount of technical information on how the markets work, which ECN has the liquidity in the stock you are trading, or which software platform performs most efficiently. Then there is information you need to know about which stocks to trade or when to enter a trade, etc.

Trading is not a team sport. Think of it like golf, singles tennis, or fishing. You can only depend on yourself. You must accept all the blame and glory for every trade you make. If you pass the blame for a bad trade selection onto a fellow trader, you are lying to yourself. If you entered the trade in your account, it is your trade and no one else's. That said, you still must take advice from more experienced traders in the beginning. Naturally, using information gained from others about which ECN to use or listening to an explanation of the intricacies of electronic trading or the way orders are routed over the Internet takes nothing away from your accepting full responsibility for your trading. On the contrary, there is so much to learn about how these new markets work, it usually pays big dividends to attend a reputable school.

Advice on trading is another thing. You will definitely need some in the beginning. Trading advice is like guidance on walking on ice on a deep lake. If someone told you the ice was thick enough to walk on without going through, the first thing you would do is consider the source. If the kid telling you it's okay to go out on the ice was your best friend, you might give it a try. If it were someone else you didn't trust, you would be much more cautious. In other words, taking advice can be dangerous. No one wants to fall through the ice.

This is one of the strongest reasons to find a mentor you can trust. If Tiger Woods has a swing coach, why shouldn't you? You need someone to second-guess your plans and trading strategies, someone you trust to get straight answers from as you begin your trading career. For example, one typical question of newbie traders in stocks, commodities, or options is, Where should I begin trading? If you begin trading on a trading floor, you will find that many of the regulars trade securities you are completely unfamiliar with. The reason is the more experienced you become, the more volatile issues you will trade. These are often thinly traded securities that do not make CNN's headlines. If you try to emulate the experienced traders, you can get yourself in trouble fast. This is the kind of mistake a good mentor will help you avoid. If you specify in your written plan the securities or the type of securities you plan on trading, you can save yourself time and money.

In your written plan, include a list of the specifications of what you plan to trade. For example, a stock trader may say, "I'm going to trade Nasdaq stocks that are priced from $10 to $30 per share, with a daily trading volume of at least 500,000 shares that are in the hottest sectors." After reading this, your mentor may strongly recommend you start with stock with a higher daily volume, perhaps 1 million or even 5 million. The reason is that thinly traded stocks are easy to get into but not always easy to get out of. There is always someone willing to sell you a stock at the market, but sellers have a habit of driving the market lower. If you are a new trader and your initial objective is to make some good trades, you may have some problems with your selection. Besides the stock being thinly traded, you also selected the most volatile sectors. The combination of low trading volume and high volatility is a recipe for disaster for a new trader. Prices make large incremental moves, which are often difficult for even experienced traders to navigate.

Your mentor might suggest, depending on your past trading experience, that you begin trading on the New York Stock Exchange rather than the Nasdaq. The NYSE uses a specialist trading system, which is different from the market-maker system the Nasdaq uses. Specialists act as referees on the trading floor. They have broad authority to regulate the trading in the stocks they are responsible for. For example, they normally have an inventory of the stocks they manage, allowing them to add to liquidity when demand overpowers the market or to buy when supply weights down the market. They can halt trading mid-market or delay the opening. Their function is to maintain an orderly market. As we have seen in recent years, the NYSE has not been the model of decorum. Nevertheless, there are some old, widely traded issues that trade rather dependably, and your mentor might suggest you begin with them just to get some experience entering and exiting trades at a lower risk than you might face on the Nasdaq.

The Nasdaq is known for its volatility for a couple of reasons. First is the market-maker system. Market makers do exactly what their name suggests—they make markets. They are on both sides of the markets that they trade at the same time. For example, the market makers have a bid and an ask in the market for anyone who wants to sell to them at their bid and to buy from them at their ask price. That sounds like a specialist, but for every stock traded on the Nasdaq there are multiple market makers making a market in the same stock.

Now all these market makers are competing against one another and against all the traders, professional and amateur, who are actively trading. While there is only one specialist for each major stock on the NYSE, there are several market makers for each stock on the Nasdaq. Some of the market makers trade for themselves; some trade for clients; and most do both, thus the name broker-dealer. When they throw out a bid and ask into the market, an order size is included. Suppose, for example, Goldman Sachs is making a market in ABCD and is showing 1000 × 32.25 and 500 × 32.27. It will buy 1000 shares at \$32.25 and sell 500 shares at \$32.27. What this does not tell you is how many shares it really wants or needs to fill customer orders. GSCO may need to buy or sell 10,000 or more shares, meaning that it will keep working the market higher or lower to execute the order. Or it may only need to buy the 1000 shares showing and will exit the market or put out the next bid at a price that is below the market so it will not have to buy any more shares of ABCD.

The same is true for all the other market makers of ABCD or any other issues. In other words, the Nasdaq is a giant electronic poker game where you only see your own cards. Since there are no referees, as there are on the NYSE, there tends to be more volatility. You see much of this at the open. Market makers may get orders after or before market hours, even though there is some trading going at these times via ECNs. So during the first 15 minutes after the open, all these orders are entered into the market. Prices may gap up or down at this time. A good mentor will caution you, if you are a beginner, to avoid trading the open for this reason. It really is not indicative of anything but what happened overnight on foreign exchanges and any news released after yesterday's close. You should have a written statement in your plan that details how you will trade the open or that specifies that you will not trade the first 15 minutes after the open.

You will find a similar situation at the close, usually the second most volatile time of the trading session. Volatility begins an hour or so before the close. Traders are balancing portfolios to avoid taking any more risk home with them than they absolutely must. What will your plan say about the close? Will you be flat or carry some positions into the next session? If you do decide to hold overnight, what will your criteria be? Will you trade after hours?

Between the open and the close, breaking news usually is the catalyst for volatility. There are basically two kinds of news—preannounced and unannounced. The most common example of preannounced news is earnings releases. Earnings are made public quarterly, and you know years in advance when they will be made public for the stocks you trade. Meetings of the Federal Open Market Committee are another good example, as are financial reports on the state of the economy, e.g., employment, unemployment, GDP, CPI, consumer confidence, etc. On the commodity side of the aisle, the USDA alone makes over 300 monthly reports on the state of just about every commodity produced and traded in this country. Unannounced news is any unexpected story or rumor that sweeps through the trading community like a gentle breeze or a gale. News can additionally be classified as market-sector-, or issue-specific.

A variation on unannounced news is the quasi-unannounced event.

This is a market-moving event that the perpetrator attempts to keep secret from the market. Traders are usually tipped off when they notice a stock or a futures contract moving higher on high volume. In other words, someone in the trading community has insider information or suspects something clandestine is afoot. For example, a company with a history of splitting its stock has a particularly good quarter and its price is at or near new highs. That company calls an unscheduled board meeting. Some astute traders smell another split, which usually means a bull rally, and begin to accumulate positions early. If an individual in this case were considered an insider, using this information would be illegal in the United States. This type of event, as was discussed previously, is even more common in the futures market because there is not the traditional concept of insider information. For example, one of the major grain companies discovers an impending shortage of corn due to a weather pattern over the Midwest and begins accumulating long positions.

Therefore, in your plan you need to address these concerns. You must decide what entities you are going to begin trading, what information sources you will rely on, and which strategies best suit your time, temperament, training, ability, and pocketbook. How do you plan to progress up the trading food chain? In later chapters, I'll provide some insights and suggestions on sources you should review to complete this portion of your plan. All I am doing here is calling your attention to some of the areas that must be covered in your written plan.

Money management is also a vital section in any plan. The first consideration, if you are hoping to become a full-time trader, is how are you going to support yourself during the transition period, which could last 6 or more months? If you have family responsibilities, you should additionally have in place the basic financial foundation to meet them. This means life insurance, a retirement plan, and a nest egg for emergencies. Those with young children must also be concerned with future educational expense. And every person or family needs food, shelter, transportation, and a sense of security. All these needs must be addressed in your plan, and you need to include what your backup plan will be if trading does not work out. Remember our sniper friend never took a position without having multiple avenues of retreat.

There is an age-old adage in the financial community which states: "Scared money never wins!" I sincerely believe this axiom as it pertains to trading and all aspects of life. In sports you refer to it as choking or pressing too hard, when a player has to make a play to win and doesn't. The individual tries too hard or has too much pressure on him or her to do something perfectly. I have seen the same condition in traders who are not sufficiently financed, either in the long term or in the short term. If you cannot comfortably afford to lose your entire risk capital or you cannot afford to exit a losing position for whatever reason, you should not be trading. With some people, it is more psychological than monetary. They cannot reconcile themselves to the fact that they did something stupid, that they selected a bad trade, or that their analysis was faulty. The result is the same—too much pressure forcing the person to hold on to losers.

Therefore, part of your written plan must contain your acknowledgment that you could conceivably lose all the money and more that you put into your trading account. Let this be a wake-up call to your spouse when you read your plan aloud to him or her. Don't gloss over or sugarcoat this reality. I have seen hundreds of traders open accounts, only to watch them close these trading accounts 2, 3, or 6 months later after a series of margin calls totally emptied the account. Welcome to the real world. I hope it never happens to you, but it could, just as you can have a serious drawdown in a mutual fund, real estate venture, or new business startup. My point is to acknowledge the possibility up front and in writing. Somehow it sinks into your psyche deeper and becomes more real when you put it on paper. If it is any consolation, my life experiences have taught me that if you prepare for the worse to it usually doesn't happen. It's when you don't prepare, you get taken to the cleaners.

Just like an operational plan for a brick and mortar business, one of the most important functions of your plan is to help you determine the feasibility of trading for profit. If you prepare your plan well, you will have every contingency covered. Plus you will have a tool that will allow you to make a very rational decision about your future.

A big part of your plan should be a budget. What expenses should you prepare for? How much might it cost to become a full- or part-time trader? As referred to earlier, you must plan for at least 6 months without any appreciable income. Next on the list is risk capital—how much is enough? If you are going to be a day trader or what the security regulators refer to as a pattern day trader, you must maintain $25,000 in your account at all times, as mentioned in Chapter 1.

What is sometimes overlooked is that you must budget for the commission you will pay each time one of your orders is filled. You can lose all your trading equity by overtrading just as easily as if all you picked were losing trades. Very active traders can do 100 trades a day and more. Newbies can easily execute 10 or 20 trades a day. Brokerage commissions have dropped substantially in the last decade, but they are still there, ranging from a cent or 2 per share to between $5 and $15 per transaction (one side of a trade). Someone must pay the clearing firms, which match up the tens of millions of trades executed each day in all the markets. Someone must sell you the entity you buy or buy whatever you sell. Ownership of the stock representing all the buying and selling must be matched and balanced. Then there is all the accounting that must be done so your account is ready to trade the next day. There is a lot of expensive work to be done overnight. It makes the job of Federal Express look simple.

There are other fees besides commissions you must include in your budget. One that can be a real surprise is the ECN fees, which can range from a quarter of a cent per share to over 1 cent per share. If you trade Nasdaq stocks heavily via ECNs, you can get hit for some stiff charges each month. Always ask about these fees when you first go shopping for a broker. You will also be hit by the SROs (or self-regulatory organizations), i.e., the New York Stock Exchange, NASD, NFA, etc. These tend to be minor. And interest on the money borrowed from your broker—the margin money—can add up, depending on how long you hold positions. One nice thing about being a pure day trader is that you are not charged for positions that are bought on margin but not held overnight.

In your budget, you'd also need to account for your tools, bandwidth, office space, Internet service provider connections, and any other support equipment necessary. The software needed to trade is usually available for $200 per month or less. It is usually free if you execute 25 to 50 trades a month. If you trade on a trading floor provided by a brokerage firm, you may have to pay a seat fee. That might run $500 per month and would provide a desk, computer, multiple monitors, high-speed Internet connectivity, and news wires. All or part of this may be rebated based on your trading activity. If you trade at home, you would still need to account for your Internet provider and connectivity. I would also recommend anyone trading from home or a private office to have a cellular phone available just in case power is lost and you need to call your broker's trade desk to go flat and cancel any open orders until power is restored. If you trade remotely, also budget the actual costs of your Internet connection (cable, DSL, etc.) and Internet service provider, or at least $100 per month.

Perhaps the most important budgeting may be personal or family expenses. What will it cost you in living expenses if you plan to trade full time. You should budget for a minimum of 3 months without any profit.

Six months might be even more realistic. The worst case is you trade for several months, lose money, and give up. You must support yourself until you get a job and your first paycheck. At the same time, you may have lost $5000, $10,000, $20,000, or more trading. This is the reality of the professional trader. Ask yourself, can I, or do I want to, trade part time first? Can I get a leave of absence from my job for a few months to try it?

Your trading profits must exceed your expenses. For example, if your cost per share for brokerage, ECN, and SRO fees is just 2 cents per share and you executed 5 round-turn trades per day of 1000-share lots, you would generate $44,000 in commissions if you traded 220 days in a given year. If half your trades are losers and you lose an average of 5 cents, or $50, on each 1000-share-lot trade, your losses would be $27,500 per year on 5 trades a day over 220 days a year. Therefore, you would need $71,500 in profits to break even before paying living expenses and any loss of trading equity. This may sound steep, but I know many franchise fees that are as high before all the overhead and equipment are paid for. To make that much from trading means the other half of your trades of your 1100 trades must pay all your bills. To just cover your out-of-pocket trading expenses, the winning trades must average $0.13 per share. Having a win-to-loss ratio of over 2:1 and batting 500 on your trading the first year is not bad. As a matter of fact, it would be exceptional.

Create an equation like this on an electronic spreadsheet and run several variations. Get a feel for what you would actually have to do to break even and reach the reward level that would satisfy you and repay you for the sacrifices you and your family will have to make.

The numbers above are just to give you some figures to work with as you develop your own profit and loss proforma and to act as a reality check. Success in trading rarely comes in a steady fashion. You will learn it is more feast or famine. By that I mean you will make your month on one or two days' trading. The market will get hot, and you will be in the right place at the right time. This is what makes money management so very critical. Think of trading as fly-fishing. You spend hours and hours waist-deep in cold water making one cast after the other. You get tired, cold, uncomfortable, and frustrated. Then there is a hit. Adrenalin flows. The fish does everything in its power to get away. You finally land a trophy trout. It is all worth it. The risk, of course, is doing something stupid and drowning as you wait to hook the big one that belongs over your fireplace.

How can you reduce the time line and cost of learning how to trade?

I would sincerely recommend attending a trading school like the one I am associated with, i.e., the Market Wise Trading School. Keep in mind that there is only one way to learn to trade and that is by actually trading. There is no substitute. What a good school will do is substantially increase your learning curve. It will provide you with a lot of good information and share with you the insights of veteran traders so you can avoid some of the most common pitfalls.

Let me give you a few examples of what you should expect to take away from class at a respectable trading school:

1. Active traders must understand and practice safe money management. What are some of the options? What tips and tricks have experienced traders developed? How do you evaluate and select a dependable money management system?

2. Active traders cannot succeed without liquidity. They must have a willing buyer for every sell order and a willing seller for every buy order. Finding where the liquidity is for the specific stock or commodity they plan to trade is fundamental. Which exchange? Which ECN? What type of orders are accepted? What is the most effective and cost-efficient routing? Where is the liquidity before or after normal trading hours?

3. Active traders must have fast, dependable order execution. Which software platform is best? Which Internet provider? What connectivity options are the fastest and most reliable? What hardware is needed?

4. Active traders must know how the electronic markets work from the inside out. How do you trade to avoid MIC (market impact costs) due to poor fills, order delays, slippage, etc.?

5. Active traders need to know all the players and their vested interests. How do you to avoid paying for order flow? How do you read what each key player is really doing? How do you avoid or take advantage of bull or bear traps?

6. Active traders function as their own order desk and must understand the intricacies of order routing. Which of the several order routes available will be most effective? What types of orders are accepted, and which one is most appropriate depending on market conditions?

7. Active traders must primarily depend upon themselves to do research and select trades. What web sites are most reliable? Which

are not reliable? Which ones deliver the news fastest? Which provide good, sound, tradable information? What software scans sectors, stocks, or commodities best? What sites or software should be used to alert you to tradable ideas?

8. Active traders must understand and use technical analysis. What is the best way to get educated? What are the best sources for continuing education and daily insights?

9. Active traders must choose one or more trading strategies. How do you do this? Where do you get ideas, insights, or training?

10. Active traders must have a working knowledge of telecommunications, Internet connectivity, and computer hardware and software if they plan to trade somewhere other than a professional trading floor.

These are just a few of the skills and just some of the background information you need to begin a career as an active trader. A good trading school can supply much of this, and it can point you to where you can find more. Always keep in mind two things. First, anything you read in a book is dated. If I or someone else recommends anything, check it out to see if it is still as good as it once was. Second, trading is a very personal, individual enterprise. Everything you read and learn must be modified and adapted to your specific trading persona.

That is why you must have a section in your written plan regarding how you are going to educate and constantly reeducate yourself. Learning how to trade is a journey, not a destination. The markets are evolving—they are always in flux. Trading is like navigating the Mississippi River. It clearly flows from north to south. It is wide and is even visible from space. Anyone would think you float down it without a care. But if you try to pilot a riverboat from St. Louis to New Orleans, you better know where all the sandbars are and how they continually shift—or you will find your boat, crew, passengers, and cargo hung up on one of them.

Guidelines for a Written Plan

Trading Philosophy and Psychology Section

> As a trader . . .
> - What will I be attempting to accomplish?
> - Why do I want to trade?
> - What within me makes me want to trade?
> - What is my single most important material goal I expect to accomplish?
> - What is my single most important psychological goal?
> - Are these goals compatible?
> - What are my weaknesses and how will I deal with them?

Educational Section
- Where is my knowledge weak?
  - General understanding of how markets work?
  - Trading skills? Analysis? Selection of entity to trade?
  - Trading software, connectivity, Internet, etc.?
  - Psychology of trading, self, etc?

Discipline Section
- How am I going to stay on track and stay the course?
  - Trading rules that specifically apply to me?
  - Selection of mentor, attitude coach, etc.?

Tracking Section
- How will I evaluate myself?
  - Trading log, journal?
  - Statistics to track, analysis, etc.?

Money Management Section
- What are my budgets? Personal? Trading? Etc.?
  - Can I afford to start as a full-time trader?
  - What are my loss limits per trade, day, week, etc.?

Your trading plan must be all-inclusive. It describes every aspect of your life and being—personal, social, work, trading, financial, psychological, and even recreational. You must answer all the key questions: How, when, where, what, and, most importantly, why.

6

DEVELOPING AND PERFECTING YOUR TRADING SHTICK

In my youth I lived in Ohio on the shores of Lake Erie, one of the Great Lakes. Boating—on the open water or on ice—was king. Everyone and his brother had some sort of sail or power craft. One would imagine sailing on a lake to be a safe sport, but I learned differently.

More ships and boats have sunk in Lake Erie than have gone down in the famous, or infamous, Bermuda Triangle. The reason is simple. The lake is very shallow compared with the size of the surface area. When a squall blows up, you can be caught in waves that are 6 feet and higher in a matter of minutes. I was once caught in such a predicament as a teenager. Three classmates and I had taken a 12-foot Chris Craft run-about to Cedar Point to enjoy the beach and the mermaids. We were heading home about dusk. As we entered Sandusky Bay, the winds picked up and it began to rain. Minutes later we were engulfed in waves ranging in height from 3 to 6 feet. The 25-horsepower Johnson outboard motor could barely make headway. Our small boat was tossed around like a bobber at the end of a fishing line. Eventually this very shaken quartet reached shore. We could have just as easily become one of the members of the Lost Souls Club of Lake Erie.

Years later, I was again on the water. This time it was on a man-of-war in the North Atlantic. A very similar storm blew up out of nowhere, but no one took notice. The difference was that the size and depth of the ocean allowed it to absorb the storm's energy, and the ship's tonnage gave it stability in heavy weather.

The moral of this tale is that you must pay as much attention to where you are trading as you do to where you are sailing. If you are trading a blue-chip security, let's say IBM whose daily volume is in the millions of shares, you are in an ocean. If you decide to trade a stock like MROI (MRO Software) with daily volumes of less than a half million shares or a thinly traded futures contract, let's say O (oats), you are in a lake or just a pond. And shallow-water markets can become extremely volatile faster than most new traders can react, making them very dangerous.

The challenge of trading in lakes is volatility and liquidity. One or two large orders can become a white squall that has enough energy to capsize your account. For example, you can watch a sparsely traded security for a week or two. You notice a pattern that you think you can take advantage of. You jump in and make a few successful trades. This is not unlike how my gang got into trouble on Lake Erie. We had successfully run over to Cedar Point on many occasions without mishap. We thought nothing of it. Then out of nowhere we were surrounded by white-caps, with our lives on the line.

Thinly traded securities must be entered with care. The odd thing about them is that you can almost always get into these markets, but you cannot always get out. There are always sellers, but there are not always buyers—at least not at the price you want to, or have to, exit to keep from drowning in red ink. Someone is always willing to sell you the entity, but your offer may go begging for hours. Between high volatility and low liquidity, the thinly traded markets should be avoided until you become trained and have developed substantial experience as a trader.

To our parents' credit, they insisted that all of us take a course in the handling and safety of powerboats (education). Additionally, we were not permitted to take the boat out alone until we had spent many hours in it under close supervision of an experienced boat handler (mentor). Life-jackets were a must (stop-loss order). The training and precautions saved our lives. When I first began trading futures, I had that same feeling of helplessness when I plunged recklessly into a thinly traded lumber contract. Luckily, my mentor was there to bail me out before I took on too much water or ran aground on shallow liquidity.

When you begin trading, particularly if you are on a public trading floor, you will see the floor "leaders" popping in and out of very thinly traded stocks. I strongly caution new traders against this. Many a novice has been blown out of the market attempting to mimic the style of these more experienced traders during the first weeks of trading. Instead, work at your own speed. In the Marines, Sergeant Ross used to say, "Never grab a hold of anything you can't let go of!" This is particularly true in trading, because there are stocks and futures contracts you can't always sell easily. Some mentors will want you to begin trading New York Stock Exchange issues or the major grains on the futures markets. The reason for the NYSE, of course, is the size of the float of these stocks and the specialist system. The grains, particularly corn and soybeans, tend to have sufficient trading volume, and so entering and exiting trades is normally not a problem and the size of the contracts is not prohibitive. Nevertheless, you will have to deal with volatility with any futures contract and the possibility of limit-up/-down trading sessions. You might consider beginning when the grains are seasonally not so volatile.

GET A SHTICK

Another consideration regarding market perspective is your "shtick." You know what a shtick is. It's a comedian's or actor's unique style or routine. For example, George Burns always played the straight man to Gracie Allen. Lucy constantly got herself into trouble. Jackie Gleason was "The Great One." Rodney Dangerfield never got any respect. Tom Cruise plays the troubled hero. No one gets more out of pomposity than Frasier, and we all wait up late for Dave Letterman's Top Ten List. How will you approach the market? What will your shtick be?

A few years back, I was representing some commodity trading advisers (CTAs). Before I took anyone on, I spent a considerable amount of time conducting an in-depth evaluation—due diligence—of the person's trading style and organization. I did not want to recommend any CTA to my clients that I did not believe in and whose trading style I did not totally understand. (In the process, I collected enough information for a book, *Winning with Managed Futures: How to Select Top Performing Commodity Trading Advisors.*)

One thing became clear to me as I studied these successful CTAs. They each had a unique approach to the market that they relied on. And they did not vary from it. For example, one CTA I represented had been a computer programmer for NASA before entering the futures market. He wrote programs that predicted when and which asteroids might hit the earth. His programs had to take hundreds of random variables into consideration and predict the most logical outcome. He put this experience into predicting the futures market. Another had been a classical musician and composer before entering the trading arena. His mind grasped the ever-changing, yet repetitious, nature of the futures price activity. When I read Jack Schwager's three books on market wizards, I noticed that the people he chose to interview for his books also had a unique approach to the markets they traded. Two of Schwager's books are primarily on commodity traders, and the third is on stock pickers. You would do well to read them as you develop your own style.

The first step in your development, in my opinion, is to become a specialist—an expert in one aspect of trading—or at least plan to learn one aspect at a time. In this chapter, I am going to discuss one specific trading strategy or approach to the markets that utilizes moving averages. There are many, many more—thousands. I dare say there are as many as there are successful traders. New traders usually borrow a strategy from a veteran trader and in time develop their own as they become more experienced and competent. Or you can begin with an area, a stock sector for example, you currently have expertise in and expand on it

For example, one student I came to know at the Market Wise Trading School had traded a group of 10 to 15 blue-chip stocks. The person had watched and traded the same stocks for years, make that decades. Upon retirement, he wanted to become a more active trader. Thus he attended our trading school. Once he graduated, he began day- and swing-trading the stocks he had been investing in and holding for months and years previously. At the time, it worked very well for him since these stocks were trading nicely in a 5- to 10-point channel. He bought when they bounced off the bottom trendline and sold as they approached the upper one. The beauty of this approach is that it gave him time to become technically competent and experiment with other strategies and software trading platforms until he was ready to sail into uncharted waters. I think it is critical to begin with a single strategy, perfect it, and then move on to others. Never be in a hurry to get rich trading and always remember . . .

A BUS LEAVES EVERY 15 MINUTES

If you miss a trading opportunity at 8:15, another will be coming down the pike by 8:30. If you want to learn to scalp or swing-trade, or milk stock splits, earnings plays, IPOs, futures unbalances, option spreads, or whatever, write down those strategies in your trading plan. Put them in order of priority. Which is most important to you? Which is easiest to learn? Which is most in tune with the complexion of the current market? Which will get you making money the fastest? Then go after them one at a time. Focus on developing a whole bag of profitable plays.

Think for a second how the professional golfer differs from the happy hacker at the driving range. The pro takes multiple buckets of practice balls and one club to his practice session. The pro hits bucket after bucket until he becomes expert in a single club. The distance the pro can hit with that club must be uniform to within a meter each time. The pro must be able to curve the ball to the left and right at various degrees. He must be able to hit it well with a low and high arc, off uphill and downhill lies, out of traps and roughs, etc.

The weekend duffer picks up multiple clubs, usually the whole bag, and one bucket of balls for his practice session. He hits a few five irons. Then he hits a few drives, followed by a slew of short irons. He perfects none of his shots. The amateur never leaves the flat, well-manicured range area. Is it any wonder the pro shoots scratch or better and the amateur has an 18 handicap?

Hackers in the professional trading world are known as losers. Losers of respect. Losers of confidence. Losers of money. The saddest part of this analogy is that there is just a very thin line between the winners and the losers in golf or trading. Jack Nicklaus, in one of his best years, had an average score for tour events only four strokes better than the average pro making the cut that year. When he lost a tournament, he was often at the back of the pack. When he won, he set records. Remember the little girl with the curl down the middle of her forehead? When she was good, she was very, very good. When she was bad, she was horrid! You will find the same pattern with trading. When a trader makes money, he or she usually makes BIG money. I call it a wide spot in the road to success. The key to trading is surviving between tournament wins—in other words, not blowing out when your "A" game does not show up. This is another big reason to develop patience and discipline if they are not part of your nature.

All it takes for the trader to be a big winner is a little more education. A little more passion. A little more mentoring. A little more discipline. A little more money management. And a lot more patience and planning. In other words, a *lot*. Trading professionally for a living is almost as tough as making and staying on the PGA tour. But a lot of people become scratch golfers, and a lot of traders do pretty well without turning pro.

Let's get back to what it means to specialize. You can become an expert in a particular stock or stock sector or in a particular commodity or commodity complex, or you can master a trading technique or even a single chart pattern. For example, Linda Bradford Raschke, who was written up by Jack Schwager in *Market Wizards* and is coauthor of *Street Smarts*, has said in some of the public appearances she has made that if a trader only can master bull flags, he or she can made a good living trading. Linda has been a successful S&P futures trader for over 20 years. She knows of what she speaks.

I know another trader that does well just trading a single stock, AMAT (Applied Materials). He usually only trades the first hour or two after the open and knows how that issue responds to the premarket trend of the Nasdaq futures before the open, the trend of the Nasdaq itself once the market opens, and the behavior of the stock after the first 15 minutes of trading. His day and profit objectives are often met by 9:00 or 10:00 a.m. How's that for a life?

What some specialists look for is called a setup. This can be a set of circumstances or a technical signal that indicates with a high degree of reliability what a stock or commodity may do next. The key phrase is "with a high degree of reliability." It is at this point that money management protects the trader's equity. When I mention money management in this context, I think specifically of protective stops (real or mental), risk versus reward, size of positions, and time in the market. Remember, the only aspects of the markets you have absolute control over are on which side of the market you enter a trade (long or short), what the size of your position is, when you enter the market, and how long you stay in the trade. Everything else is totally out of your control. Therefore, all your focus must be on those elements.

The best way to explain the concepts of control and specialization is to review a few examples. I'll cover a simple strategy that has worked for those new to active trading. To even touch on all the possibilities is impossible. As I am sure you recall from Chapter 3, literally hundreds of technical studies can be used to trade successfully. A trader developed each, and it became his or her shtick. At some point the trader or an associate wanted some publicity and published a book or started giving seminars. In other words, you have access to plenty of possible trading signals generating strategies to adapt as your own. Plus hundreds of web sites offer ideas. My advice is to start simply until you have mastered the software you will be using and you are absolutely sure how orders are routed electronically. I don't get into order routing in this book because order routing is changing so quickly. By the time you would read about it here, it would be different. Get it off the WWW or at a trading school.

From our previous discussion of technical analysis, you know it deals with history, even if the chart you are looking at is only a moment old. Additionally, to accept technical analysis you must be prepared to live by two other axioms. First is an old law of physics you learn in high school. A body remains in motion until another force influences that motion. In other words, a trend—be it up, down, or sideways—continues trending in the direction it is going until something, often news, causes it to change direction. The reason for this is simple. I call it the lemming reflex in humans. When dealing with the unknown, humans tend to herd together. In the markets, the great unknown is what will the price of a certain security be 5 minutes, 5 hours, 5 days, 5 months, or 5 years from now? Therefore, if a stock or commodity is trending up, the majority of the crowd of traders interested in it will continue to buy. The greater fool theory prevails as each buyer looks for a greater fool to sell to at a profit. King Greed rules the pits.

At some point, more news seeps into the market that scares some traders. It is time for fear to move to center stage. This news may not be known to the entire trading community. Or the entity being traded just gets too expensive, or the influential advisers convince the crowd it is too expensive. It could be stocks with no earnings trading at $200 or $300 a share. Did you hold Enron at its highs? A lot of folks did. Or pork bellies when they soared to $1 per pound? Sugar over 45¢ per pound, or when crude oil was over $25 per barrel? Looking back at these prices, we are dumbfounded to think we would not have seen a bubble was about to burst.

Trading is all in the timing. Who wanted to be left out of a very good thing and stop buying Amazon at just $100 per share? Almost no one! When greed dominates the market, we are all too human. Of course, greed is usually followed by fear. That trader who uncovers some negative news regarding the stock making new highs begins selling. At first, it is called profit taking. Pretty soon we all know the bubble has burst, and it looks like pandemonium in the pits.

It is these abnormal swings that technical analysis is supposed to alert you to and protect you from. And in my opinion, it can—if you stay rational. Nothing can help you if you give in to greed and fear. When a high is peaking, the trading volume can be your guide. It will give you a sign to exit. But it does not mean volume will not pick up again after a top and the entity will go to even higher highs. That happens, but it can just as easily crash. As noted earlier, you can get rich selling too soon. But you can't by selling too late. Let technical analysis rule your normal instincts of greed and fear. Remember, human beings create the price patterns you see on the charts.

Now I would like to give you a brief description of a professional trader's shtick. First I must apologize to Brian Shannon, a professional trader and instructor of technical analysis at the Market Wise Trading School for oversimplifying his approach to the market. As with any trading approach, many subtle aspects go by virtually unnoticed. My objective is to offer a simple overview of one of the ways Brian trades to illustrate how it can be done simply and efficiently. Keep in mind, it is only an overview of one of the many strategies Brian has learned and used over years of trading. Brian's approach to the market changes as the market does. As you become more experienced, you will see many of the strategies you initially learned become obsolete. The market is like the ocean, always changing while always being the same. Your "old" setups are replaced by new ones as you and the markets evolve.

TRADING IS A LONG, ARDUOUS JOURNEY

Here is a concrete example of how fast a trading strategy can vanish from the trading floors. When I first became involved in day-trading stocks about 5 years ago, one of the most popular and reliable strategies was called "following the ax"—the ax being the dominant market maker for a specific Nasdaq stock. It might have been Bear Stearns or Merrill Lynch manhandling Cisco, for example. When you saw the ax on the bid, you joined the bid and let the ax run the stock up a quarter point, a half point, or more. Traders would often join the ax by SOESing it for 1000 shares. SOES is basically Nasdaq's ECN and stands for Small Order Execution

System. Market makers were obligated by exchange rules to honor the first SOES order received. They could not "back away." It was common knowledge among the pros who the axes were for all the active issues. You could always check one of Nasdaq's web sites for a list of the major market makers by share volume for whatever stock you are interested in trading.

The ax was often trying to buy (or sell) a large amount of shares for a customer. For example, the ax might need 50,000 shares to fill an institutional order, say a retirement or mutual fund. The ax would sit on the bid as long as needed to get the order filled. The client might give the ax as much as $2 (plus or minus) discretion in price, which would give the ax some wiggle room. If too many traders hit the ax, it might back off for a while or even join the offer, but not at the inside bid. Sooner or later, it would be back on the bid moving the stock higher. It was a great cat and mouse game to match wits with the ax by reading the Level 2 quotation screen and the buy-sell tape. The objective was to piggyback the bid for a $500 or more gross profit on 1000 shares.

Following the ax has gone the way of the once famous SOES bandits, the boys who put electronic day trading on everyone's radar screen. The culprits that did away with the following-the-ax trading strategy were revisions in the SOES rules in favor of the market makers and decimalization. New SOES rules set up tiers of stocks, which reduced the number of shares a market maker must buy or sell on a SOES order. Therefore, a trader could not always SOES for a thousand shares. Decimalization substantially reduced the amount a market maker must increase the bid to stay on top of the inside market, thus offering the best price. The market maker now only has to go up a penny to stay on top, whereas previously it was a sixteenth ($0.0625) or, more commonly, an eighth ($0.125). Multiply these fractions by 1000 shares and you get $62.50 and $125, respectively. The financial incentive is no longer there for day traders since the market makers can head-fake the trades more easily, with less financial risk, by moving their bid or ask up or down a penny at a time.

It is for these and other reasons I'll mention as we go along that I strongly recommend you begin your trading with a mentor at your side. Look to the mentor to fill you in on how the markets you trade are in flux before your very eyes and how you must adapt.

Now let's get back to Brian's trading shtick. First of all, he carries around a list of stocks of interest to him at the moment, called a watch list. This is a list of securities that match a criterion he has devised for himself that will offer him multiple trade opportunities every day on either the long or short side of the market. He carries this list on his person whenever he is not trading. It is attached to his money clip. My point is that you cannot underestimate the value of developing a good watch list of your own. To Brian it is just as much money as the actual greenbacks in the clip.

When you first begin, what are you going to use for your watch list? More importantly, what will your selection criteria be? This is an area that you may need some professional assistance developing. The criteria will vary depending on the complexion of the market you will be trading and your experience level. For example, Brian has many years of trading behind him. He is at his trading station an hour before the market opens, all through the daily sessions, and for another hour or so after—every trading day. That's 220 or so days a year. He trades a lot of stocks that are way too lightly traded for my taste and experience. But he has the skill to handle these skinny minis. Because these stocks have low daily volumes, they tend to be volatile, as we have discussed earlier. Volatility leads to opportunity, but the flip side of the opportunity coin is risk.

Therefore you must devote much thought to the selection of the stocks or futures contracts you put on your watch list. With futures, it is not as difficult because there are considerably fewer choices than with stocks. To begin with, I would recommend only trading on exchanges in the United States. It is not patriotism, but liquidity, that prompts this remark. Plus you get some regulatory protection from the Commodity Futures Trading Commission and the National Futures Association. Second, there are fewer sectors or complexes to evaluate. Here is a brief summary of your choices:

- *The grains complex.* Corn, oats, soybeans, soybean oil, soybean meal, and wheat

- *The meat complex.* Live cattle, lean hogs, pork bellies, and feeder cattle

- *The food and fiber complex.* Coffee, cocoa, sugar, FCOJ (frozen concentrated orange juice), cotton, and lumber

- *The energy complex.* Crude oil, heating oil, gasoline, natural gas, propane, and electricity

- *The metal's complex.* Gold, silver, palladium, platinum, aluminum, and copper

- *The financial complex.* Currencies, bonds, single stock futures, and the major and mini stock and futures indexes

Trading interest in futures tends to move from trading pit to pit depending on volume, volatility, and seasonality. Some pits, like the bonds or the S&P, are always full and humming. Others, oats or lumber for example, can slow down substantially at times. There is a more predictable seasonality to futures than stocks, in my opinion. The reason is simply that the tug-of-war between supply and demand is more real because many of the futures contracts represent real commodities that can only be produced at certain times of the year and used for human and animal consumption, directly or indirectly. If the world is low on food, it gets all our attention, not to mention if there is a shortage or surplus of chocolate or coffee. On the demand side of the equation, physical commodities are required, regardless of the cost, at certain times of the year, heating oil being an example.

My recommendation for beginning futures traders is to trade short term, use technical analysis, and start with a very liquid contract that has, at the time you begin, a relatively low volatility. Grains or metals might be a good place to start. Once you hone your skills, you progress to the more volatility-prone, higher risk-reward sectors, such as bonds, stock indexes, currencies, etc.

Stock pickers have a much broader menu to select from. You can find approximately a hundred sectors tracked by *Investor's Business Daily.* Studying the various rankings of the sectors and stocks in *IBD* is a good starting place.

Another possibility is starting with stock you are familiar with from your days as an investor. Earlier we discussed a trader who began day- and swing-trading a list of stocks he had held and traded long term before he retired. It worked for this specific trader because he was very analytical and disciplined, but this strategy has a fatal flaw. All too many traders who have traded stocks they knew well were emotionally attached to them. This is a distinct handicap. Short-term trading must be coldly rational.

Losing positions—and more importantly positions that appear to be losing—must be eliminated. Notice the emphasis on positions that *appear* to be losing. The reason for this is that you never know what the market is going to do next. Or what piece of news or rumor will hit the pits to accelerate the movement of the current trend. Your first concern must be survival. Trade with stop-loss orders in place at all times. If they are hit,

you are out. You may get whipsawed, but that is part of the game. If you
are emotionally attached to a certain stock, when it is apparently losing,
you will have the inclination to hold instead of fold. Sooner or later, this
will cost you dearly.

It is very common for professional traders to have memorized a list
of a hundred or more stock symbols and never have a clue to what the
full names of half of them are or what the companies behind the symbols
do. Trading by symbol only is a good way of keeping professional de-
tachment. I have run into the same problem with commodity traders. Try
to get a corn farmer to cut loose of a losing long corn contract when his
own fields are being decimated by a drought but while the worldwide
crop is setting records. Sometimes we just can't see over our psychological fences.

How should a new short-term trader approach the question of selecting stocks for his or her watch list? One answer could be recommenda-
tions of professional analysts, but as I noted in the introduction, the
amount of financial information on the Internet will, in time, render professional stock analysts obsolete, not to mention the conflicts of interest
and scandals they don't seem to be able to transcend. A better answer is
filters. A filter is simply a tool to sort stocks or scan trading activity to
locate special circumstances. If you go to www.google.com and search
for "stock filters," you will find a list of more sites than you will ever
need. The hard part for the new trader is to determine the most meaningful
criteria to sort by. That comes with experience. Here are a few examples
of common criteria:

- *Price levels.* Stocks trading at or less than $25 per share
- *Volatility.* Stocks whose volatility increased 20 percent or more in
  the last 5 trading days
- *Volume.* Stocks whose daily volume averages over 1 million shares
  per day and is above the daily average by 10 percent or more
- *Sectors.* Stocks by sector with high volatility and fastest-growing
  volume, etc.
- *Value indicators.* Highest price-to-earnings ratio, etc.

You decide what kind of stock you think you want to begin trading.
A stock that trades over a million shares per day generally has enough
volume that you will not have problems exiting when you want or have

to. The next selection criterion might be price. You should begin trading small quantities, say 100 shares. As you become more skilled and experienced, you will move up to 1000 for day and swing trades. Therefore, you will scan for price at a level where you can trade 1000 shares and not be risking an inordinate percentage of your equity on any one trade.

If you have a trading account with $30,000 ($120,000 in buying power with a day trading margin) in equity and you will eventually trade 1000-share lots, what will your maximum stop loss have to be? Here you have to make some rough estimates, which will become easier to calculate as you become more experienced and begin to places stops below areas of support or above resistance, depending on if you are long or short. A stop loss that is 10 percent below a $30 stock on a short-term trade amounts to $3, which is on the high side of a risk-reward ratio. If your risk-reward ratio is 1:2 or 1:3, you would be risking $3 to make $6 or $9, respectively. While this risk-reward ratio is in line, the chances of catching a $6 or $9 move is not likely on a daily basis, except in very volatile times. More commonly, the stop would be set at less than a dollar.

But setting the stop and taking profits is more a function of where support and resistance is, as we will see shortly. It is common for experienced traders to set multiple risk-reward targets. For example, on a long trade the first reward level might be at the first resistance level. If the price sails through it on strong volume, the trader would hold out for at least the second resistance level. And for the third, if price action and volume were steady as the second one was reached. The greater the reward, the more heat you will take on a trade. Therefore, let's say our criterion is stocks trading for no more than $30 per share.

Volatility would be the next criterion. Should you start with low, medium, or high volatility? Again, this goes back to experience. If this is day one of your trading career, you might go with a calm stock as you work out the mechanics of the trading platform you are using and gain confidence in reading the tape or Level 2 market-maker screen. Most important is the pressure of trading real money, your real money! That takes some real getting used to.

The filtering tool will ask over what time frame you wish to search. For the short-term trader, the last 45 to 60 trading days is a good length of time to filter for price, volume, and volatility. Additionally, you would specify which exchange to scan, the Nasdaq being the most likely, and you could additionally narrow the search to a sector you are familiar with. The choice of sector varies depending on economic and political conditions.

Keep in mind, this is a trial-and-error process. You rarely get a list of acceptable candidates on the first try. Additionally, this is not a new tool. When you visit the web sites originally generated by your search on Google.com, you will find a plethora of ideas of what others have already developed. One very popular site to visit is Tony Oz.com. Tony is known for his filters, which he calls scans, and you may well decide to test a few on that site. Here is a description of a few of his most popular scans.

- *10-1/2 Weeks*. It searches for stocks that are on the move higher and isolates candidates that are making new 53-day highs with accompanying volume increases.

- *The Gapper*. Here Tony Oz scans for stocks making opening gaps that continue to trade above the gap. Higher volume is a key determinant. Trading gaps is not for the amateur because the opening gap can signal increased strength, or it can just be the result of something that happened unexpectedly overnight. Once that news is out, the stock plunges, closing the gap.

- *Bottom Fisher*. This scans for stocks that are trading lower over several consecutive trading sessions. It seeks stocks that have hit bottom or resistance and are poised to move higher.

- *Sky Scraper*. It is the opposite of the Bottom Fisher. It seeks out stocks that have slammed into resistance and are headed lower. Like most of the other Tony Oz filters, it takes volume into consideration.

These are just a few. You need to spend some time on Tony Oz's web site and other similar ones. Then test a few of the scans. Are they for you? Can you make trading filters your shtick? You will find Tony Oz scanners built into trading software platforms, such as RealTick® by Townsend Analytics, allowing you to easily drag and drop stocks from the scan into the watch list window of the software trading platform. Another scanner available through RealTick® is Hot Trends. It constantly scans the Nasdaq during trading hours alerting traders to opportunities, such as stocks showing unusual price or volume activity. It has had good results as well.

PARALYSIS BY ANALYSIS

A word of caution: Try to avoid paralysis by analysis. It is all too easy to get caught up moving from one great web site to the next and never make a decision. Here is another job for your mentor. Follow his or her lead in the development of your initial watch list.

Returning to Brian's shtick, he does not use filters or scans. He has developed his own list over time by studying the technical factors of stocks. Each day before the market opens, he searches several news sites, The Drudge Report being one of his favorites, looking for news that will impact the overall trend of the market. He prefers stocks that are not going to be affected by things like earnings reports or news stories. When he spots one, he does some technical analysis. Never take stock selection casually or do it haphazardly. It is one of the most important parts of the ritual you must perform before trading, equivalent to the sniper assembling his gear before heading out. If you have to stop trading, after the market opens, to figure out what stock to trade, immediately stop trading for that day because you are not properly prepared.

TRADE BY THE 7 P'S

"Proper prior planning prevents piss-poor performance," as Sergeant Ross used to tell us. There are a few things I just can't stress enough. One of them is preparation. Once you begin to trade, nothing should be allowed to distract you.

Each morning, Brian pulls out his watch list and reviews each stock on the list. He does this by pulling up a 45-day chart. He is looking for setups (Figures 6-1 and 6-2). To him, a setup is a chart formation that indicates that the stock is about to make a move that day which may last from a few hours to a few days. In this example, let's say he is looking for a breakout setup. That is one in which the stock (or commodity) has moved lower (phase 1) for a few days. It has reached an area of support and has traded sideways (phase 2). Trading volume has increased and the stock has started to move higher (phase 3). The next area of resistance is $2 higher. In other words, the stock has room to run up another dollar or two. On a thousand shares, it could be a nice profit opportunity. If it is Friday, Brian might pass on this trade, depending on how strong the volume increase is, and wait to enter the trade on Monday. He only looks for day trades on Fridays because he wants to be flat over weekends. Holding short-term positions over weekends is not for stock market survivors. One survives by being cautious and avoiding all unnecessary risks, like the possibility of news about another Enron-type scandal taking the whole market down when you can do nothing about it. Holding positions

FIGURE 6-1. Phases of the Market
Markets move up, down, and sideways. Traders must know what phase the over-all market, the sector of the entity being traded, and the entity itself are in. If any of these are out of sync, the risk of a reversal in trend increases.

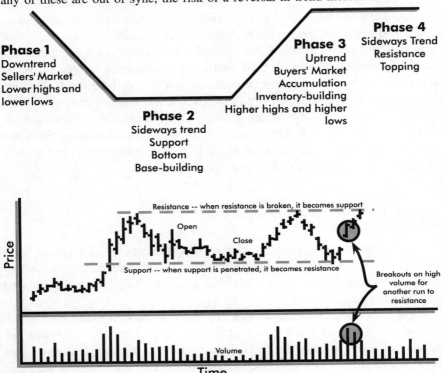

overnight, as you do with swing trading, is as risky as you want your short-term trading to get.

When Brian sees the breakout setup on the 45-day chart, he will look at other views of the potential trade. For example, viewing a daily chart of the last 5 months shows him where the most reliable areas of support and resistance are located. He'll note or memorize them. Remember from our earlier discussion of technical analysis, support holds prices from going lower and resistance restricts prices from going higher. He also determines from the 5-month charts which phase the stock is in long term (i.e., base building, bullish, topping, or bearish—see Chapter 4) and what the long-term trend is (up, down, sideways), and this view provides a reading on average daily volume and volatility. Naturally, Brian will plot the 10- and 20-day moving average to get a feel for what long-term investors may be thinking so he can get a fix on the supply-demand situation. He is always in touch with the direction of the Nasdaq 100 futures and the strength or weakness of the sector the target stock is in. All this analysis only takes a minute or two for an experienced chartist using a trading platform like RealTick®.

Once satisfied that there are no potential problems on the long-term charts, Brian switches back to the short-term charts. He must orient himself to whichever short-term phase is in play. He is considering a long position, and this stock is in the bullish phase, which is perfect. The chart preference for the day or swing trader is the 60-minute-interval chart. Each bar represents 1 hour of trading. You need to be able to generate a chart that provides at least 45 days. A chart with 65 days is even more preferable because it represents 2 weeks of trading on the major exchanges. (This is a function of the software platform being used.) The major exchanges are open 6½ hours a day, 5 days a week, or 65 hours over 2 weeks. As was discussed in Chapter 3, the moving averages tell you the trend and alert you to changes in the trend.

On the 60-minute chart, Brian plots the 65- and 130-minute moving averages. These will be the moving averages that indicate the longer-term trend in this example. When trading short term, just as you would when investing for the long haul, you must keep the trend at your back. Brian plots the 8- and 17-minute moving averages to monitor the short-term trends, and he uses them for entry and exit signals. When you first begin trading this way, it helps to mark the areas of support and resistance on the chart on your trading software platform. You can easily do this with most trading platforms. In time, recognizing them becomes second nature to you.

Also keep in mind that all technical analysts do not use the same moving averages. Some will use longer or shorter-term averages, such as the 10-, 20-, 50-, and 200-period moving averages. Brian developed his own (the 8, 17, 65, and 130) to more closely match the fact that the trading day is 6½ hours in duration. Halting trading on the half hour means that over a normal trading session there are 390 minutes (6½ × 60 minutes). Therefore it is impossible to divide the trading session into even increments, and that is why he uses moving averages of 8, 17, 65, and 130 for the hourly charts. As you develop as a trader, you will learn what works best for your style and experience level.

The next step would be to compare the 60-minute chart with the daily chart, noting at what points the trends and support-resistance are in sync.

This gives you a better perspective. As you become more adept in technical analysis, you discover that the more directional indicators that are aligned, the stronger and more reliable the signal. Brian also checks 10-minute–10-day, 5-minute–5-day, and 2-minute–2-day charts using 10-, 20-, 50-, and 100-minute, 20-, 40-, 100-, and 200-minute, and 10-, 20-, 50-, and 100-minute moving averages, respectively.

Prices rarely move up or down smoothly. They usually move in stair-stepping patterns up and down in a jerky, sometimes erratic, motion. Price momentum swings from overbought to oversold and from bullish to bearish. Rarely does any stock or futures contract have supply and demand in balance for any period of time. If the price is above one of the long-term moving averages, it is considered bullish. If below, bearish. Naturally if the signal is bullish, you prepare to open a long position or buy. If bearish, you look to short.

The short-term moving averages are the most sensitive to price changes. The 10-interval moving average turns direction first, followed by the 20, 40, 50, 60, 100, and 200. Or using Brian's moving averages, the 8, 17, 65, and 130. (Commodity traders may find the 4-, 9-, and 18-day moving averages more common.) For a signal to enter a stock on the long side, look at your support levels. Is the stock in one or approaching one, either on a downtrend or a pullback during an existing bullish move? Does the support hold? If support holds and the shortest moving average begins to turn up, load your weapon. You do this by moving to the order entry window on your computerized trading platform; entering the stock symbol, number of shares, type of order (I recommend you almost always use limit orders), preferred routing, and marking the buy box.

Before squeezing off a round, calculate the risk-to-reward ratio of the proposed trade. This is a two-step process. Step one is determining where the stop-loss order should be placed. It should be in the neighborhood of the next support level for a long trade. You also take recent volatility into consideration when picking a stop-loss price. If it is a long distance to the next support level, let's say a few dollars south and the daily trading range is approximately $1, consider placing a stop at $1.05 or just below the daily trading range. Some traders have a fixed percentage, usually 5 percent or less, that they use. Your stop limit order becomes a market order when hit, and you will be out of the stock with not much more than a dollar loss under normal conditions. Commodity traders must also consider limit trading days when evaluating volatility and setting stops. On a 1000-share-lot stock trade, the loss is $1000, or 3⅓ percent of the equity in a $30,000 account. A worse case, the stock gaps to the next support level, $2 down, and you take a $2 hit. This, or even worse, can happen if the stock, the sector, or the entire market is extremely volatile. If the trend of the sector and the market as a whole is up, the risk of a downside gap diminishes geometrically. This is the rationale for constantly tracking these factors.

Now determine the upside or reward potential. If you expect a 1:2 risk-to-reward ratio, you must see that there are no price resistance areas preventing the stock from moving $2 higher. If there is no resistance for $3 or $4, it is all the better. For some a 1:2 ratio may sound minuscule, but we are discussing day trading or very short-term trades. The expectation is to execute multiple trades over single trading sessions. Tiny drops of water can fill a large bucket over a trading session.

As you do these calculations, also estimate the amount of time you will be in the trade. The longer you expect the trade to last, the greater the risk and the more that can go wrong. You must always be rewarded for accepting risk or at least have the potential of an adequate reward. Therefore, if you think the trade will take 4 days for the stock to increase $2, or a risk-reward ratio of 1:2, you might want to pass. Estimating the time for a move to materialize is speculation at best. With experience, you can look at average daily moves of the last 30 days, volatility, and volume trends and make a good estimate.

At this point, you should have a pretty good idea of how the trade is expected to unfold. One of the keys to survival is visualization. You run the trade though your mind's eye. If the trade does not begin to unfold as you imagined, you bail out. For example, you get in the trade and the stock futures indexes make an about-face, heading south. The uptrend of the stock being traded stalls, and volume evaporates. Run for the exit marked survival or discipline.

I would like to spend a moment on volume because it is usually one of the key factors, at least for me. If volatility is the speed of the market, volume is its power. It is your signpost alerting you to how strong or weak the change of direction will be. Spend some time just studying price charts. Begin by looking for points where the trend of any stock or commodity made a substantial change in direction. Use long-term monthly charts at first. Then check out the volume bars at the bottom of the charts. Notice how volume changed. It could have increased or decreased, but it did change compared with the previous few trading sessions.

Think back to our discussion of supply and demand. It just stands to reason that if there are a lot of buyers clamoring to get a hold of a stock or futures contract, they will increase volume. This, of course, results in an uptrend. The opposite is equally true. If everyone in the pits decides to sell, volume goes up and prices go down. Prices also fall when volume dries up and there are no buyers left in the market. The market is said to "fall of its own weight." Pay close attention to places where prices have gapped higher or lower or made limit moves. The beauty of paying close attention to volume is that you will often notice a change in volume before the change in direction occurs. This is because not everyone with a strong enough opinion about a stock or futures contract gets the word (news) at the same time. It is for this reason the Securities and Exchange Commission is so sensitive about insider trading. A classic example is Enron. Key executives were selling, knowing things were not as they seemed to outsiders (including employees), while telling the public everything was copacetic. Trading volume increased while per-share price stalled and then began a free fall.

Once you get a good feel for the big moves on long-term charts, move to weekly, daily, and eventually hourly and minute charts. Volume and trend changes tend to be more noticeable on the longer-term charts at first. Next start looking for subtle changes on volume, which are harbingers of ½-, 1-, or 2-point moves. At the same time, pick the spots you would put your stop. Mark up these charts and discuss them with your mentor.

Traders of real commodities, such as the grains, metals, softs, meats, etc., that have commercial hedges supporting their markets should combine their analysis of volume with open interest and the Commitment of Traders Report (COT). Commercial hedgers are somewhat equivalent to the institutional buyers in the stock market. Open interest quantifies the number of futures contracts outstanding long or short at the end of every trading day. These are contracts held overnight. The volume of open interest shows the bullish or bearish conviction of a large segment of each market. The COT, made available by the Commodity Futures Trading Commission (www.cftc.gov) every Friday at 3:30 p.m. EST, contains a breakdown of the previous Tuesday's open interest for all futures markets with 20 or more traders holding reportable positions. A second COT Report that includes options is also worth following. It is released every Monday at 3:30 p.m. EST. You are looking for two things: Who is holding what, and is the open interest increasing or decreasing? It's important to know who is holding the commodity, because if it is a commercial hedger that will take physical delivery to use the commodity in its manufacturing, say copper in electrical equipment or corn and beans in a feeding operation, you then know that a bottom in prices may be imminent or at least an area of support.

GOOD TRADERS ARE LIKE SNOWFLAKES!

Although most traders are very similar to one another, the top performers seem to have something unique about their approach to the market—some call it an edge on the market. Our friend Brian, for example, uses the short interest indicator as a way of predicting or anticipating trend changes and runaway markets. He likes to keep tabs on the shorts for two reasons. First, the professional short trader often has stronger opinions than the average trader. More importantly, Brian knows from experience that many big moves occur because of a favorite Wall Street play, i.e., the short squeeze.

Short players take naked short positions when they are convinced a particular stock is headed lower. The objective is to buy it back at a lower price and keep the difference. But what if they are wrong and the stock moves to go higher? How long do they hold on? When do they cry uncle and buy back the stock at a higher price and take a loss? Tough questions. When the shorts try to offset losing short positions, the market makers and specialists become like sharks that catch the scent of blood in the water. They buy, buy, buy, driving prices even higher and squeezing all the shorts out of the water, often missing important limbs.

Brian makes a point of knowing the price and size of the short positions in the stocks he shepherds. This gives him some early warning about when a short squeeze might take place. Naturally, he wants to be in position to take advantage of the opportunity, and he does it by monitoring web sites that track short selling. This approach is not unlike the commodity trading tracking done by the Commitment of Traders Report.

As you do your analysis and study the charts, think of your trading plan. What are you going to be looking for in a trade? Is your plan to make 5, 10, or more half-point trades each trading session for a net profit after commissions and losers of $500, $1000, or more? Or do you want to be a swing trader and take large per-point profits utilizing a weekly time frame? Hone your chart reading skills to the time and profit frame you anticipate. Do not begin trading without committing your plan to writing. Your plan should never be vague. You must write explicit objectives you expect to reach on a daily, weekly, quarterly, and annual basis. It is the only way to know if you are on track and when you must make adjustments.

Please do not think the above discussion is anywhere near a definitive discussion of volume, volatility, trading strategies, or anything else. Not just a few books—but libraries—are full of information on each of these subjects. The purpose of this chapter is just to point you in the right direction.

ENHANCING
YOUR SHTICK

By now you should be thinking about what your trading shtick will be. This is a good time to explore in a little more depth the ways you can enhance your success—and also note some areas you might want to avoid, at least in the beginning of your career.

Initial public offerings (IPOs) come to mind as an attractive, yet dangerous, trading opportunity. These are stock offerings made to the public for the first time. For example, a privately owned company may be in business for a period of time. It could be months, years, or even decades. The owner(s) decides to take it public. This is done for a variety of reasons. The owner might want to get his or her money out of the company before retirement. Or that person might want to divide the company among family members or employees, which is easier to do if stock certificates can be distributed. Some companies go public as a last-ditch effort to raise money before bankruptcy. The most exciting IPOs are usually the ones where the company has a big idea or opportunity that management wants to take advantage of and needs some serious financing to do it. A common recent variation of the above is the dot-com begun on a shoestring, grown with venture capital, and now primed for a big-time payout to the owners, investors, and employees.

Companies traditionally go public through brokerage firms that underwrite the initial stock offering. Underwriting the cost means fulfilling all the legal requirements, which can be staggering and expensive, plus organizing, funding, and promoting the sale of the new stock issue to the public. In return, the broker-dealer is reimbursed out of the proceeds for its expenses, and it controls who gets access to the new shares before the public does. This is done using an offering memorandum reviewed by the Securities and Exchange Commission containing all the information an investor should know before investing. The lead broker-dealer may form a selling syndicate. You, as an investor or a trader, may be able to obtain access to shares of the stock in one of two ways. First, if you are a big customer of the underwriting firm or a brokerage firm that is part of the selling group, you may be offered an allotment of shares at a set price, the offering price, before the IPO is launched publicly. Some of the initial shares of some public offerings were also offered through major online brokerage firms when IPOs were very hot items a few years ago, but this is not the traditional venue. If you don't get an allotment, you can buy shares the day the IPO begins trading on an exchange. Trading publicly on an exchange is called the secondary market.

This whole process gets exciting when the stock becomes a "hot issue" the day it begins trading. A hot issue is one in which price takes off like a bear being chased by swarm of bumblebees. During the famous dot-com years, the action was nothing less than astounding. VA Linux Systems set a 1-day record by opening at $30 per share and closing the day at $250, while hitting an interday high of $320! The record holder for the year (1998) was Red Hat Software, skyrocketing 1837 percent by year's end. IPOs that merely doubled or tripled on their Nasdaq debut were commonplace during these times of irrational exuberance. If I remember correctly, neither of these hot issues ever made a penny, at least for the first few years. During that period, earnings meant nothing— growth was everything. For an investor this is not necessarily the best environment, but for a trader it was a dream come true. This is part of what is meant by understanding and becoming attuned to the complexion of the market. There are times to day-trade. There are times to make swing trades lasting several days. There are times to hang on to positions for weeks and even longer. And there are times to buy and hold. Experience will teach you the difference.

Does it make sense for you to trade IPOs on the secondary market? My answer is no. It is gambling, not trading. My reasoning goes like this. Traders should always be looking for an edge, not giving one away. An IPO on day one has no technical history—no charts, no moving averages, no price history whatsoever. Therefore, there is no trend to follow, no setup chart formations to look for, and no way of anticipating which way the stock is headed once it comes out the chute. You don't know how to read volume because there is no baseline.

There are two kinds of IPOs—the hot and the not. When IPOs are hot, a feeding frenzy occurs among amateur traders, as we saw during the dot-com heyday. The energy and excitement are overwhelming. They can't be contained and they are not rational. Manias in financial markets are common and have occurred for as long as there have been markets. We all have read about the South Sea island and tulip bubbles. The Internet and dot-com craze was no different. When these bubbles occur, everyone and his brother launch IPOs. Traders can't wait to get in on the action. There isn't enough time or solid information to judge the jewels from the junk.

Then comes an even tougher question, how do you trade or day-trade a bubble? Weeks before the launch date, the Internet is abuzz with wild rumors about how hot the next IPO will be. Amateurs hound their broker to get them in on the allocation, which is usually severely restricted. They then give the broker market orders to get them in on the open. The day a hot IPO finally goes public, there are a ton of orders backlogged. The price gaps higher two or three times at the open, and the market orders get filled at prices two or many times higher than the offering price, which is the price you would have gotten it at if you had been allocated some shares. The stock price continues to explode to the upside, and greed rules the trading floor. Everyone wants in; no one seems to want out. But someone must be selling into the storm in order to get the buy orders filled. And those someones keep jacking the price higher.

Then out of nowhere prices deflate like a punctured balloon. The stock closes lower than the opening price. What happened? How could this be? There are a couple of things happening behind the scenes. First, stockbrokers of the underwriting firm got their best customers a portion of the stock allocation. These lucky investors were in before the open. Their brokers then sell them out as the great unwashed rush into the market. A worse situation, in my opinion, also occurs when the underwriter or members of the sell group allocate stock to hedge fund managers or large traders. They flip the stock as soon as they can for a healthy profit. In return, the hedge fund runs other trades through the broker-dealer at an unusually high commission rate as payback. To my way of thinking, the game is rigged in favor of the house when it comes to the hot, or the most attractive, IPOs.

The other kind of IPO, the not hot one, is strictly luck of the draw.

Without any trading history to go on, you lay your money down and hope for the best. At times, it goes well, and the price moves up 5 or 10 percent. But how much is high or too high? Without areas of resistance to alert you to what previously cooled enthusiasm for the stock, how do you know when to get out? More importantly, if the price moves against you, when do you bail out? Zero is the only support level on the chart on that day.

This is gambling if I ever saw it, and gamblers, or traders acting like gamblers, are not going to retire rich and famous or make it into the next edition of *Market Wizards*. The gambling mentality has a basic flaw. It makes the assumption that past trades will have some impact on future ones. Gamblers are known to double up after losing a string of bets. Theoretically, if you double up your bet each time you lose and do it until you win, you will be ahead. I suppose this may be true if you have enough money and time to stay in the game—and if the game stays open until you finally score. Besides the stress of getting farther and farther behind the eight ball, there are too many "ifs" in this approach for me. Trades per se do not have any memory, nor do they feel any obligations to the trader. Each trade is unique unto itself. It stands solely on its own merits. There is no law of physics dictating that if you make five losing trades in a row, the sixth will be a winner. The opposite is equally true. If you make five winning trades, the next might or might not be a loser.

Think back to your high school math class when you studied the probability of flipping a coin. No matter how many times you flipped it, there was only a 50-50 chance of a head or a tail. If you flipped 10 heads in a row, you were not guaranteed a tail on the next flip. Trades are the same. Each one is unique. If you are in a losing streak, don't start thinking the market owes you a winner. It does not owe you diddly-squat. After 10 straight losing trades, you must put the same work and thought into the next trade. You won't get any freebies from the pits or the floors.

Good traders do play the odds, but in a different manner. The odds you should be studying are the odds of each trade being a winner given its own set of circumstances. Along with this you should have a plan of action if the trade goes sour. Survival—means getting out of losers as fast as you can. Trades are not bets. With a bet, you normally cannot cut your losses short. If you take the Lakers over the Celtics, you cannot cancel the bet at halftime if the Celtics are up by 10. You are in it to the end—win, lose, or draw.

This is an area that options traders must learn to manage more efficiently. It saddens me to think of all the clients of mine that bought calls over the years and just let them expire worthless. No matter what I said or did, these people played options like gamblers would—buy, hold, and wait for the outcome of the game. Many did not even care about getting updates until just before the options expired. For some reason, they were convinced that their options would be most valuable at that time. Anyone who follows the markets knows the fallacy of this thinking. Calls made to these customers during the life of the option telling them that the underlying entity was up and they could get out at a small profit or break even fell on deaf ears. Hope of a big winner at expiration was the expectation. If you have that mentality and are not willing to change, burn this book now and stuff all your money underneath your mattress. You will be better off that way when you retire.

Just buying options, particularly ones with months to expiration, is a sucker's bet in my opinion, unless they are being used to hedge risk. Granted, a trader who is totally convinced the market is headed one way or the other may buy a call or a put to take advantage of his or her analysis. It is considered a conservative approach because that person can absolutely define the downside risk, meaning the premium paid for the option. It also provides excellent leverage. Nevertheless, I question the soundness of the strategy. My experience has convinced me that buyers of these types of options do not have good enough intelligence about where the market is headed to profit from the strategy. There are some good stories about winners, even a Chicago legend about a Woolworth's clerk who became a millionaire after he bought several calls as the Hunts attempted to corner the silver market in 1979–1980. I have even seen a handful of winners, but I have seen a bushel basket full of losers. It is my opinion that the size of the price move needed in the underlying entity to pay back the premium and commission, and then drive the option far enough into the money to make the risk-reward ratio attractive, is not sufficient 99 percent of the time.

Think for a moment about the risk-reward potential of the buyer compared with the seller of a call on IBM or COMEX silver. The buyer has unlimited upside potential and fixed downside risk, the premium. The seller has fixed upside potential, the premium, and substantial downside risk, from the strike price to infinity. Now it is very rare that any underlying entity increases infinitely in value. Nevertheless, the buyer sure seems to have the better deal.

If this is so, why do most options expire worthless? Why would a seller of options be willing to take a theoretically infinite risk to pocket a limited gain? What is wrong with this picture? I have sold more options than I care to admit, and my experience has been that the seller has a much better chance of success than the buyer.

I sincerely believe the reason is the work, attention, and thought the seller puts into the strategy compared with most, make that just about all, buyers, save hedgers. A seller of options, with so much more at risk, must determine how to price the option so the reward matches the risk. Then he or she follows the price activity and is ready to buy back the options (to offset the position) or acquire the underlying entity (to cover the position) if the sale becomes a mistake. The buyer, in all too many cases, sits passively waiting for the option to leap deep into the money. The buyer may even leave it up to his or her broker to signal when it is time to sell or the expiration date approaches. A good broker will do this, but no one pays better attention to your money than you do.

The seller is a trader of options—constantly on top of the market, buying and selling as market conditions warrant. The buyer is a gambler, betting on the future without trying to get an edge. The seller is trying to make a living, while the buyer is often betting on a tip from a broker. The seller has the edge and will prevail in the profit-and-loss tug-of-war.

While we are discussing things not to do or to guard against, let me mention another. This one has to do with how our memories work. I call it the gambling casino syndrome. I really admire, yet avoid at all costs, gaming casinos. The reason is the same one that makes me admire good traders. Casino managers have mastered the art of putting the edge in their favor. I mentioned earlier the fact that the roulette wheel has a zero and a double zero, which gives the house an ever so slight edge. With proper volume, a slight edge is all that is needed.

But there is another edge that the house or a public trading floor has, and it's at the basis of the casino syndrome. It has to do with human nature. All of us enjoy pleasure and shun pain. It is enjoyable to be around excitement and winners. Casinos have learned that people put more money into slot machines when there are a lot of slot machines in one place, rather than a lone one out in the lobby. Why? It is the constant noise of players and the excitement of someone winning, even if the lucky person hit a $100 jackpot after dropping $1000.

Keep in mind, the odds are the same—remember the coin-flipping exercise. For each dollar dropped, the slot machine is preprogrammed to win or lose at a given rate set by the house in its favor. You would have the same chance of winning if you were in the middle of the Sahara Desert at the Camel Stop Oasis by yourself as you would at the Bellagio. The difference is that you might not continue tossing tokens in the slots if it was dead quiet—if there was no noise of winners hitting jackpots and none of the other excitement that takes place in a well-run casino.

The same phenomenon occurs on a public trading floor in the middle of New York, Houston, Los Angeles, or Denver. As a matter of fact, there is even a physical resemblance. In place of rows of slot machines, there are computers. Traders replace gamblers; at least they *should* be traders. Unfortunately, you may well find quite a few gamblers on trading floors. When you do, avoid them.

There is certainly excitement and winners, which is what I wish to warn you about. Trading floors are a mixed blessing. They can be an important part of your maturation from novice, to journeyman, to master trader, or they can be your downfall. One of the most serious pitfalls for the newbie is a tendency to overtrade when on a floor with a number of experienced traders. One of the worst things you can do is take a seat next to someone who has been momentum-trading for the last 5 years and is knocking off 50 or 100 or more trades a day. If this is your first experience or even if you do have some experience, it will plum drive you bananas. You will find yourself constantly peeking at that person's screens, trying to find out what he or she is seeing, trading, and doing. Like most of us, you will assume that activity is progress and that this person has the key to the kingdom of trading. It may or may not be true, but this is not where to begin your trading career.

You must protect yourself from overtrading, which can bring your career to an abrupt end. If you put yourself in the wrong atmosphere, meaning the casino atmosphere, you will be caught up in the phony camaraderie common to soldiers or contact sports teams. Members worry about appearing weak if they show fear of getting injured—in this case, of losing money. They appear to shrug off losses as immaterial, but a day or two later their chair is empty or someone else is using it.

Should you begin trading on a public floor? And if so, how should you go about selecting the right floor? As I see it, you have 2½ choices about where to trade. First, of course, is on a public trading floor. Choice number two is at home, or at an office, by yourself. The last one, which I characterize as half a choice, is with a group of friends or a trading club. I dub it a half choice since there are not many trading clubs that are successful.

I'll discuss each choice briefly, but first let me review what is required to trade using computerized direct access to the stock or futures market via the Internet. For short, I'll refer to this type of trading as direct access to distinguish it from online trading, such as E*trade or one of the many other online brokerage firms. With online trading, the trader emails an order to his or her brokerage firm. The order then goes into some type of order routing system. The order may actually be sold to a wholesale broker, called a broker's broker. If that occurs, the trader automatically loses the spread between the bid and the ask, allowing the wholesaler to make a risk-free trade at a small profit. This used to be a big deal when spreads were a sixteenth, an eighth, or more. Now with decimalization, it is not as big a deal on the highly liquid stocks. Nevertheless, there are still times when the spread can be a nickel or more. If you trade short term for SIPs (small incremental profits), it can still be a problem. Losing all the spread might be the difference between a profitable trade and breakeven.

This is one of the reasons most active traders switched to direct access trading when it became available. But what was more important to these traders was transparency and routing. Transparency means being able to see behind the market. Direct access trading venues have Nasdaq Level 2 windows that display all the market makers and most of the ECNs that are making a bid or an offer on the stock being traded. Even the New York Stock Exchange now shows the specialists' limit order books.

Personally, I call this opacity, rather than transparency. Having access to the Level 2 window and the New York limit book is great and important, don't get me wrong. But I refer to it as cloudy or murky because you still aren't seeing the whole picture. For example, a major market maker, say GSCO (Goldman Sachs & Co.), is on the inside bid. It is buying INTC (Intel) at a given price and showing that it is willing to buy 1000 shares. How many more shares are behind that bid? Remember the "follow the ax" strategy mentioned earlier. GSCO may need 5000, 10,000, or 50,000 or more behind what is showing. You don't know. Therefore, it is still a little murky. The same goes for the NYSE limit book. What about the orders the specialist is personally holding or the orders in the crowd around the specialist's booth? How would you characterize it— transparent or murky? The new ARCHEX plans to change all that.

Transparency also means access to a full array of trading tools on your computerized trading platform. I will briefly describe the platform from RealTick® by Townsend Analytic because it is the most mature, the most widely used, and the one I am familiar with since I have an affiliation with the company. That is not to say there are not other trading platforms available that will provide the level of services you need as a trader. It is just that I personally think RealTick® is the industry leader.

Barron's ranked it the best for order execution in its 2002 article entitled "The Best Online Brokers."

The trading tools you need fall into three general categories: basic information, decision support, and trade execution. A typical direct access trader would need all of the following functions at his or her fingertips:

Basic Information Tools

- *Level 2 window(s).* Bids and asks, including size (number of shares), for all market makers and ECNs active in a Nasdaq market.

- *NYSE limit order window(s).* Limit order held in an electronic order book on the New York Stock Exchange.

- *Time & sale window.* Streaming quotes of every buy or sale executed, time-stamped.

- *Interest or watch window.* Trader stores symbols of stocks or indexes that he or she wishes to track throughout the trading session.

- *Price tickers window(s).* Streaming prices of exchange activity, which can be customized to suit the trader's needs.

- *Internet browser access.* Allows the trader to gather news or other information (chat rooms) useful during trading.

- *Alarms and alerts.* Functions that can be customized to give the trader notice that important price levels are being reached (new highs on price-volume-volatility on key stocks, curbs kicking in, etc.) or that key news is breaking (interest rate increases or decreases).

- *Specifically programmed windows.* Setup for options quotes, spreads, news, spreadsheet interface, forex markets, scans, filters, etc.

Decision-Making Tools

- *Charts.* Bar, candlesticks, tick by tick, bid-ask, overnight markets; technical studies can be overlaid; any time interval can be utilized; customizable color and scaling; daily, weekly, monthly; stocks, futures, options, indexes, etc.

- *Technical analysis.* Over 40 available—for example, moving averages, envelopes, oscillators, MACD, directional movement, stochastics, volume, open interest, statistical moments, point and figure,

Gann, Fibonacci, trendlines of all sorts; all studies are dynamic and can be overlaid on charts and are easy to use; all of the most common are easily accessible.

- *Options.* Deltas, vegas, gammas, thetas, theoretical values, profit and loss price calculations, etc.

- *Market montages.* Nasdaq trends, shares bid and asked at price levels, etc.

- *Market profiles.* TPO or tick profiles, split profiles and collapse prices, calculator and key prices detail box, etc.

- *Multiquotes windows.* Prices and fundamentals, etc.

Order Execution

- *Order types permitted.* Market, limit, IOC (immediate or cancel), stops, trailing stops, conditional, reserve, discretionary, short, PNP (post no preference), direct preference, etc.

- *Enhancements.* Quick cancels, hot keys, cost estimates in order confirmation, automatic position entry (drops symbol and other details automatically into order entry window).

This is just a quick overview of what a good trading platform provides. RealTick® has grown and developed since I first became familiar with it about 5 years ago. By the time you read this, I am sure many features will have been added. To find out what is new or to see what it really looks like, visit the web site at www.realtick.com. Once you have a feel for this platform, compare it with other systems, CyberCorp, Watcher, TradeScape, etc., and decide which one suits you best. This is important if you are going to trade on a public trading floor because it may only provide access to one trading platform.

As you can imagine, accessing all the data on today's stock or futures trading platform takes some serious bandwidth. This is a key part of your decision about where to trade. If you trade at home can you get the bandwidth you need to support the system you plan to trade? It is becoming more and more common for traders to utilize two, three, and more monitors to manage all the information they feel is necessary.

When direct access trading first got under way, many people opted to trade at home on a single-monitor system. Many were able to function with a POT (plain old telephone) line, which is 56K in bandwidth. But as software became more sophisticated and bandwidth requirements grew, people turned to DSL or cable Internet access. Public trading floors generally provide multiple T3 service, which is more than sufficient. Therefore, plug into your plan which platform(s) you are considering, the number of monitors you think you will need and the bandwidth you have where you plan to trade. Then get a professional opinion about whether the bandwidth available to you will be sufficient. I would get that opinion from more than one source, i.e., from the provider of the software, your equipment vendor, any traders you know that are using similar systems under similar conditions, and an independent consultant, if available and practical. Bandwidth is that critical a consideration. If you can't operate the way you think you should be trading, it will erode your confidence, one of the most critical elements of successful trading. It will also provide an excuse for failure, poor fills, and missed opportunity—and excuses don't feed the bulldog.

One more tip on software selection: Most of the major platforms will allow you to download a simulator version. This provides you with an opportunity to try out the features of each, giving you a better idea of which one best suits your specific needs and trading style. For example, you might rely on a specific technical study, say Bollinger bands or Wilders' %R. If that is not available to you, you could have a problem with the software. Or you could find out that one system is much more intuitive, faster, or easier to use or learn, which might be the determining factor for you. Also, having tested one or two of these platforms, you can talk more intelligently with the manager of the public trading floors in your area.

A big word of caution when experimenting with simulators now and when you first begin to trade: Simulated trading is to actual trading as thinking about winning the lottery is to actually winning the lottery. Simulators naturally do not actually enter orders into the market. It seems like they do, but in reality the practice orders are matched via an algorithm with streaming real-time data, giving the impression the fill you get is about what you would get in real life. Not so. First off, on the simulator you always get a fill. Second, that fill is fast and usually favorable compared with what happens in real trading. Now I do not think the software companies are trying to trick you into believing trading is easy. Simulators just cannot duplicate real price action, such as someone's order getting ahead of yours and getting the last stock offered at a certain price. Nor can a simulator mimic the order routing possibilities; for instance, would an order routed via Island get filled before one sent through Archipelago? The answer to this question in real life is that it depends on which one has the liquidity to fill the order. On the simulator both get filled in the same amount of time.

There is one other key difference, which is the most important. I call it "buck fever." You use cyberdollars on a simulator and your hard-earned cash when trading for real. Which makes you more nervous? If your money is on the line and the stock you are trading plunges 3 bucks against you, how cool are you? Can you deal with it, just as you would when you had cyberbucks on the line? Needless to say, there is a difference. I don't know how many newbies have come strolling onto the trading floor and proudly told me they had been on the simulator at home all last week and were up 5000 bucks and were ready to trade live. By the end of the day, they were in the hole.

Trading on a simulator is important for learning how to operate the software. You must be able to pull up a chart, fire orders to the floor, cancel orders, change routing preferences from Island to Archipelago, review open orders, check news, overlay studies, etc., and do it all in nanoseconds. But whatever you do, please do not confuse it with live trading, which it ain't!

After getting a background in the hardware, software, and bandwidth requirements you think you might need, it is time to do some legwork. It is hoped that you will have a choice of public trading floors to pick from. A key consideration is what kind of training and how much do you need before attempting to become a direct access trader? Most floors offer formal and informal training. An outline of a formal training program presented is below and is best suited to someone who has not actively traded in the past:

- History of the Stock Markets: How They Developed into What They Are Today

- The Markets and the Market Participants—Specialists, Market Makers, Broker-Dealers, Brick'n'Mortar vs. Electronic Exchanges, Professional vs. Amateur Traders, Hedge Funds, ECNs, Market Analysts, the Fifth Estate, the Internet, Pranksters and Con Artists, etc.

- Types of Securities: Common Stocks, Preferred Stocks, Options, IPOs, etc.

- Keys to Trading Economic Data: Before, During, and Immediately After Release

- How to Trade the Supply and Demand Swings of the Float
- Introduction to Level 2 and the Discipline Required to Make the Most of It
- NASDAQ Level 2: Market Breadth and Volume Theories
- Other Advanced Level 2 Trading Skills and Strategies
- Trading News from the Internet, TV, Print, Beepers, and Radio
- Using Fundamental and Technical Analysis
- Day Trading Announcements: Earnings, Splits, Rating Changes, IPOs, and Secondary Offerings of IPOs
- How to Successfully Electronically Route and Execute Trades
- Managing Trading Risk
- The Internet and Connectivity: How to Get a Good Connection
- The Psychology of the Market, Professional Traders, and Third Party Influencers
- Advanced Trading Strategies: Dancing around the Post, Swing Trading, Midterm and Longer-Term Trading, Trading Thin and Thick Markets, Loaded Spring and Other Approaches to Complex Markets
- How to Get the Most Out of Using a Trading Simulator with Real-Time Price Quotations
- Finding the Right Brokerage Firm and Opening an Account
- Developing Your Personal Trading Plan and How to Get Started
- Taking Advantage of Mentoring Programs for the First 3 Months of Trading

If this sounds like a lot to learn, you are absolutely right. It is also the curriculum of the Market Wise Trading School's 4-day stock trading school, which I am affiliated with. Use the list to evaluate the other schools you will be see as you visit the trading floors in your area and the Internet.

On your visits, ask about mentoring and costs. Are mentors available? What other costs are involved? Is there a seat fee? Is a minimum number of trades per day required to hold a seat? What account size is required? How much are commissions? Are there education charges? Are any tui-

tion rebates available? Software leasing? ECN fees? Is there a daily briefing for traders? Ask about the daily routine. Some floors have a lot of
hidden fees that you might not think of the first time you trade on a
public floor. Ask for a list of all services available and the charges. You
may think ECN fees are insignificant, for example, but you could be
wrong. Next request to see a sample account statement. Have the floor
manager or his or her assistant explain the statement in detail. Find out
if trading activity is credited against any or all of the charges.

CAVEAT EMPTOR!

It is common if you generate a certain volume of trades per month, probably 50–100 round turns, that most of the charges will be credited back.
If this is the case, the floor most likely would be affiliated with a broker-
dealer since it is paying the bills with the traders' commissions. That
means the employees are registered with the NASD Regulations, Inc. This
is important because the registered individuals are held by the NASD
(National Association of Security Dealers) to a high standard of ethics
and are compelled to arbitrate disputes with customers if a problem occurs. This is just a little extra protection since you have all the other
avenues of recourse any customer would have. You also know that the
registered reps have passed at least entry-level proficiency examinations
conducted by the NASD. Naturally it is by no means a guarantee of any
level of trading, teaching, or management skills. Let the buyer beware.

EDUCATION AND MENTORING

By now you have prepared a written needs assessment, part of which
covers education and mentoring. I personally think there is some advantage to trading at the same place you attended classes. That is the way
the firm I am affiliated with does things. This gives you direct access to
your instructors after the course is complete, and one or more of the
instructors may be mentors as well. Therefore they have a good understanding of what you know, which is always an advantage in the beginning.

Graduating from a trading school does not make you a trader. Most
schools can only teach you the mechanics of trading, i.e., they can teach
you how the electronic markets work, show you how to use software, and

give you some insights into strategies. At best, you watch actual traders trade, train on a simulated program, and maybe even execute a few live trades. All this takes place in less than a week. To become a trader, you must trade.

More correctly, you must survive the first 3 months of trading real money to trade enough to become a novice trader. Getting you started is one of the key things a mentor can do. A good mentor can be a great help. Think of your mentor as a personal trainer who can help you determine what you need to do to lose 20 pounds and improve your definition, but he or she cannot do it for you. It takes discipline and determination to show up at the gym three times a week and go through the routines. It takes even more grit to maintain a healthy diet and work out on your own. Your personal trainer cannot lose the 20 pounds for you any more than your training mentor can make you a millionaire.

Mentors are coaches. Coaches stay on the sidelines. Even the best players have help. How many times have you heard that Tiger Woods has spent the week before the major with his swing coach, or that Tiger was the last pro to leave the practice range after the day's round. Think about it. The best contemporary golf pro, maybe the best ever, has a mentor and practices more than the pro who barely made the cut for the first time.

Whom do you get for a mentor? Can you afford one? What choices are available at the trading floor you are considering? My advice is to first get a feel for the day-to-day operation of the floor. Ask the manager if you can just sit in for a few days and observe. If the manager insists you pay a month's fee, consider doing that if you do not have a lot of options to choose from in your locale. If you attended a school there or plan to, spend as much break time as possible observing the floor and the interaction of the traders with the people who run it.

Start by finding out the daily routine. Many floors offer a morning briefing that makes the traders aware of overnight trading activity in the Orient and the European markets. The focus will then shift to the futures markets in the United States, which open before the U.S. stock markets. Particular attention will be paid to stock futures, but some time may be spent on gold, if it is making its presence felt, and the currencies, especially the U.S. dollar's strength or weakness compared to other major world currencies. You will usually get a list of announced events happening that day, such as government reports, earnings, and meetings that could impact price movement, perhaps a Federal Reserve meeting. Updates on fair value and any action from yesterday's session that might impact today's will be discussed. A list of stocks to watch, and why you should consider watching them, is usually appropriate. The meeting may end with a question-and-answer period, primarily for the newer traders.

It is important for you to sit in on as many of these sessions as possible. It will tell you a lot about the competence of the management of the floor. Take good notes. Then watch for whatever you were alerted about to see if it happens or does not happen and write your reaction. I do not, nor should you, expect the person doing the briefing to be an expert commentator or a soothsayer. All you are attempting to determine is whether that person's insight was helpful. Were the traders alerted to potential opportunities and warned about possible booby traps?

Market commentary is a lot like weather forecasting in that the short-term predictions tend to be better than the long-term ones. Therefore pay close attention to the comments about the open. Did DELL gap higher on the open due to the earnings announcement made after the bell yesterday? Was the market exceptionally volatile as predicted? For each day you attend these meetings, grade the performance of the presenter. This duty is often shared by several staff members. Who in your opinion is the best? Which one answers questions the best? Shares the most information? Remember, you are shopping for a mentor.

Your mentor does not have to be one of the instructors or staff members. It could turn out to be one of the traders. Part of your observation of the floor includes the traders. Which ones appear the most professional? The least emotional? If you can, try to get a feel for the trading style of the traders that you think might be good mentors. Attempt to sit near these individuals and engage them in conversation before and after trading sessions.

Traders generally don't mind talking about their trading with other traders. But it is not always clear what their words really mean. Some of what you are looking for is quantitative, but the most important is subjective. For example, the quantitative part has to do with the amount of time someone has been trading. You would probably want a mentor who has been at it for over a year and has been trading substantial volume daily. At least this person has shown some survival skills. You also want a feel for the level of trading in terms of trades per day, week, or month and the size of the trades. It is one thing for a trader to be at it for 5 years, executing one or two trades a day for 100 shares. Then you find out the person is retired and the spouse wants him or her out of the house, and it is just a hobby. That person may be using the floor as a club, compared to the person who has only been trading full-time for a year but is very active.

Then there is the question of profitability. The floor manager knows or can find out exactly how profitable any trader is by reviewing his or her monthly statements. But that would be unethical since it is confidential information. If a manager offers to do it without the written permission of the owner of the account, run, don't walk, from that floor. On the other hand, if someone working for the floor makes a comment about the success of one of the traders, don't put too much credence in it. First, the floor personnel want to make it seem that everyone on the floor is making money. That's good for business. Second, it is often hard to determine if the winning streak that person is referring to is occasional or sustained. It is one thing to have a very good day, week, or month. It is quite another to be profitable year after year after year.

Most brokerage firms, or their clearing firms that do the accounting for the trading accounts, have a built-in function to generate profit-and-loss statements. So the information is usually available, although this does not mean it is sharable. You want to be sure this function will be available to you, as you will see when we get to the chapter on evaluating your trading.

You may have to do a little detective work. Determine if the trader who interests you trades full time. If he or she is making a living trading, that obviously is a good sign. How does that person's standard of living appear? Does he or she panic when a losing day occurs? If you hear statements like "I won't be able to make the house payment if I don't have a good week," you know things aren't all roses and clover. You also want to determine if trading is a major contributor to that person's lifestyle. On our floor, we often have several successful entrepreneurs who sold their business at a large profit and have taken up trading as a hobby. This is not necessarily a disqualifier. That kind of person could be a good trader and have the time to mentor you, plus they may have time to spend with you.

You can often tell a lot from the attitude that other traders have toward your mentor candidate(s). Do they ask him or her questions about trading techniques, strategies, or individual stocks or futures contracts? For example, you will hear questions like "What are you trading today?" Or "What do you think of Cisco as a short today?" If other traders are trying to key off of that person's trading, it is a good sign. Observe how much respect the other traders display for that person's opinions. Is he or she one of the floor leaders? Does that person take the time to answer questions and share experiences?

It is not uncommon for an experienced trader to take a novice under his or her wing. It can be an ideal situation for the newbie, since the mentoring is free and the person doing the mentoring obviously wants to do it. But it can also be dangerous if you do not get a good fix on the type and quality of the mentor candidate's trading. The worst case scenario is that you learn a lot of bad habits.

I caution you to take your time finding a good mentor. Pay for the service if you have to. You certainly would not expect a professional personal trainer with a degree in the field, several years' experience, and a solid book of clients to offer to train you for gratis. So why would you expect the same from a trader?

In Europe, students are encouraged to attend more than one university in more than one country before their education is complete. I don't think this is a bad idea for a trader. You might go to a school run by one firm and then attend one or more mentoring sessions conducted by another. There are also a variety of Internet-based mentor opportunities utilizing interactive trading sessions where you watch and listen to a pro trade. These can be extremely useful. Take a look at www.innerworth.com.

At about this point, the question of cost comes up. How much will all this training set you back? The classic answer is how much will it cost not to learn as much as you can before beginning to trade? Some of my brightest students took the time to thoroughly explore active trading as a vocation and chose not to attempt it. This is something you hope a mentor will help you with, but it often never occurs to the mentor because the student shows so much desire to trade. I'll go more into detail about this subject in the last chapter.

If you decide not to trade on a public trading floor or one is not available in your area, what are your alternatives? I said earlier that you have 2½ choices and we have discussed one in detail so far. The others were trading on your own or trading in a group, a club.

It takes a special type of trader to handle trading by himself or herself, especially if it is done at home. Most people are social animals. We all need some human contact. When I am writing at home for prolonged periods of time, I find it lonely. I also keep finding things I need to get done around the house that draw me away from my primary pursuit. Other traders I have discussed this with also said the same thing. They have a bad trade, and the next thing they are doing is cutting the grass. Their spouses even have the nerve to schedule carpet, window, and other cleaning services since they were going to be home anyway. Go figure?

To trade at home, you need the equipment and Internet connection described earlier. Most of this is available in most areas of the country these days. The only question mark is bandwidth—not so much the availability as the dependability. It has historically been unstable where I live, the Denver area. As a backup, the home trader must have a cellular phone and a back office to call for support. A *back office* is a brokerage term meaning an office where licensed brokers are available to assist remote traders. The back office also has the responsibility of assuring that all the accounting, clearing, reporting, and account updating is complete before the opening of each trading session. The back office is the place you would call if something appears wrong in your account.

A good back office will be able to see your account in real time. This means that if you are in a trade and your cable, DSL, computer, or electric power crashes, you can call the back office for help. The back office will, for example, be able to see that you just fired a limit order to Archipelago and that it has not been filled yet. It can cancel that order for you, the prudent thing to do under these circumstances, or it can let you know when and at what price your order gets filled. You can trade through the back office until you are up again. That is if you are used to flying blind!

A more serious obstacle may be discipline. When you are alone, discipline can be your downfall. For example, I have a friend who trades very well in crowds. If other traders are around, he follows all the rules. But let this person trade alone, and he will hold losing trades longer than he should and it will often cost him serious money. Just the thought of another trader looking over his shoulder and saying, "Why are you holding all that Titan? It is down big!" is enough to keep him following the rules. When he is faithful to them, he is successful. You must have enormous self-knowledge and iron discipline to be a loner, as I'll explain in the last chapter.

An alternative is to trade out of an office where others are around. The other inhabitants may not be traders, but they may be able to offer the human connection needed. It can be a big ego trip to be able to leave the office mid-afternoon each day, while the rest have to stick it out to 5:00 p.m. Plus having people around when you take an occasional break or decide to go out to lunch sometimes helps. Just knowing that someone might ask about your trading can help discipline. Personally, going to the office makes me work better. I put my game face on and know others expect me to crank the whole day long. At home, I am tempted to play a little hooky.

I rated clubs as half a choice because my experience has been that they have half a chance of succeeding. This is particularly true if the expenses are shared, i.e., rent, equipment, utilities, Internet connections, bandwidth, etc. The cost of a club can easily be several thousand a month. If the members are not professional or semiprofessional traders with a long-term commitment, it probably will not work out. The worst case is a group of newbies getting together to start trading together. Chances are good that a few will be blown out of the market in a matter of weeks or months. Then what do the remaining members do, especially if they are strapped with several long-term leases for rent or bandwidth?

It can be tricky. I have seen cases in which a brokerage firm set up an installation where individuals could meet and trade. The trick was to have enough demand that when someone left the group, others were ready to fill the open seat. To do this, the firm needed to have some commitment regarding the minimum amount of trading that could be expected to occur. If you can put something like that together, it might work. But it will be the exception, rather than the average setup.

Now let's move on to the next chapter and start discussing some specific rules that will improve your chances of success.

8

DEALING WITH ONE OF THE TOUGHEST PARTS OF THE GAME: DISCIPLINE

In the last discussion of trading alone versus on a floor and with or without a mentor, I deliberately left out a few key considerations that clearly separate the winners from the losers. Those considerations are discipline and focus. To paraphrase Warren Buffett, The first rule is discipline. And the second rule is to obey the first rule.

Grabbing hold of the true concept of discipline is like trying to pick up liquid mercury—just when you think you have it cornered, it squirts from your grasp. The reason is that people have their own idea of what it means to be disciplined, and they often have a poor understanding of how disciplined they really are. This is particularly true of traders because of the irrationality of the markets. A trader can be rewarded for doing something really undisciplined and punished for following the rules to the letter. The good feeling that accompanies the rewarding trade dulls the senses to the fact that some important rule might have been over-looked or bent.

SEMPER DISCIPLINE

To me the only way you can develop discipline in any activity is to learn the rules and create a system to force yourself to follow them. Once the rules are ingrained and mastered, you develop a sixth sense of when you can get away with stretching or even violating a rule on occasion. But if you attempt to outsmart the trading rules in this book before you reach that stage in your trading career, just as God made Marines to party, you'll bring a premature end to your life as a trader. In the second part of this chapter I discuss focus, which is the key to following the rules.

WINNERS VERSUS LOSERS

Here is a typical example of how and why so many traders fail in the first 3 months of trading. The most basic rule of trading is to let winners run and cut losers in the bud. Sure sounds simple and easy to follow. Unfortunately, it isn't. All too many undisciplined traders cut their win-nings short and let their losers run wild. Say, a trader is long Ariba. It jumps 5 points for no known reason. There is no good news on the cable or Internet. Earnings aren't due out for another month. Just about every-one on the floor picked it as a short. Now our typical new trader is long a 1000-share position and the stock is up 5 sticks. Guess what sweeps through his soul? Fear! Fear of losing $5000 that he never expected to make. He got in the trade before he got the word it was a short, and he was right and no one knows why. Fear motivates him to cut his winner instead of placing a tight trailing stop.

When the fear dissipates, he can't admit to his fellow floor traders that it was just dumb luck. Rather, he tells them he saw some technical signals they didn't and it was just a dazzling move. If he tells the story long enough and hard enough, he will believe it himself. This is the beginning of the erosion of his discipline. He is now the boy genius of the floor.

The next time he is in a trade, the opposite happens. He is long Ariba again. He is looking for a modest move higher to the next level of resistance, which is $1.50 above his entry point. This time the stock drops a buck. That is the point at which he should have a stop loss order placed, but he doesn't. Human nature emerges from the primordial swamp. He can't admit he is wrong, neither to his floor mates nor to himself and certainly not his mentor. He tells himself it is just a head fake. Ariba will dip another half dollar and make a spectacular recovery. He believes he is still the whiz kid that made the previous call netting 5 grand and that everyone on the floor will now have to admit it if he's right again. If it happens twice, it couldn't be just luck.

As Ariba sinks, so does our trader's hope for another winning trade. He is now concentrating on just breaking even, and he is still not able to admit he is wrong. Pride goeth before major losses. The trader is now wrestling with some very complex emotions,—fear, hope, and pride. He is doing this while under the pressure of losing money and face.

His wrong thinking revolves around the assumption that a losing trade is a mistake in judgment. This is incorrect. More times than not, a losing trade has to do with timing, being in too early or too late. The art of speculation is not about hoping for small profits. You don't get rich making a lot of small profits. It is about making large profits. When a trade goes right, it usually goes very right. When a trade goes wrong, you get out as soon as possible. You place real stops in the market, not mental ones. Trading is all about surviving so you are still in the game when you hit a series of big winners. Until then you play defense.

THE PARABLE OF THE FLY FISHERMAN

Think with the mentality of a fly fisherman. He stands waist-deep in cold water for hours, constantly casting his line. Mosquitoes and other airborne pests torment him, and yet he perseveres because he has a mission. If a fish does not snap at a cast, he reels the fly back in and repeats and repeats and repeats the exercise. Periodically, the fly comes back with a small fish, which is pitched back into the stream. Then out of nowhere

the fisherman lands a trophy. That is what speculation is all about. That
is what the rule about cutting losses short and letting winners run means.
You won't thrive unless you learn to survive.

Just as you never know when a winner will strike, you never really
know when it will stop running. Thus some brainy trader invented the
trailing stop. It is simply a stop that moves higher and higher and higher
as the price of the entity being traded long moves higher. On shorts, the
process is reversed. When I say stop, I mean a plain stop. Not a stop-
limit order. A plain vanilla stop becomes a market order when hit, while
a stop-limit order becomes a limit order upon activation. For this conditional order to get filled, the limit price level must also be satisfied. If for
some reason this condition cannot be filled, you might give up all your
profits, as can happen when a futures market limits down for a day or
two and does trade until your limit is long out of range. This is where
greed joins the other two wicked witches of the north, hope and fear, to
ruin your trading career.

Stop-limit orders have legitimate uses, but not as stop-loss orders for
speculators in my opinion. A buy stop limit is great for getting into a
market at a certain level. You might want to buy a stock or futures contract after resistance has been pierced and the stock does not retrace. For
example, you don't want to own the entity unless it stays about the area
of resistance. That is a job for a stop-limit order, so use one.

TO SHORT OR NOT TO SHORT?

That is the question. So far most of what I have said and the examples I
have used involved taking long positions. The reason is that most traders,
particularly new traders, favor the long side. Shorting seems foreign to
many. How do you sell something you don't own and buy it back later?
The proponents will tell you it allows you to always make a good trade
even when the markets are bearish. They'll also tell you that markets tend
to fall faster than they rise, offering outstanding profit opportunities for
the short traders. Lastly, trading schools and instructors insinuate you will
never be a true pro without learning to play on the south side of the street.
All of this is basically true.

Unfortunately for me, I am a Libra. Since I see both sides of any
argument, my advice to you is to take the time to learn to short if, and
only if, you are comfortable with shorting or really think it will offer you
a profit opportunity. The breadth of the market, the number of stocks up

compared with the number down, on any give day is never 100 percent one way or the other. This simply means that even in down markets there will be opportunities to be bullish and there is always something to short on up days.

Second, it is even more important for you to truly understand that you do not always have to be in the market. There are days you should not trade. For example, avoid trading when you are ill or extremely tired. If your judgment is impaired in any way, have the good sense to pass. Even if you really want to trade, don't. To trade or not to trade is a decision you must consciously make. Never allow someone to bully you into trading or force you into a trade when you are not physically, emotionally, or financially prepared. The great risk you take besides losing money is losing confidence. Be careful to understand why you have chosen not to trade on any given day, because it can lead to procrastination. This in turn can eat away your confidence, leading to inaction. I will talk more about this side of trading in the last chapter.

There is also a pesky mechanical problem with shorting. It is called the uptick or plus-tick rule. Security regulations require a short to be initiated on an uptick or a zero uptick. An uptick merely means the previous trade was higher than the one before it. A zero uptick is one where the previous tick was the same as the one before it, a zero change in price, but the one before that one was an uptick. The software platform you use is normally programmed to prevent a trader from making illegal trades, such as shorting on a downtick. If you have the stock in your account, the software will know that and will allow you to sell it, but it isn't a short. The reason for the rule was to help slow down negative moves. The regulators thought that slowing traders from jumping on a falling market would put more order into trading.

What if you just throw a short into the market and hope for the best? If you are using a computerized trading platform, it should reject your order unless there is an uptick. Even with an uptick, you might not get filled if there is "stock ahead" of you, meaning there is a backlog of orders. If you get in a falling market too late, you take the risk of getting caught in a short squeeze if any positive news about the stock hits the floor. This could be costly. Remember stocks tend to swing from overbought to oversold and then back again. It is normal for the pendulum to swing too far one way and have an immediate adjustment too far the other.

My answer whether or not you should learn to short is that you must make up your own mind. I certainly would not recommend you make learning to short a high priority, particularly if you have never done it previously. I have seen a few new traders place learning to short as a top priority only to watch them go into the hole and become very frustrated in the process. You can make money without shorting. But if you decide to accept the challenge, do nothing else for a month. Run scans daily to find targets that are in a declining phase and short, short, short. This goes back to how a pro golfer masters a new club. He hits enough buckets of balls to be able to hit with consistency under virtually any condition.

SCARED MONEY NEVER WINS

This rule is as old as trading. If you can't afford to take losses, the pressure to win is often just too great for you to be able to function. First, losing is an integral part of trading. You will lose at the beginning of your trading career, in the middle of your career, and even on the day you retire from trading. That is all there is to it. Not having some reserves makes losing all the more trying, and you will find yourself breaking basic rules to stay afloat, to force the market to give you a winner. As you might guess, breaking or bending too many rules too often is a recipe for disaster.

RIGHT PLACE, RIGHT TIME

Another old trading saw is that on your first day of trading you will be as bad as you are going to get. I don't agree with this because the markets are not logical, nor are they predictable. You might have a great day on your debut. This in itself should cause you to pause and make some psychological adjustments. If you make money on your first day, look out. It will lead you to think trading is easy. It is not. The markets giveth and the markets taketh away. Some days are easy. Some weeks are easy. Even some months are easy. In the 1990s we had a decade-long bull market that some considered easy. Chimpanzees, throwing darts to select stocks, outpaced the S&P. There were times when it was more like horseshoes than rocket science, since you could make big money by being near right. We used to teach traders to select a stock's first cousin to trade if they missed a move on the cousin—if Amazon.com skyrocketed 20 points so fast you could not catch it, trade Barnes and Noble.com because it would be sucked up in the updraft. Believe it or not, this was a strategy we taught traders because it worked, but not indefinitely.

Trading is timing; timing is trading. If you are in the right place at the right time, it is more important than all the skill, experience, or research you can muster. But you will never always be in the right place at the right time, and you will rarely know you are in the right place at the right time until it is over. That is why you must follow the rules in this book to survive—so that you are still able to trade when you are in the right place at the right time.

AIM FOR THE MARKET'S BELLY, NOT ITS HEAD

New traders often try to get too much out of a trade by entering too soon and exiting too late in an attempt to do what is commonly referred to as picking tops or bottoms. The danger of course is being whipsawed. You enter a trade too soon hoping (a bad word for a trader to think or speak) to be in at the bottom only to watch the market tumble lower of its own weight. The same type of price action can punish your greed when you keep holding and holding a long position waiting for a top to be put in so you can sell at the apex. As you try to pick the top, the bottom falls out of the market and you give back half your gain.

With experience, you will be able to better size up these market movements. Most of your successful trades will come out of the middle of a move. For example, you don't enter a trade when the 10-interval moving average flattens out and begins to move higher. This is usually too soon. A better time is when the 20-interval crosses the 10, giving some confirmation of a trend change. But do you fire off your order then if volume is weak? The answer is no. Remember, volume is power, and it takes power to keep a trend moving. At the top, you exit the same way by following the moving averages, particularly if you see volume waning.

In the majority of trades, you are trying to take a nice chunk out of the center of the move. This is just like our sniper friend from Chapter 3, who aims for his target's belly if he is shooting from a marginal distance with turbulent wind conditions.

You simply take what shot the market gives. In most cases it is just part of the overall move. The best thing is that when a big move comes— you are long silver as it limits up, or you are short Lucent as it drops like a lead balloon—it moves so fast in your direction, you don't even have to make a decision. Boom! The trade hits, you are in, and it's an express train to the bank. Between these gifts, you work damn hard trying to eke out a living and preserve your risk capital. Don't ever forget this.

BATTERS WHO AVERAGE 300 MAKE MOST ALL-STAR TEAMS

If you follow the advice above and use stop-loss orders, two-thirds of your trades may be breakeven or losers, small losers that is. Most of the rest could be small and medium winners, but a few will be trophies. You'll want to get your monthly statement framed when the biggies hit. The objective of trading is to be a net winner. The objective of speculating is to be a very big winner. The objective of investing is to become wealthy. Avoid confusing these objectives. Trading and speculating are for income—short-term income. Long-term holds, with proper asset allocation, build your net worth. Because you pile up more losers than winners in day or swing trading, do not let that buildup increase the pressure on you. Once a week run a profit-and-loss tally on your trading. The facility to do this is built into most accounting software your clearing firm will give you access to. Take advantage of it. Run a P&L after the close on Friday, and study it Saturday morning. In the next chapter I'll get deeper into performance evaluation.

Another smart way of adding to your losers is to never meet a Regulation T margin call. If you get one, your position has obviously deteriorated substantially. Another conclusion you can draw is that you don't have enough money in your account to continue to hold the position. A margin call is your wake-up call to close out the position and reassess your situation. You may find it difficult to admit you are wrong on this trade, but, on the other hand, you can't in all honesty say you planned the trade to generate into a margin call. The trade obviously has not worked out as you visualized it. From my experience, it will get a whole lot worse nine out of ten times if you sweat it out. You can always wait until the entity bottoms and get back in at a lower price if you are still convinced it is a good trade. Mortal beings, you and I, were not built to face margin calls on any kind of regular basis. They just scream at you that you screwed up and the money is still bleeding into a bottomless trading pit. Get out! Get yourself together! And get back in if it looks good later! End of story!

AVERAGE INTO HEAVEN, NOT HELL

Another corollary to this axiom is never average losing trades. Averaging positions is the practice of entering or exiting trades at specified intervals. You might plan on putting on a 5000-share position in Microsoft or going long 100,000 bushels of corn or soybeans. Instead of buying the entire position at one time, you slowly buy and add to the original position. You might acquire 1000 shares at a time over five intervals. The intervals may be price levels. For example, you buy each time Microsoft goes up a dime or two corn contracts (5000 bushels each) each time corn inches up a nickel until you have your 5000 shares of Microsoft or your 100,000 bushels of corn. You can exit positions the same way. For example, Microsoft spikes up a half dollar, yet it is still looking strong, so you unload a thousand shares, generating $500 profit. This reduces your overall price for the 5000 shares by a dime. Each time Microsoft or corn moves higher, you take more profit, thus lowering the per-share price until you are out of the trade. As the price goes up and the size of your position gets smaller, the pressure on you is lower and you can take more heat from the market.

Averaging in and out of trades can reduce the stress of trading for some people. What you don't want to do is average down. This would be when you buy a few thousand shares of Microsoft, it drops a half dollar, and you decide to buy some more, obviously at a lower price. In this case you are buying more and more in a falling market. Yes, the price is getting cheaper, but at the same time your overall position is losing more money.

NEVER GIVE LOSSES CPR

There are bound to be times when traders find themselves in a losing position. For some traders, when it's a big loss, it will arouse the demon fear. Or they just can't admit they have been so wrong. Instead of dismantling the position, they attempt to devise a strategy to miraculously change it into a winner. How do they go about working miracles? They may try to straddle their position with a put, or they may try to sell calls above a losing long position. As me poor old Irish grandfather used to say, "Laddie, never try to turn a sow's ear into a silk purse." The more you attempt to convert a bold-faced loss into a world-class winner, the deeper you dig yourself into financial trouble. Go back to square one and drop a loser like a gold digger would in Las Vegas. The consequence is booking two losers versus one—not the kind of odds that will make you a rich person.

YOU'RE NOT A WAITER, SO DON'T RESPOND TO TIPS

For the newbie, avoiding tips can be a confusing rule. First you are told to get a mentor and let that person guide your first steps into the trading jungle. You count on that person to teach you how to avoid trip wires and how to spot tiger pits. Now you are told to disregard trading tips. This becomes even more confusing if your mentor is an unofficial mentor you meet on a public trading floor, meaning just another trader who has considerably more experience than you and has befriended you. This is common. The floor manager might deliberately seat you next to this person because he knows the person has a history of helping new traders. Your de facto mentor shares with you what he plans to trade each day and tells you his rationale, research, and strategy. Is this a tip or is it training?

That is training. The difference is that a tip is totally a barebones recommendation. "Short Dell today." "Jump on Sprint. It's going to the moon!" There is nothing wrong with taking a tip and doing your own research to come to some kind of a rational confirmation that the tip is a legitimate trading recommendation. Maybe you've been thinking about Sprint too as a possibility. You check the overall market to see that the trend is up. You look at the telecom index and the Sprint long-term, midterm and short-term charts. The stock has just retraced, and its short-term moving averages have just begun to head higher while the longer-term moving averages are flattening out. Volume even looks good. That is no longer a tip but a trade. To just take the tip and trade it is gambling and stupid.

Here is a classic example from the heyday of day trading. One of the hotshots on a trading floor always sat in the back of the room. He traded very thinly traded stocks. Every once in a while, he would shout out that a certain stock was making a spectacular move higher. He pretended he was talking to himself, "Go Sepia! Wow, up 2 sticks! Going to the moon!" Pretty soon most of the other traders were looking at Sepia since this character had a reputation of making big trades. Next thing the whole floor was pushing the stock higher. It shot up another $5. As the floor ignited a rally, the guy in the back seat sold into this volume exiting his multithousand-share position, with a substantial profit taken in part from his trading buddies. As you probably guessed, the new rally failed and many of these traders took a bath in red ink.

Did he do anything wrong or illegal? If this trader were a licensed broker, this would be called front running, which is a serious security rule infraction. It occurs when a broker takes a position in a stock and then sells his customers on the stock. As they buy into it, the price rises and the broker exits with a profit. Technically, this punk did nothing illegal. He was not licensed, and he did not recommend the stock. He just conned his fellow traders into running his position higher. Morally he was a lizard, but the floor should have had the discipline to avoid being suckered.

There are two lessons in this story. The first is to carefully select whom you associate with on a public trading floor. Joining a floor is no different from becoming part of any other group or clique in that there are good members and there are harmful ones. When our kids start a new school or join the armed services, we all sweat how they will change. Will it be for the good or not? Will they take up with a crowd that cuts class to smoke or do much worse things, like drugs? Or will they join the group headed for an Ivy League school? On any floor you have the same mix of good and bad influences. Care must be taken.

Initially trading on a floor can substantially reduce your learning curve. If the manager and the traders share, it can be a fast track and help you avoid many pitfalls. But if you team up with the sycophants who are just there to brag or make a quick killing, you will pay dearly for nothing. I have met several successful traders who spent some time on a floor and then decided to trade from home or an office. They learned what they could, but did not like the atmosphere or having to explain or defend their strategies. One told me he left the floor because he did not like other traders trying to talk him out of what he wanted to do. A public floor is not for everyone.

SELL INTO RALLIES

The second lesson to learn from the evil little gremlin in the back of the room is a good one to remember. I don't like the way he created the rally, but I do like the fact that he knew enough about when to sell.

Always sell into strength. You will retire a happier and richer trader if you learn to exit trades too early. Those who try to take the very last penny from the piggybank get caught when the market reverses.

The old Wall Street proverb "All the good news comes out at the top and all the bad news at the bottom" is worth heeding. The same goes for "Bull markets climb a wall of worry." My point is always watch your technical signals. Trading news is akin to trading tips. It's a sucker's bet at best when unaccompanied by research to back it up. The technicals will tell you what is actually happening, not what a lot of people are guessing. The more excited and bullish a market gets, the more likely it is about to reverse. Or if a trend is up, continue to be long, no matter what the analysts are saying or worrying about.

LISTEN TO THE STREET, BUT BE PARANOID

In a previous chapter we discussed the specialists on the listed exchanges, primarily the New York Stock Exchange. They are the guardians of order and sanity. But never for a minute think of them as benign. The same goes for the analysts.

The specialists are extremely powerful. Their position is so regal that you almost have to be born into it. Think for a moment what authority and power they possess. Besides being able to halt trading as mentioned earlier, they can buy and sell for their own account and for omnibus accounts, which might be friendly banks or wealthy investors. They can make the price of the stock they control rise or fall, almost at their whim. For example, if good news hits the floor, the specialist can sell from his own account or an omnibus account into the strength. Once the price is high enough, he can begin selling, putting enough pressure to halt the move. Then, if he wants to, he can short the stock, driving it down. He can offset the short positions by buying and just enjoy a profitable roller-coaster ride. Since he is the only one who can see at what prices and size the big buy and sell orders are in his book, he can spot trends and profit opportunities before anyone else on the face of the earth. Some fun, what?

Did you ever see an analyst working for a major brokerage firm that didn't like a stock? Analysts are not paid to learn why stocks should be sold. They are, in my opinion, as much a part of the marketing team as the sales manager. When Enron took its dive in 2002, how many analysts were touting the stock, and how many were recommending it as a short? If I remember correctly, there was only one analyst warning that something was not quite right. The terminology used by analysts reinforces the bullish slant of their advice. Everything is a strong buy, a buy, or a hold. An analyst with a sell on his or her list is as rare as an ethical politician.

ALL TRADERS ARE ISLANDS

John Donne probably wouldn't like this last rule, but it is true. You begin your career by assimilating as much as you can of what has been learned. I call them the rules. From there you must develop your very own trading system. You have two basic choices, intuitive or mechanical. Intuitive traders are spontaneous. They trade by instinct and hunches. The most successful intuitive traders have years of experience behind them and most started as mechanical. Once they mastered the rules and developed a keen instinct for certain markets, they "became" intuitive traders. The most common ones you will run into on a trading floor are momentum day traders. Their shtick is to find the fastest-moving stocks and just jump from the long to the short side or bounce in and out of a market as the momentum ebbs and flows. This type of trading was very profitable before decimalization and during the blow-off top of the bull market of the 1990s.

The trader with a mechanical system is most likely a technical trader. This is what I would recommend for starters for any short-term or swing trader. Once you have developed a repertoire of trading strategies and have mastered all the basic trading skills, you can begin to go out on your own. This is when you really become a trader. You develop your special technical signals, much like Brian Shannon has developed moving averages that may be unique to him. These modifications of an existing and proven approach put Brian on his unique island. When you get to this stage, your confidence soars, permitting you to occasionally bend the rules. But please don't break them, at least not often—it won't be a pleasant experience to try to fool Mother Nature.

Let's talk a little about swing trading rules since a good percentage of short-term traders use this technique. I define swing trading as holding a position from one trading session to at least another. That could end up to be only a few hours of actual trading—from the end of one session to the beginning of the next. Theoretically, a day trade could last longer. The distinction I make is holding the trade between sessions.

One big question that often comes up is what do you do if a weekend occurs between the sessions. If you totally rule out holding positions over weekends, you can only day-trade on Fridays. Holding trades over weekends is a personal decision. I tend to let the systemic volatility of the market, combined with the beta of the stock being traded, make my decision for me. In other words, if the market as a whole is unsettled and I feel there may be some possibility that an event could occur over the weekend that could cause the market to go against my position, I would just as soon be flat over the weekend. This is particularly true if the entity (stock or commodity) had a high beta, meaning it was very responsive to the market or index it was a part of.

The most striking example of this approach is the terrible acts of September 11, 2001. A massive terrorist attack shut down most markets for a week. Other worldwide markets traded down. Then the United States markets opened and they crashed. This is a horrendous example, but it can repeat itself on a much smaller scale. On a Friday of a week that has been especially volatile, I just think it is foolish to open swing positions. On the other hand, if the market being traded has trended in my direction for all or most of the week, it may make sense to hold a swing trade over the weekend. The big risk between a swing trade that occurs during the trading week, Monday through Friday, and one that goes over the weekend, a Friday through the following Monday, is that there is substantially more time for something to happen that can negatively effect your position when you cannot do anything about it. Stop-loss orders will not protect you on a weekend, nor can you exit a trade in after-hours trading. Again, experience rules. For the first 6 months or so of trading, you may want to be flat on weekends.

Much also depends on how the trade you are in is going. For example, the general rule about holding a position overnight is to do so if it is making you money. Remember trends, like rocks rolling downhill, continue in motion in the direction they are going until they meet resistance. If you are long and the trend is up, you have the edge that it will continue up the next day. If you get a gap on the next day's open, take your profit and run. Why? Because a gap is an unexpected event, and it has changed the complexion of the trade. You are in no-man's-land.

STRONG CLOSE, STRONG OPEN—AND VICE VERSA

Another possibility is you get a weak, lackluster close. What do you do? Exit the trade in after-hours trading? This is a judgment call based on experience with the stock being traded and its after-hours liquidity. Many traders will exit the trade and look for a better position the next day. By now, I think it is clear that the opening and the closing are the most important segments of any trading day. It is not uncommon for traders who cannot be in front of their trading screen all day to make arrangements to trade either the open or the close, or both if they are lucky. That way they have a good chance of catching 70 or 80 percent of all the opportunity. By open and close I mean from approximately 7:30 a.m. to 10:00 a.m. and 2:00 p.m. to 4:00 p.m. EST, respectively.

Let me state a word of caution regarding the open. The first 15 minutes can be erratic. Prices often bob. and weave. The reason is that retail brokers all over the country get thousands and thousands of orders before the market opens. Their customers call before going to work and set their trading up for the day. Online traders email orders to their firms at the same time. You often have to wait for this backlog of overnight orders to be flushed through the system before beginning to trade. This activity is easy to spot with a little experience.

The close can also be very tricky. In the industry we say, "The open belongs to the amateurs and the close to the professionals!" Therefore it is key to watch the close very carefully for a hint of what will happen the next day. How many times have you seen a market go south for most of the day and then recover just before closing? That's the pros (meaning institutions, mutual funds, hedge funds, and brokerage firms) adjusting their portfolios for the evening. It is common for the specialists or the market makers to put a short squeeze on just before the close, especially on Friday. There is no better time to put the fear of God in the hearts of those negative-thinking short sellers.

Getting back to that gap opening, many traders expect gaps to be filled. Therefore if a trade gaps higher at the open, there is a group of traders that may short it looking for the gap to be filled in, particularly if volume is average or low as the gap reaches its apex. The energy that caused the gap is likely to be short-lived, and the odds now call for some kind of retracement to follow the gap. Once the retracement occurs, you may have another buying opportunity, but that is a whole new trade and must be treated as such.

How long should you stay in a swing trade? Like any other trade, you must plan your exit before you enter. Actually, plan two exit moves. The first move should be your response if the trade does not begin to move in your favor as soon as you enter it. Don't wait around very long for a trade to develop, especially if it is a setup trade. If you have to wait, you most likely got in too early or your analysis missed its mark. Visualize your trade; as soon as you lose the vision, exit. This could be in a minute, an hour, a day, or days, depending on your time frame and style.

If the trade develops as you visualized, exit at your target price. At the same time, you are monitoring volume, futures indexes, the stock's sector, the Nasdaq or whichever exchange the stock trades on, and news. Keep asking yourself, "Is anything changing that will impact reaching or exceeding my price objective?" If nothing spooks or encourages you, close the position at your objective or place a tight trailing stop.

When swing trading, use stops, just like you would at any other time. If the swing trade is a setup-type trade, keep the stop pretty tight. But if you are trading a trend and it has been consistent for a few days, you can take more heat and use a little wider stop. Keep it a few pennies larger than the largest daily move over the past few days or just below the last support area on a long trade.

ANTICIPATE! ANTICIPATE! ANTICIPATE!

Like the old joke about what are the three most important characteristics of a good retail store—location, location, location—what are the three most important characteristics of a good trader—the ability to anticipate, anticipate, anticipate. You must be thinking ahead of the market. It is like playing chess. No one becomes a grand master by not being able to anticipate what his opponent will do over the next 10 moves. Obviously if any of us could anticipate any market with a high degree of accuracy, we would keep our mouths shut and rake in the millions. My point is that you must constantly try to get a jump on the next move. If you don't, you will miss it.

Additionally, you must always be protecting yourself from being wrong, thus the use of hard stops. Hard stops are stop orders that actually exit, not mental stops that may or may not get activated. Always keep in mind the biggest difference between professionals and amateurs. Professionals make a living through their trading by acting before all the facts are known. Amateurs wait for confirmation.

The pros sell into the amateurs, which they refer to as dumb money when they take a profit. This is most clearly seen during a stock split. The pros will be watching a stock. Let's say it has a pattern of splitting. This company calls an unexpected board meeting. The company's sales and earnings have been strong. The share price is up. The pros start buying, and anyone who closely watches or scans for these market indicators sees that volume and price are creeping up. Next there is a rumor of another split. Price and volume go even higher. A split is announced. The next trading day the stock is up strong on the open, only to fall sharply shortly thereafter.

How many times have you seen this? If the split is a sign of strength, what causes the retracement after the open? The answer is that the professionals buy the stock on the anticipation of the split. The dumb money waits for confirmation. When the amateurs rush in, the devils take them out. The pros sell into strength and buy into weakness, which is what you must learn to do. There probably isn't any clear distinction between the pros and amateurs. The pros do it every day by being able to decipher the technical signals and understand the market's mood simply by sensing if there are more buyers than sellers or more sellers than buyers.

All this sounds simple as you read it, but it takes a lot of experience and effort. It is what is most commonly referred to as a passion, specifically a passion for the market. Another way of saying it is that the successful trader has an ever-unsatisfied need to learn what makes the market tick. The answer is complex and revolves more around the psyche of the trader than the inner workings of the market. This is the subject of the last chapter.

LOSE FOCUS; LOSE MONEY

Now let's talk a little about the second key consideration mentioned in the first paragraph of this chapter: focus. I'll start by telling you a little story about a trader I worked with. Let's call him Frank. He was intelligent and attended the Market Wise Trading School. Upon graduation, he began trading on our trading floor. We would meet before and after the markets to discuss the day's trading, a sort of unofficial mentoring session. One day, I had to run an errand and ducked out the back door. There was Frank smoking and talking to some of the other traders. I stopped and asked if any of them had positions on. The only one who did was Frank. I told him in no uncertain terms, many of which I had learned while at sea, that you cannot leave a trade unattended. This was during a period of high volatility on the Nasdaq, which everyone was trading.

To make a long, sad story short, Frank blew out of the market. He lost two sizable amounts of risk capital. The reason was not that he didn't understand the market or that he didn't have a talent for it. The reason was focus. He could not sit for hours at a time and keep his mind on the nitty-gritty.

Can you? Are there any tricks of the trade that can help? Just the fact that traders have a trade on in which they could easily lose a grand or two should be enough motivation, I would think. Nevertheless, I feel it is important that traders interact with the market in an active way. Trading can be more successful and even enjoyable if you can keep your head in the action.

For example, before the market opens, as was mentioned earlier, you need to listen to Bloomberg, CNBC, or whatever to get a feel for the mood of the world. Was the rest of the world bullish or bearish while you slept? A whole ritual was laid out. Now let's take that a step further and through the trading session.

Create a daily trader's log. Record all the pertinent facts and developments that are expected and that occur during each trading day. You should even include weekend events of note. Think back to Chapters 2 and 3 for a second. You were asked a lot of questions about your passion for the market and were told to ritualize your preparation for trading. Now formalize those concepts into a written log. This will be a history of your trading that allows you and your mentor to talk through every trading day. As you first begin, this interaction is more critical. As you mature as a trader, you may only meet with your mentor weekly. Eventually, your mentoring sessions may become monthly, quarterly, or on an as-needed basis—when one of you feels it is important to meet because something has changed. Go back to our golf analogy. When does Tiger Woods call in his swing coach? Whenever he feels he needs him. And if the coach sees something that concerns him, he calls Tiger. You need to grow into that type of relationship with your mentor.

Below is some of what might make up your daily trader's log. I use the word *might*, as opposed to *should*, because you must tailor the log to fit your specific needs. Most logs will have some common areas, such as:

- Overnight markets, i.e., European, Asian, other.
- U.S. futures markets opening before U.S. stock markets, i.e., bonds, Nasdaq, other.
- Futures traders would check Globex's overnight activity.
- What is the overnight market sentiment?
- Stocks to trade today—yesterday's activity and close.

- Trading plan for today—orders, entry, exit, target, stop loss.

- Visualization—how do you expect the trade to unfold?

- Psychological reflections on your state of mind.

- Summary of sectors of today's trading candidates.

- Summary of major indexes of today's candidates.

- News—overnight and planned stories (reports, earnings, Fed meetings, etc.) for today and anticipated impact.

- Any other influencing factors to track.

- Trading day:

  o   Premarket trading

  o   Preopening—0600–0730

  o   Opening—0730–0800

  o   Postopening—0800–1030

  o   Noon—1030–1330

  o   Preclose—1330–1530

  o   Close—1530–1600

  o   Postclose—1600–1500

  o   After hours trading

- Recap day's trading.

Futures traders will naturally have a different timetable depending on the markets they trade, many of which open at different times. Nevertheless, the objective of maintaining a daily log is to force you to keep your head in the game, build good habits at the very start, and give you and your mentor hard information to talk about. You will not get the real help you need from your mentor without being able to point to hard facts and without taking good notes about how you are trading and how you are feeling while trading.

9

STAYING THE COURSE

My first trading rule, as stated in the previous chapter, is to become a very disciplined trader. That is easy to say, but how does one enforce self-discipline—the very toughest type of discipline? I think there are some important steps you can take once you begin trading. I also suggest that you do as much of the calculations as you can personally. It is the only way to get the focus on your activity that you need to really improve.

Remember one of our first keys is survival. You want to be alive and trading when you find yourself in the right place at the right time. Call it what you like: staying in the game, preserving your capital to be ready to take advantage of opportunities, surviving until you're thriving. How do you measure how well you are doing as a survivor?

Survival depends on cutting losses short. Here is a technique to help you evaluate how well you are doing with this most vital area. To begin, you need to understand the concept of standard deviation from the mean. It is a way of quantifying random occurrences. You must also accept the fact that your daily losses are as random an occurrence as flipping a balanced silver dollar and picking heads or tails in advance. You skew these random occurrences in your favor, meaning financial success as a trader, by efficiently controlling the risk and preserving your capital.

Actually all the trades, not just the losing trades, you make are random occurrences, as was discussed when distinguishing gambling from trading. Each one is independent of the preceding one. Fully accepting this concept also helps you deal with a losing streak, and the hope is that it will prevent you from doing something stupid, like doubling up after you have had several losers in a row, with the idea that the slot machine is due to pay off.

To grasp this concept, it is helpful to walk through a few basic statistical concepts. One that we have discussed often is volatility, particularly of the markets you may be trading. You learned that the more volatile a stock, option, or futures contract was, the more profit opportunity it presented and the more dangerous it was. This basic idea is true for the losses you experience. The more volatile your losses, the less control you have over your trading.

What I recommend, especially for the first 6 months of trading, is that you measure the volatility of your daily losses. Just look at your losses, not your winning days. To illustrate how this works, let's evaluate 2 months of trading by a hypothetical trader: the first month and the sixth month. We'll use 20 trading days per month to make the math simpler (there are approximately 22 trading days a month over any given trading year). In month one this trader had losing days equal to 60 percent, or 12 days, and in month six he reduced the percentage to 50 percent. Keep in mind, we are evaluating the volatility of his losing days only. This has nothing to do with overall profitability. No matter what his percentage of losing days is, he could still be a net winner if he let his winners run and cut losers short. Table 9-1 shows his losses on the days he was a net loser.

On a gross basis, month one looks better because the loss is lower. On an average basis, month one again appears to be better because the daily loss is about $250 less. But the most meaningful method of comparing the two months is calculating the standard deviation of the two.

To understand how standard deviation is calculated, let's go back to the example of flipping a coin. From thousands and thousands of experiments, it has been proved that a balanced coin will have an equal chance of landing with its head's side up or with its tail's side up. By quickly running through the math, you'll be able to see how the same process can be used to determine the standard deviation of your daily losses and the value of being able to calculate it to determine if you are controlling them.

The classic example, which you may remember from high school math or college statistics, is flipping a balanced coin 225 times, or 15

Table 9-1

Month One	Month Six
($355)	($500)
($267)	($467)
($100)	($605)
($799)	($555)
($99)	($465)
($1345)	($524)
($67)	($444)
($36)	($489)
($299)	($588)
($169)	($857)
($88)	
($22)	
($3646)	($5494)
Average $304	$550

separate series of 15 flips each. This exercise produces the theoretical results shown in Table 9-2.

Every time you do this experiment, the results vary some, but oddly enough they will be more similar than different. We all believe that flipping a coin has a 50-50 chance of coming up heads or tails. If it didn't work randomly and fairly, we would not make so many important decisions, like who will kick off first in a football game, by flipping a coin. Would you do it if you had four captains from two professional football teams—a ton of four steroid-taking, weight-lifting athletes who make their living pounding each other into the ground—crowding around you as you do the flip if you didn't think it was a fair way to decide?

The next step is to calculate the arithmetic mean or the average value of the series of flips. After that, we will calculate the value of what 1 standard deviation from the mean will be as a measure of volatility. Before you get too worried about all this math, I will walk you through how all this can be done in seconds using Microsoft Excel or a similar program. It is as simple as pointing a mouse and making a few clicks.

The mean is calculated by multiplying the number of event results on one side (heads or tails, winning days or losing days) by the number of flips and dividing the total by the number of event results. Table 9-3 shows the results of all the flips that landed on heads.

Table 9-2

Series #	# of Heads	# of Tails	Total
1	1	14	15
2	2	13	15
3	3	12	15
4	6	9	15
5	8	7	15
6	7	8	15
7	10	5	15
8	11	4	15
9	9	6	15
10	5	10	15
11	6	9	15
12	4	11	15
13	2	13	15
14	1	14	15
15	0	15	15

Table 9-3

Flips		# of Heads Event Results
1 × 1	=	1
2 × 2	=	4
3 × 3	=	9
4 × 6	=	24
5 × 8	=	40
6 × 7	=	42
7 × 10	=	70
8 × 11	=	88
9 × 9	=	81
10 × 5	=	50
11 × 6	=	66
12 × 4	=	48
13 × 2	=	26
14 × 1	=	14
15 × 0	=	0
Total number of flips = 75		Total number of heads = 563
563 divided by 75	=	7.5067

As predicted, the mean is approximately 7½, or over time and thousands of flips, every other one is a head. Does that make you feel a little safer if you're the one who has to flip the coin in the middle of a football field before a championship game?

Our next step is to calculate 1 standard deviation from the mean. This will tell us where two-thirds of all random occurrences can be expected to fall. For example, our objective in this exercise is to determine how consistent our losses are, which are random occurrences. The closer they are together, the more consistent we are. Consistency in losses is critical because it illustrates control. Therefore the lower the standard deviation for the mean is, the more consistent we are.

As I mentioned earlier, the calculation is simple using a program like Microsoft Excel. Here are the steps:

1. Open a spreadsheet and input the daily losses for the period being evaluated.
2. Input the numbers in a column. Use column A for the first month, B for the second, etc. Since we are evaluating the first and the sixth month, we would be using columns A and F. It would look something like this:

A	F
355	500
267	467
100	605
799	555
99	465
1345	524
67	444
36	489
299	588
169	857
88	
22	

3. Highlight the first column (column A).
4. Move your mouse up to "fx" or select "functions." Click on this

and select "Statistical" functions. Scroll down to "STDEV" and click.

5.   Repeat the process using the second column (column F).

In this example, the answers are

$$391.8186 \ (3.9\%) \qquad 120.6401 \ (1.2\%)$$

This trader made substantial improvement. The standard deviation of her losses dropped from almost 400 to approximately 120, an improvement of over 300 percent. In other words, she is over three times more consistent in controlling her losses.

Controlling losses is critical to survival, but it has nothing to do with profitability. As a trader you must know how much you can afford to lose per trade, per day, per month, and totally. If you lose too much, you are out of the game, period. On the other hand, there is no need to measure the standard deviation of your winners. Why? Winning trades do not have to be consistent. You take what the market gives you. In one case, you go long and hold the position until it reaches some serious resistance. You see volume dropping and the moving averages flattening out. You exit with $500 profit. Another time, the same stock blasts through the resistance on stronger volume for a profit of $5000. In each case, you took what was available.

With losses it is different. You must control them. You must set a limit of some sort. Losses must be consistent if you are cutting them short. As we discussed when we were talking about stop-loss orders, it is common for traders to set a maximum dollar amount or percentage. If you set a dollar amount, measuring standard deviation can be very helpful in measuring how consistent you are—or are becoming. Using a percentage can fluctuate depending on the price of the entity being traded. Nevertheless, if your trading pattern is consistent, which it should be in the beginning, calculating the standard deviation of your daily losses will give you a better feel for your performance.

Remember back when we began talking about technical analysis. We said there are only five outcomes for any trade—large or small win, large or small loss, or breakeven. Using the two tools we discussed so far—the average size of the losing trade per day (or whatever period is under review) and the standard deviation of the losses—we can now quantify and evaluate how well we are obeying the rule to cut losses short.

In our example, the average loss for the first month was $304, and for the second month it had jumped to almost $550. But the standard deviation, or the volatility of the daily losses, dropped from 392 to 121. What has taken place? Is this positive or negative? The information only describes one side of the equation. The ultimate answer always resides on the profit side of the ledger. Nevertheless, this trader has eliminated the wild swings in her losses. Note that when she experienced a loss of over $1300, she appeared to cut her trading back. This is a common reaction and another reason to work hard to maintain low, consistent losses. By month six, it appears this trader settled in on limiting each loss to approximately $500. That is where you can now find her stop-loss orders.

Simultaneously, you would expect the level of trading to have substantially increased. This accounts for the much higher gross loss, $3646 versus $5494. I also use gross loss of equity, which includes commissions and fees. Some mentors do not include these two entries in their accounting. The way I look at it is that the money has been taken out of the account due to trading activity. You cannot trade without paying commissions and fees. Therefore any accounting that ignores them creates a pro forma statement, which to me is bogus.

Besides taking into consideration the average size and the standard deviation of your losses, you also need to think about duration. How long has your account been trading in the red? This concept is generally referred to as a drawdown. In the beginning, meaning the first 3 to 6 months of trading, I recommend you measure it in days down and dollars lost. In our example above, month one had 12 losing days and month six 10. It is important to keep track of how many of those days were consecutive, what was the longest period, and what was the percentage of losing days.

Results for month one might be figured out like this. First, you use the number of days traded in the period being measured, not the total days the market was open. If there were 22 trading days and the trader missed 2 days, that month would be considered a 20-day month. The stats for month one are shown in Table 9-4. The percentage of losing days for the month is 60 percent (12/20). The longest drawdown is 3 days, which occurred twice.

The information we are looking at may appear to be meaningless because it is sketchy and the conclusion that can be drawn may not hold up, but this will be a good start if you are serious about becoming a professional trader. Every journey starts with the first step. Data like the above become more and more valuable the longer you trade. If you al-

Table 9-4

Day	Loser	Winner
1	x	
2	x	
3		x
4	x	
5	x	
1	x	
2	x	
3		x
4		x
5		x
1	x	
2	x	
3	x	
4		x
5		x
1	x	
2	x	
3	x	
4		x
5		x
	12	8

ready trade, go back and try to recapture some of this information. If you are just starting out, please build good habits of collecting and monitoring your trading activity. If nothing else, it helps you focus on the results of your trading. This is a key to success.

Once you collect 6 months or a year of statistics, you will start seeing important patterns. One of the most critical is how long it takes you to recover from a losing streak. You are going to have losing streaks. If you cannot deal with them, you need to know early on or you will blow out.

As you review the facts you compile, ask yourself the following questions on a monthly or quarterly basis, depending on your volume of trading. Better yet, have your mentor ask them of you. (By the way, at the Market Wise Trading School, we usually say it takes about 1000 trades or 3 months to really get the feel of the Nasdaq and the software platform.

Even then, there are many valuable subtleties built into today's software that take much longer to master. The mechanics of trading is a very key aspect.)

1. What is your largest drawdown in dollars?
2. How long did it take you to recover from the drawdown?
3. What was your largest single day's loss?
4. What was the longest number of consecutive losing days?
5. How often do you go on losing binges?
6. What is the trend of the standard deviation of your losing days? Go ahead and chart these data points.
7. What is the trend of the percentage of losing days per week? Again chart the data.

Whoever acts as your formal or informal mentor should be a close confidant of yours. You should respond to these questions and spill out your guts about the impact of each loss, or the effect of accumulative losses, on your psyche. For example, let's say the answer to question 1 is a real heartbreaker. You lost more than you can afford on one trade; let's put it at 25 percent of your trading equity. How does that make you feel? How will you deal with it? Answers to these types of questions will determine if you survive as a trader. Therefore, they should be discussed with someone who is more than just sympathetic. That person must have the experience to help you prepare a recovery plan.

Are you beginning to think I am paranoid about losing money? Am I taking it too seriously? Or am I spending too much time on the subject? My answers are yes, no, and no. I am very paranoid about losing money, and the reason for this is summed up in the loss recovery table shown in Table 9.5.

The deeper the hole you dig for yourself, the longer and tougher it is to work your way out of it. It is like climbing up a steep sand dune. You can rationalize some losses by categorizing them as tuition paid for learning a new profession. That is legitimate. But you must be careful with too much of this type of thinking because you may find yourself in a hole that is too deep to climb out of. Also note that it only takes 5.25 percent to recover from a 5 percent loss. That is why many professional traders place their stop loss at 5 percent below the entry price on long positions or 5 percent above on shorts. One of the very best traders of our times is Paul Tutor Jones. Jack Schwager, in his excellent book *Market Wizards*, quotes

Table 9-5

% Loss	% Needed to Break Even
5	5.26
20	25.00
30	42.86
40	66.67
50	100.00
70	233.33
90	900.00
100	Impossible

Mr. Jones as saying, "The most important rule of trading is to play a great defense, not a great offense." I concur. If you don't get yourself in financial trouble, you don't have to get yourself out. If you can stay on the merry-go-round long enough, you'll get a brass ring.

You may be thinking that if I am going to lose as much as this guy says, what do I have to do to win? Winning as a speculator is like hitting in baseball. Aren't many of the greatest home run hitters also known as strikeout kings? Aren't the players with the most hits and highest batting averages also the ones who hit the most home runs? As noted earlier, it only takes a lifetime batting average of 300 or so, if the career is long enough, to make it into the Baseball Hall of Fame. With the right mix of winners and losers, you can get rich by winning every third or fourth trade. The key, of course, is small losses and medium and big winners. A successful trader might have a trade distribution something like this:

Total trades	100
Winners	30
Losers	70
Winners	
Small	15
Medium	10
Large	5
Losers	
Small	50
Medium	19
Large	1

The big winners may account for only 5 percent of the total trades, but they could easily be 70 or 80 percent of gross profits.

While careful monitoring of losses is critical to successful trading, the overall profitability of the account is always the final arbiter. At the height of day-trading the dot-com bubble, there were many aggressive traders who spurned the idea of nursing losses. They felt they could overpower the market, overcome any losses, and end up as winners in a big way just by trading their brains out every day. A few actually did, damn few. Most became what are referred to as blow-out traders. Eventually they sustained a crippling loss.

It is much better to practice safe losing from the beginning. Even in the best of times—during raging bull markets—you will be big dollars ahead. More importantly, the complexion of the market will change. It always does. The raging bull becomes the bleeding bear. If you take the time to learn how to harness your emotions and losses, you will survive and thrive in either.

A corollary to managing losses is to avoid overmanaging them. You manage losses by using stop-loss orders and doing sound technical analysis. You know in advance how far the next support area is on long positions and resistance on shorts. You constantly monitor the trend via moving averages. And you do all the other important things that are part of your trading system. What you do not do is hide. I have seen traders who became so paranoid about taking losses that they trade stocks or futures contracts that have flatlined, as far as volatility is concerned.

Let's go back to the parable of the fly fisherman. In order for him to put himself in a position to catch a few trophy trout, he must do his homework. He must read the sports section of the local paper to find out where big fish are being caught. It also wouldn't hurt to call the state's wildlife commission and find out what streams are well stocked. Learning how to tie flies or where to buy the best ones should be on his list. Visiting fishing web sites is certainly a must. Knowing how to select the best places to fish might help. If he is afraid of the water and fishes only in slow-moving, shallow rivers, he is going to be a loser.

My point is that you must put yourself in volatile's way to make big profits. But you must ease into it. If our friend the fisherman attempts to fish in a very deep, fast-moving river on day one and drowns, he will never make the fishermen's hall of fame. The same fate awaits any trader who thinks he or she can bully the market on day one and not worry about managing losses, learning the mechanics of electronic trading, and determining how he or she will react psychologically when faced with losses and margin calls.

Your average loss, your drawdown, and the standard deviation of your losses are only three of the many numbers you should be monitoring daily, weekly, monthly, quarterly, and annually. Now I would like to give you some background on how professional traders are evaluated, specifically commodity trading advisers (CTAs) and hedge fund managers (HFMs). I use CTAs because I believe more thought and research has gone into evaluating them than their equivalent on the stock side of trading, i.e., registered investment advisers and market analysts. Once you have an idea about how the CTAs and HFMs are scrutinized, you can borrow some of those techniques that will give you some excellent insights into how you should be tracking and evaluating yourself. Then we'll take a look at updating and improving your trading plan.

I feel very strongly about self-evaluation, particularly if quantitative measures are in place. Sad to say, it is way too easy to lie to oneself. Our equity will be down and our win-lose ratio tanking. But what we think about is the last big winner and how good it felt. "All I need to pull out of this rut is a 10-stick blow-out!" On the other hand, if we are carefully tracking and watching the standard deviation of our mean losses and see it climbing, we know our discipline is waning. Time to recharge our batteries and tighten our discipline. Take a day off and review the basics. Screw your head back on tight and follow the rules you know will eventually get you back on the sunny side of the market.

PORK BELLIES TO PORK BELLIES, SYSTEMS TO SYSTEMS!

Professional managers of mutual funds, proprietary traders, commodity trading advisers, and hedge fund managers measure their performance against a standard that resembles the market they trade. For example, I am sure you are familiar with some of the better-known mutual funds that compare their performance with that of the S&P 500. Ideally an actively managed basket of stocks should outperform one that is left on its own. But that isn't always true, is it? I also believe that many of the indexes that are considered "unmanaged" are indeed managed, since any issue that falls too far behind the group or goes out of business is replaced by the strongest candidate available that matches the criteria of the index. Is it any wonder the stock market gets credit for generating returns of over 10 percent a year since the Great Depression?

Mutual funds that specialize in a particular sector, such as gold or technical stock, are measured against their respective subindexes, i.e.,

XAU or the SOX. There are enough subindexes to cover just about any specialty. Additionally, you will find ratings from investor services such as Morningstar or Value Line, some volatility indicators (standard deviation, mean total return percentage, beta, alpha, R-square, and maybe even a Shape ratio), the expense ratio, fees, and overall performance over various periods.

CTAs are compared with indexes as well. Some of the more well-known ones are the MAR Qualified Universe Indices, the Barclay CTA Index, and the Norwood Index. Or CTAs might be weighed against a subindex that matches the commodities and futures contracts being traded or even the trading style of the manager. For example, the CRB (Commodity Research Bureau) is broken out by major categories of commodities, i.e., grains, metals, petroleum, food and fiber, etc.; and both the Managed Account Report (MAR) and the Hedge Fund Report categorize funds and advisers as discretionary or systematic. The latter traders adhere religiously to a system, and the former are more intuitive in their trading. These reports also compare currency or stock index traders against other similar programs.

Knowing how some of these indexes are constructed will give you insight into how to classify your own trading and decide which yardstick best matches. The MAR is a monthly report on the performance of managed accounts. Each year, it selects 25 prominent CTAs with over $30 million under management as a sampling of the industry. The performance of this group becomes the index. The Barclay CTA Index is more democratic in that it includes all CTAs with over 4 years' performance history. It adds the CTA to its index at the beginning of the CTA's fifth year of trading. A third index, the Norwood Index, uses the net asset value of the funds under management, rather than being VAMI-based as the other two are.

For those not familiar with the analysis of the track record of professional traders such as CTAs, I'll quickly review the concept of VAMI. This acronym stands for value-added monthly index. The Commodity Futures Trading Commission (CFTC) and the National Futures Association (NFA), the self-regulatory bodies of the futures industry, require CTAs to include a current VAMI table in their offering documents. They have done this to keep the evaluation of trading track records uniform for investors. The standard table contains nine columns: "Month/Year," "Beginning Net Asset Value (BNAV)," "Additions," "Withdrawals," "Net Performance," "Ending Net Asset Value (ENAV)," and "Annual Rate of Return."

One of the criticisms of VAMI is how the additions and withdrawals are handled. I only mention this because it could be a problem for you if you plan on calculating the rate of return of your account. The rate of return is figured by dividing the ENAV by the BNAV. Sounds simple, doesn't it? The problem the CTAs have is when they receive a large investment, an addition, after the trading month begins. The trader only has use of the money for a few weeks. Or the money arrives on the last day of the month, and so the trader has no use of it for that period. When does it have to be added into the BNAV? For example, adding an additional million or half million to the BNAV without being able to trade it reduces the trader's return on investment. Or leaving it out of the BNAV because the trader only had use of the money for half the month could make the rate of return look better than it is.

Conceivably you could run into the same type of problem and feel the tendency to make your rate of return look a little better than it really is. You might get some money, a big commission or bonus, and decide to deposit it in your trading account. When do you do it? Immediately? At the beginning or end of the month? What about a large margin call? You have no choice when it gets deposited. Any large addition can impact the rate of return.

The same problem, of course, occurs when funds are withdrawn. If 5 percent, 10 percent, or more is pulled out of a trading account at the beginning of a trading period and winning positions must be closed prematurely, there is a definite negative impact on the return calculation. Or if funds are returned to a large investor at the end of a particularly good trading period, the next period may be artificially skewed to the high side due to the lower denominator. Obviously any substantial change in the numerator or denominator of an equation severely impacts the results. Just be honest with yourself. You must make adjustment for these changes and avoid pulling the wool over your own eyes.

Earlier I mentioned a few important ratios that are used to evaluate investments such as mutual funds and managed futures funds. These formulas are also an excellent way for you to judge yourself as an investment. Are you a good deal? If you compared yourself with a Nasdaq 100 index fund, how would you rate? At the end of your second year of full-time trading, will you be an attractive property for a complete stranger to invest in? This may sound silly at first, but if you aren't, you may have some tough investment decisions to make. Should you continue to invest in yourself?

Selecting the right analytic tool is not easy. It reminds me of a group of guys around the scuttlebutt on Monday morning arguing about who the best quarterback is. What do you use as a yardstick? Pass completion percentage tells nothing about games won. Nor does the touchdown-to-interception ratio. Winning percentage is key, but no quarterback does it by himself. What about the defense and the running backs? Football is a team sport; trading isn't.

When you put a trader under the microscope, you find similar problems selecting just one statistic to measure. For example, rate of return tells you nothing about the trader's volatility. If you have a decent rate of return, say 30+ percent per year, but your volatility is off the charts, I would begin to get nervous. Volatility here means monthly returns, positive or negative. Let's peg it at 10 percent. This indicates you have the capability of making a fortune or blowing out completely. That's the risk of high volatility. If I then looked at the standard deviation of your losing trades and it was low, indicating you had control of them, I would begin to feel better. Finally I would check your drawdowns to find that your largest over the last 12 months was less than 5 percent. My conclusion? I would get in line to invest in your trading program. In other words, the combination of generating profits while controlling risk is a winner. That's the profile you want to develop. Therefore you need to maintain good statistics on your trading to make these calculations.

Since it takes multiple indicators to make accurate evaluations, analysts have developed various ratios combining those indicators they felt were most important and representative. One popular ratio is the Sterling ratio, devised by Deane Sterling Jones. It attempts to resolve the risk-reward syndrome. If you ran it on your own trading, you would need 3 years of performance. Your objective would be to see if the risks you have been taking are being adequately rewarded.

The Sterling ratio compares your, or a trader's, average rate of return (ROR) over 3 consecutive years with your average largest drawdown in equity during the same period plus 10 percent. Here is the formula:

$$\text{Sterling ratio} = \frac{\text{3-year average ROR}}{\text{average largest drawdown} + 10\%}$$

The 10 percent was tacked on to the largest drawdown to adjust for the fact that short-term calculations of drawdown are understated compared with the annual drawdown figure.

An example will make this ratio much more meaningful. You and your cousin Vinnie have been trading for the last 3 years. Uncle Ralph wins the lottery and decides to invest with one of you. To be objective, he says he'll trade with the one with the best, and best meaning highest, Sterling ratio. Your cousin has an average return of 35 percent over the last 3 years, but his largest drawdown is 20 percent. You, on the other hand, have a somewhat lower return of 30 percent and an impressively low average drawdown of only 12 percent. Who gets to trade the lottery money?

Vinnie	**You**
$\dfrac{35}{20 + 10} = 1.167$	$\dfrac{30}{12 + 10} = 1.364$

Although your cousin's track record seems 5 percent higher than yours, yours is really better when adjusted for risk. You get the lottery money.

Another consideration for you as you do an annual or semiannual self-examination is the volatility of your ROR. In the examples above, how widely dispersed are the annual returns. Yours was an average of 30 percent over 3 years. Was that a solid 30 percent, 30 percent, 30 percent? Or was it 10 percent, 80 percent, and 0 percent? See the difference? I always valued a low standard deviation of the mean return on investments of traders.

As a self-employed trader, it is to your advantage to become consistent for two reasons. First it is easier to budget your expenses. Second, it is much easier on your psyche. Put yourself in the trading chair of the person who just came off a year that generated an ROR of 80 percent. Great momentum! High confidence! Then he or she begins to struggle. For the rest of the year that person is just trying to stay afloat. What does that do to momentum and confidence?

Trading results are seldom consistent. You must come to deal with ups and downs. Much of it is the result of the systemic risk of the markets in general and subtle changes in its complexion requiring traders to modify their approach. It is for this reason you should treat each year as a wholly new period, much the same way you must attack each day or trading session as something completely new. The ritual you perform before each trading session to prepare yourself for that unique trading session must be done on a grander scale as you enter every new year of trading.

I mentioned the systemic risk of trading, or the intrinsic risk of trading, above. Markets also have systemic momentum. By this I mean, as a trader, you get a certain amount of help from the market itself. If you are trading long and the market you are trading is in an uptrend, this overall momentum is to your advantage and helps propel your positions higher. That's why you always try to stay with the trend. But what if you want to evaluate yourself and see only what your skill as a trader contributed to your success?

Evaluating your trading using the Sharp ratio attempts to address this. This ratio endeavors to extract from a trader's monthly or annual return on investment that portion that can be attributed solely to the trader's skill. You accomplish this by subtracting from the trader's rate of return the rate of return that could be generated by investing the trader's risk capital in a risk-free investment. The most common substitute for a risk-free investment is short-term United States bills because they inversely adjust to the systemic risk of the markets.

Here is how the Sharp ratio works. Your annual rate of return is 30 percent. We'll keep as much as possible the same between examples so you can compare the results. From this 30 percent, you would subtract the risk-free rate of 6-month T-bills, say 5 percent, giving you a return of 25 percent. This figure is divided by the standard deviation (SD) of your monthly returns. We will give you a SD figure of 5 percent, which would be considered low to medium for a stock trader. This gives you a Sharp ratio of 5 (25 percent / 5 percent).

A minor variation of this is called the efficiency ratio. The only difference is you do not subtract the risk-free rate of return from the annual rate of return before dividing by the standard deviation. In your case, it would give you an efficiency ratio of 6 versus a Sharp ratio of 5. The efficiency ratio is more commonly used by futures traders than stock traders because it is considered by professional money managers to be more representative.

A couple of other ratios you may want to run on your trading results are the win-loss period and the gain-to-retracement ratios. With the win-loss period ratio, you are simply measuring the number of winning periods against the number of losing ones. In the beginning the period measured may be weeks. As you mature as a trader and get into your second year, I suggest you run this one monthly. You simply divide the number of winning months by the number of losing months. The higher the ratio, the better. For example, let's say in year one you have 8 winning months and 4 losers. So you would divide 8 by 4 and get 2. If your next 2 months are winners, you divide 10 by 4 and your ratio has improved to 2.5. I suggest you then plot this on a simple graph to get a visual picture of your win-loss ratio.

The gain-to-retracement ratio compares the annualized compounded rate of return with the average maximum retracement (AMR). The AMR is defined as the largest average decline in your equity since you began trading. This ratio measures actual loss of equity, rather than profits. You might want to do this one annually. The importance of it is that the loss of equity, and the implied ability to prevent losses and to recover from them, is so very, very important. I know several MOMs (managers of managers) who pay as much attention to a trader's ability to recover as to almost anything else. Why? Because for active traders, experiencing a major drawdown is going to happen sooner or later, so how they recover is vital to know.

One last technique may come in handy once you have been trading for several years. It is called window analysis. You might even think of the technique as a way of creating a moving average of your trading results. You take what you believe to be the most useful or meaningful statistics and isolate them in various time intervals (windows). I use monthly, quarterly, semiannually, 9-month, and annual periods. In each of these windows I would track such statistics as highest rate of return, greatest drawdown, and monthly losing and winning volatility. This allows you to see your worst drawdown in any quarter or year and compare it with the highest rate of return in a similar period.

Each window is calculated by rolling one month's statistics forward, dropping the last month's off, and then recalculating, which can easily be programmed on Microsoft Excel or other spreadsheet software. A year of windows breaks out as shown in Table 9-6.

You would have twelve monthly, ten quarterly, seven semiannual, four 9-month, and one annual period. The objective is to smooth the data so you can (as you would with moving averages) spot trends early. Is your trading trending up or down? Sometimes we are so hotly fighting the daily battle, we can't tell if we are losing or winning it.

So far, I have discussed statistics you can track on your own. Additional analyses are available to you from the broker-dealer you trade through and the clearing firm that actually clears your trades. Let's start with the latter. (Be aware that your broker-dealer and the clearing firm could be the same entity, which really does not make any difference.) The clearing firm handles your money. When you fund an account, the

Table 9-6

Month	Quarter	Semiannual	9-Month	Annual
1				
2				
3	1			
4	2			
5	3			
6	4	1		
7	5	2		
8	6	3		
9	7	4	1	
10	8	5	2	
11	9	6	3	
12	10	7	4	1

check is written to the firm. Since it has the money, it does the accounting. Nowadays, most clearing firms provide access to your account via a web site. On this web site, you can view the day-to-day status of your account. For example, there will be a cash history that will show all additions and withdrawals of funds. You'll also have access to trade confirmations, your trading history, and all the key accounting data pertaining to your account. Many of these web sites also allow you to run profit-and-loss statements, as mentioned earlier. My point is that much of the data you may need to analyze your trading are available on these sites.

There is also an important service that some broker-dealers, such as Terra Nova Trading (which I am affiliated with), provide. It is called a trade analysis. These reports analyze every trade you do over whatever time period you request, since the program asks you to supply the beginning and ending date. This type of service is great for updating your window analysis. An analysis of this type breaks your trading down into a variety of categories, such as:

Type of trade. Long versus short
Size of trade by share size. Less than 200 shares, 201–300, etc.
Price of shares. Less than $10, $10.01–$25, etc.
Term of trade. Day trade versus non-day trade
Time, in minutes, of trade. 0–5, 6–15, 16–30, etc.

Time of day trade took place. 9:30–10:59, 11:00–11:59, etc.

Trade by symbol. AOL, FRNT, etc.

Trade by industry sector. Retailers, drugs, telecom, oil, etc.

From here the report does an overall profit-and-loss analysis followed by a breakdown by subcategories. You will know which stocks, sectors, time frame, trader type, etc., you trade most profitably. The report even shows you the best and worst trade by subcategory.

Besides being an excellent source of data for your advanced analysis, the report reveals many of your strengths and weaknesses. For example, I was working with a struggling trader. One day he made money; the next he lost. When we ran a trade analysis, it was easy to see that all his losses came from non-day trades. We knocked heads together, and he finally admitted that if a day trade went sour, he would hold it in hopes of if turning around. This simple report gave him the insight he needed to turn his trading around.

You may think that I think that insights like this one are the true value of the reports and analysis you do on your trading. Not true. The lasting value of all this work is to increase your concentration on what you are doing so you realize how dangerous a lapse in discipline or focus can be.

Go back a minute to our sniper in Chapter 3. His life depends on his discipline. And your success when trading depends on your discipline. To me these are almost equal. If you do not have the ability to focus, focus, focus—if you will not follow your discipline—save yourself a lot of money and grief and find something to do with your life you can commit to.

10

ON BECOMING THE IDEAL TRADER

One of the firms I worked at utilized the ideal system for problem solving. All the managers and employees impacted by a problem got together and attempted to work out solutions. These meetings began as brainstorming sessions. Everyone would throw out ideas on how to solve the problem. No approach was too dumb, too expensive, too bizarre, or too outrageous. We were encouraged to go out on a limb and describe the most outlandish solutions to the problem we could imagine. No regard was given to internal politics or even the possibility that the company couldn't pull off the solution.

Our creative energy fed on one another. We tried to top the suggestion of whoever spoke before us. Discussions covered utilizing technologies we didn't even have access to at the time, ones we certainly could not afford, and some that didn't even exist. No limits were put on anyone's imagination. The only limitation was time. Each brainstorming session was limited to 2 hours. A moderator led each meeting to enforce the rules and to control traffic, and a recorder wrote all the thoughts on a blackboard. All the ideas were transcribed and distributed to a committee composed of key managers and employees who had the responsibility of devising the actual solution to the problem and executing it.

The beauty of this process is that many unique and creative ideas, which I am sure would not have been suggested otherwise, were uncovered. The people who had to actually solve the problem had a much broader selection of solutions to pick from than if they just met with the department manager and he or she dictated a solution.

Once the implementation committee convened, reality returned to the process. The solution had to fit within the company's structure and budget. The solution could not use technology of the future, and it had to be within the capabilities of the people who would execute it. Nevertheless, many innovative ideas were discovered and incorporated. Additionally, the employees enjoyed the creative sessions and felt they owned part of the solution. Therefore, they had an obligation to make it work.

I am suggesting you approach the art of trading in a similar fashion. You must reinvent yourself as the ideal trader. First I am going to spend some time describing my concept of the ideal trader. Then I'll discuss the seven deadly sins that prevent traders from reaching the ideal and the seven corresponding virtues that will help one perform more like the "perfect" trader. Lastly, I'll talk a little about how you can learn more about your inner self, which is truly the real key to becoming a professional trader.

For some strange reason, when I think about the concept of an ideal trader, Daniel Boone pops into my mind. I think it does because he was quoted as saying, "I explore from the love of nature."* The ideal trader must trade for the sheer love of trading.

Pure, unadulterated motivation is the single most important characteristic of the successful person and, in turn, the successful trader. Daniel Boone loved his family and strived to support them well. He was famous in his lifetime—a member of the Virginia Assembly, a colonel in the militia, a famous Indian fighter, and the subject of a biography by John Filson 36 years before his death in 1820. But he was not a financial success, despite the fact he was a serious land speculator.

Daniel Boone loved long hunts in the wilderness, lasting up to 2 years. He ventured out into uncharted territory, facing the unknown with only his wits, his rifle, and a lot of skill as a survivor to sustain him.

---

*John Mack Faragher, *Daniel Boone: The Life and Legend of an American Pioneer*, Holt and Company, New York, 1992, p. 301.

Think about what must have motivated him to be willing to confront the harsh realities of the path he chose. He had to leave his beloved wife, Rebecca, and children behind for long periods of time. He had to sleep in the forest and hunt for food. He faced the wrath of the Shawnees, other hostile tribes, bears, and even obstacles like raging rivers, mountains, and snowstorms. On one trip, his eldest son, James, was killed in an Indian fight in the Cumberland Gap. All this exploration and he doesn't end up a major landowner even though he had a Spanish land grant, which he fought for in court and lost.

The purity of his motivation made Daniel Boone a success. He is more remembered and revered than the largest and richest landowner of his time. Something inside of him directed him to constantly push himself to explore the great country before him. I have seen an inkling of this passion in a few of the great traders I have had the privilege of associating with. The single most important thing to them was to be in the game.

Don't we see this in the very top performers in any profession? It is more noticeable in areas that have not been corrupted with extravagant salaries. You often get a glimpse of this at the Olympics—for example, the curling team that practices every day between the 4-year cycle or the unknown runner, from some unknown country you couldn't locate on a globe if 50 bucks was wagered, making his or her third appearance without a chance of getting a medal. You also see this devotion to duty in everyday life. The SEAL who gets killed in Afghanistan and leaves a letter behind to his wife saying that being a SEAL and defending his country is worth dying for, so there is no need to grieve for him.

You see it at work all the time. Some of the best brokers I worked with worried more about doing a good job for their clients than getting commissions. I know administrative assistants who put much more time and effort into their performance than their boss, who makes a hundred-fold more money.

My point is simply this: If you are in trading solely for the money, you will blow out before you can make it a career. Trading is not about piling thousand dollar bills on top of one another. It is about participating in one of the most exciting games ever created. It is every bit as intriguing as Daniel Boone's treks into the wilds of Kentucky.

Think about it for a minute. The psychology of the trader is not that much different from that of the explorer. Boone left the known, civilization, for the unknown, the wilderness. The trader leaves the known, technical analysis of historical price charts, for the unknown, the market, which has not traded yet. To do either of these successfully, you must have a lot of courage. This is a big word and has special meaning in this context.

Courage here means total self-confidence in one's ability. It does not mean foolhardiness. It does not mean recklessness. It does not mean being a daredevil. It means knowing your limits and taking risks based on self-knowledge. Successful traders know themselves intimately. They know their limits. They also know what they do not know and admit it, if only to themselves.

Daniel Boone's first excursion into Indian country was not an extended one. He took a series of brief journeys with his father and his friends. A mentor taught him how to hunt, trap, track, shoot, and, most importantly, survive in the wilderness. Just as you must learn when to read the moves of the market makers, Boone worked hard at understanding the Shawnee, other tribes he encountered, and the new terrain he came upon. Your environment as a trader is every bit as hostile as Boone's was.

In time as his knowledge of his surroundings grew, he ventured out farther and farther. At some point, he began creating new rules of his own governing the art of exploring the American west. You, if you can trade with this same spirit of fearlessness, will come to a point where you have an epiphany of your own. That is when you begin trading as a unique individual, rather than following the precepts of others.

The evolution of a trader is one of maturation—growth, development, and the acquisition of knowledge. It simply takes time, just as it did for Daniel Boone. You don't head out into the wilds without acquiring a lot of knowledge and skills. You must be able to build a fire, forge a river, keep your feet dry, find food and shelter, and avoid becoming lost—and if you do become lost, avoid panicking and be able to find your way back. If that doesn't sound like trading, I don't know what does.

Also, just like it is in trading, discipline was paramount to Daniel Boone's survival. You just can't wander into forests for prolonged treks without a set of rules to put the odds of surviving in your favor. You must do some serious planning before you step into the boondocks. Gather all the supplies you can carry and information you can remember. Keep your long rifle clean and free of rust. Keep your powder, flints, and feet dry. Start scouting 2 hours before sundown for a safe place to sleep. Avoid traveling at night if at all possible. Keep good notes regarding your progress, i.e., distance in each direction traveled and details of landmarks passed. Take great care not to lose or damage your compass and have a replacement available. Replenish supplies, specifically food and water, often. Always wait out extremely bad weather in a safe cave. Look, think, and be patient before intruding on the domain of indigenous inhabitants. Never leave to the last minute any key function on which your survival depends.

Another interesting comparison is how an explorer like Daniel Boone expands his range. His first hunt did not last 2 years. He began small. And then he continually pushed out, continually lengthening his sojourns into the uncharted west. Traders must do the same thing. You begin with historically reliable trades in the market with low volatility. As you become more experienced and worldly, you experiment with more complex market conditions and increase the size of your trades. As you do, you develop a greater tolerance for handling stress. Staying in a safe, protective environment does not prepare you for the unexpected volatility storms that can strike any time. Nor does it let you grow as a trader or push you to perform beyond your present level.

By this stage of this book, you should have a good understanding of the key rules that will put the odds in your favor so you can survive a jaunt into the Nasdaq wilderness. But do you know how you are going to ensure you obey those rules? This is often a negative activity, rather than a positive one. By this I mean you must often learn what not to do in order to do what you should be doing. Thus we come to the subject of the seven cardinal sins—avoid committing them and you may just end up in trader's heaven.

SEVEN CARDINAL SINS OF TRADING

I don't look at the original cardinal sins as being anything exclusively religious, although they are often cited in that context. My thinking is much more secular. To me they have more to do with cataloguing and managing human nature than eternal salvation. Even the most ardent agnostic, better yet an existentialist, will admit the need to avoid becoming addicted to the behavior any one of the sins described. Within this intellectual framework, I interpret them in the context of trading and define them very literally. Later, I'll get more specific when personality types are discussed.

My most basic premise regarding trading is that success depends on understanding your emotional life. Before I discuss one of the ways you can get a fix on your overall personality type, which you will have to do if you truly wish to succeed in this business, I want to begin by discussing seven key stumbling blocks to success. Once you get a feel for how these cardinal sins of trading can trip up your trading on a very superficial level, I will go a little deeper into the source of your propensity to fall victim to one or more of these roadblocks. Not only do traders lose money because they cannot foretell the future movements of stocks, futures, and options—but they lose more often and more consistently because they lack a sound understanding of themselves and how the markets' ebb and flow manipulates their inner selves.

As we spend a little time discussing each sin, I'll attempt to point out the preventive measures you can take to guard against falling prey to its excesses. In case you haven't given some thought lately to the seven deadly sins, they are pride, greed, envy, anger, lust, gluttony, and sloth. All seven of these demons reside within each of us. Under the pressure of trading—of having your hard-earned money ripped right out of your hands by a strange, impersonal force—you become very vulnerable to giving into the worst elements in the psyche. It is at times like these that you must resist the temptation to give into your emotions. The successful trader keeps her head when all around her are losing theirs. Times of high volatility and panic are also times of great opportunities. To take advantage of them you must be the one who is thinking, as opposed to the one who is feeling.

In the final analysis, the best plan you write for yourself may well be one that deals with your emotional weaknesses. Do you have a history of losing your cool at times of high stress? Do you feel that some of your deepest emotions could get out of control just when you need control the most? Carefully think about each of these cardinal sins as they are discussed. Also consider taking one or more of the trader's aptitude tests available on the World Wide Web, in trade publications, or from some brokerage firms or trading schools. Try to find out in advance where your weaknesses are. We all have them. It is part of human nature. Don't rely on a close friend or spouse for your own analysis. You want an impersonal assessment. Some of the top traders pay psychological coaches to help them deal with their weaknesses, just like top athletes and sports teams hire motivational advisers. It is not uncommon for brokerage firms that employ proprietary traders to include psychological testing and evaluation as part of the hiring procedure. I'll get into this area more deeply soon.

Once you uncover a chink in your psychic armor, develop a plan to deal with it. A weakness, such as losing your temper when you lose money or make a mistake, never goes away. It is always there, in either the foreground or the background. It can be managed, controlled, but never eradicated. Most assessments you get will include tips to deal with the most blatant problems. Take these suggestions and incorporate them into your written plan.

Then you must make a conscious effort to make them part of your everyday trading. For example, I have seen traders with little, yellow sticky notes on their computer monitor, saying things like "Don't get too greedy!" or "You never go broke taking profits!" Other traders make it a part of their trading journal. After recording each notation, they include a word or two about how they feel at the time. It might look like this:

0945   Bought 2 corn contracts. Trend up. Bounced off support at 205. Feel confident.
1052   Sold corn after 10-cent pop. Volume weakened, approaching resistance. Feel smart.

Besides writing these notes, you should read them and react to them. In the example above, the trader appears to have made a nice day trade in corn. He got in just after the open. Spotted an opportunity. Acted promptly. Saw the uptrend fading and exited with a gross profit of $1000. More importantly, his confidence was boosted because he followed his trading rules, avoided being greedy, made good decisions, and was disciplined. In other words, a lot of positive behavioral patterns were reinforced.

If this trader had not managed his emotions, the outcome could have been much different. Therefore let's take a quick look at the seven sins that seem to have plagued humans in general and traders in particular for centuries. Before I begin, I want to state that I am a true believer that the mean is intrinsically golden. By this I mean that in themselves very few things are wrong. It is when they are carried to extremes that they become a problem. Eating moderately is good; anorexia and gluttony are destructive. Work is healthy; laziness and workaholism are harmful. The successful person, therefore the successful trader, learns to stay within the mean.

The first of the classic sins is pride. Pride challenges the first rule of trading: The market is always right. Woe to the traders who think themselves smarter than the markets they trade. The market has a way of instilling in prideful traders the virtue that is its contra, humility. Within the golden mean, pride is a key to successful trading. Pride promotes self-confidence. It gives you a feeling of satisfaction and comfort by letting you know you are doing a good job. Carried to the extreme, it leads you to overconfidence and willfulness. This leads to the god-killer, hubris, if you are a fan of ancient Greek tragedy. The synonyms of hubris are conceit, smugness, presumption, insolence, disdain, pomposity, effrontery, and arrogance. You won't read any of those adjectives describing the market wizards in any of Jack Schwager's books.

Nevertheless, you also need enough pride in your trading and self-confidence to break out on your own. Let's go back to Daniel Boone for a minute. As a youth and into early manhood, he made repeated journeys into the wilderness. At first, they were from one known settlement to another. Then he made short ventures into unknown territories. On these trips, experienced woodsmen, who taught him the tricks of survival, accompanied him. As his confidence grew, he took pride in making longer and longer forays. Eventually he had the confidence to make extensive expeditions. He was now the leader and the explorer.

Some expeditions ran 2 years in duration—that's 730 days and nights in the open! Hundreds of miles were covered on foot. Dozens of encounters with unfriendly Indians and wild animals occurred. Raging rivers had to be crossed, and blizzards had to be survived. He endured substantial losses in the process, including the death of his son. It takes a lot of confidence to face that kind of a life. Daniel Boone even became famous. He was an explorer. The difference between an explorer and a trail bum is attitude.

I think the life of a trader is every bit as adventuresome and dangerous as that of an explorer. Every day you will face an unknown and unfolding maze of price quotations. You are expected to anticipate what an irrational, undisciplined beast is going to do. Simultaneously, you are bombarded with a cacophony of impulses—news, analysis, figures, opinions, reports, data of all sorts. Some true, more false. Hundreds of Internet services are feeding you everything from earnings estimates to astrological price predictions. From all this, you must select a few of the thousands of stocks, futures contracts, or options available to trade. If this isn't enough, you have to put up with fellow traders who are as scared and insecure as you are. Last of all are the spouse, relatives, and friends. "Why don't you get a real job and feed your family?" "Who do you think you are, Warren Buffett?"

Which would you rather face, a wild bear or a raging bear market?

Not an easy choice. My advice is to follow in the footsteps of Daniel Boone. Venture slowly into the wilderness of next week's price chart. Keep trusted friends and advisers nearby until you build the confidence to venture on your own. Avoid getting overconfident and committing the sin of pride.

The number two sin to avoid at all costs is greed. Its associated virtue is generosity. We spent some time on greed as it pertains to wanting more than your fair share of a trade—in other words, holding onto trades hoping for more and more profits while all the technical signals are telling you the party is over. But there are many more aspects of greed to contend with.

Greed manifests itself in the characteristic of always trying to get more—pushing the limit on what is rightfully yours, or just plain selfishness. Believe it or not, having this characteristic makes it hard for other, more experienced traders to help you or share with you. On some trading floors, traders will meet before and after the market to discuss what is expected or what has happened. Every group has a leader, but all are expected to participate. The more experienced traders usually contribute the most. These can be valuable sessions if you can separate the wheat from the chaff. But if you get the reputation as a taker only and not a giver, the group will react negatively and eventually shun you.

There really is no reason not to be generous about what you see or learn about trading, especially trading a market at a particular time. If you share an accurate insight with another trader, you lose nothing. The insight will work for you as well as whomever you share it with. The markets are big enough for all. But if you share a half-baked idea and the others in the group explain why the idea won't make anyone any money, you have advanced your knowledge base. There is an awful lot of information to share and to learn, so don't be greedy. And curb your greed by not trying to squeeze the last penny out of every trade.

Cardinal sin 3 is envy. This is one of the nastiest of the bunch. The envious trader resents the success of other traders because he inwardly feels everyone is better than he is. Instead of congratulating a fellow trader on a successful day or trade, these traders sulk over the fact others have won and they have not. This behavior eats at their resolve to become successful themselves. Valuable positive energy drains from their psyche, leaving them mean-spirited and weak. Unlike a lot of other endeavors in life, the success of someone else does not diminish your ability to succeed. It is not the Olympic Games. Everyone entered in the trading game can win a gold medal. As a matter of fact, you can win as much gold as you want and so can everyone else. Envy is just a waste of perfectly good energy.

Now the flip side of envy is a real crowd-pleaser and a valuable aid to every trader. I am referring to love. Here it means a true, unadulterated love of trading. The best traders I have ever met would rather trade than do anything else. They would trade even if they didn't make any money at it. That is the spirit needed to spend hours before a computer monitor, to study charts all weekend and still be fresh and fun to be around. Don't try to make trading your profession without loving it. You can make a few bucks now and again; you can have some fun. You can even impress friends and associates. But without loving the game you will always be classified a rank amateur.

Now, for one of the most common vices among traders and, in my opinion, the most harmful: wrath, or anger. In the ancient Greek tragedies when the gods decided to destroy a human, they got him angry and let him destroy himself. The market still does this.

What makes you angry, and how do you respond? The answers to these questions could answer the big one: Are you going to succeed as a trader?

You often see anger on trading floors. A trader will jump up and curse at his computer. Worst cases include breaking furniture and equipment, with the ultimate rampage being the shooting that took place in Atlanta on July 29, 1999. Mark O. Barton shot seven day traders at the All-Tech Investments Group trading floor and then shot himself. When someone is that sick, it is usually more than trading problems.

Most fits of rage are the result of a mixture of frustration and stress. You are risking large sums of your own money, and the market really doesn't give a damn how it treats you. Prices go up and down. You may be in sync or out of sync. No one but you really cares about you and your family. All this is compounded by the irrational sense of humor of the market mentioned previously, where it sometimes rewards you for nothing and robs you when you do everything by the book.

Can you deal with that it in a rational manner? Will you lash out at the market, your computer, or fellow trader if you become totally frustrated? Or will you internalize the pain? If so, it will eat your guts out so you will become so distracted you will miss the next gift the market offers. And it will offer one, and if you miss it, you will be doubly frustrated.

If you are prone to outbursts of anger, you need to work on ways of dissipating that anger fast. The old saw is counting to 10. Or going for a walk or for a workout in the gym. The most important thing to do is to have an emergency plan in writing. For example, you feel rage seizing you as a winning trade rolls over big time. You immediately close all day trades. Then check all swing trades and make any adjustments in stop orders or whatever. Shut off your computer and do something you particularly like. You must get good thoughts and feelings to replace the anger and frustration. Negative thinking compounds the problem. Humor defuses anger. Learning to take yourself a little less seriously helps. In time, you will dispel these negative interruptions without losing the rest of the trading sessions. But for heaven's sake, if you are prone to outbursts of anger, take up another vocation or deal with the problem before becoming a trader. Mr. Barton should never have left his job as a chemist.

The next step in anger recovery is converting the negative energy into positive, creative energy. For example, you get whipsawed in a well-planned and executed trade. A rumor that wasn't even true crept into the pits like a London fog. The floor traders bit on it, and the bid danced like a yo-yo on a long string. Instead of tossing your computer out the tenth floor window, you smile and begin to figure out how to take advantage of the chaos. Volatility is always an opportunity. What would have been negative energy, just wasted breaking expensive furniture, is now positive energy you can bank on.

Enough about anger, let's talk about something that is more fun: how about lust? The problem with the lustful trader is that he or she lacks self-control, the most important characteristic for success. Without it you have no discipline and no hope of survival. Even lusting after admirable goals causes problems because you destroy anything in your path. As a trader, this usually equates to ignoring key defensive rules, leaving you open to a total blowout sooner or later. The unbridled gambler is the epitome of lust, doubling up after every loss. Not the type you would want trading your money, is it?

Cardinal sin six is gluttony. This one is usually associated with food and gourmandism, but for trades it often manifests itself as a lack of focus. It really has a wide application. Basically it is the opposite of temperance. Traders who commit this sin cannot get enough trading or cannot trade consistently. Trading becomes an obsession. All other things in their life—family, friends, diversions, etc.—take second fiddle to their preoccupation with trading. They eat and sleep trading. They constantly try new systems and styles. It becomes their meaning of life. Since it is all they talk about, they lose their friends and often their family.

The misguided conception these people have is that if they just trade more and make more money, people will love and respect them. It is a very shallow understanding of love and the meaning of life.

If the gluttonous trader fails, all hell breaks loose. Perhaps this was Mr. Barton's problem. I have no idea. The problem for this type of loser is that there just isn't any meaning left in life if the trader is not in the center of the trading arena. Sad to say, the glutton who is successful isn't looking at a much higher quality of life. Success in trading, like success in any other field, should not be your only reason for doing it. It should not be the reason people love and admire you. Life is more than one aspect of a person's character. Who wants a father or mother who is the world's greatest trader if the parent doesn't have any time to read a good night story or go to the zoo? Husbands, wives, and children look at their loved one's heart. Is it open to them? Are they loved, nurtured, and cared for? Making lots of money is very nice, but it adds little to the development of the whole person. If you feel you are or could be obsessed by trading, "Get a life!" as my daughter would say.

I have just described the extreme manifestation of gluttony. You must also guard against becoming so involved with your trading that you can't do and enjoy other things. If you have a real knack for trading, it would be a shame to burn yourself out. There are times when you need to take a vacation from trading—to get away and do something completely different, so you can come back refreshed. One of the clues that you need time off is when you find yourself making a lot of stupid mistakes or losing track of trades. This usually means you are not paying attention or you are not focusing. For example, you forget to move trailing stops or put stops in altogether. If your mind is on something else that is important, flatten all your positions and take care of the distraction. When you are actually trading, it is okay to be a glutton, but one that is in control of his or her emotions.

And now for the final cardinal sin, sloth. A lazy, successful trader is an oxymoron. He or she just doesn't exist. You may occasionally see a trader making money who doesn't seem to be working hard. If you do, the answer is probably a raging bull market and the success is temporary. What you often run into on a professional trading floor is a trader who trades with sheer ease, a trader all the other traders look up to and admire. This trader never seems ruffled and is always in the right place at the right time. These are the gifted ones.

If you meet one of the market wizards, take a closer look. My experience is that behind that veneer of magic lies a hard worker, often with an exceptional memory. You find this out by asking a few questions. For example, you and the savant are looking at a chart of DELL. You ask what the current and historical highs are. The wonder boy blurts the answers and a thousand other facts you did not know about DELL. The same happens when you ask a technical question about ECN (electronic communications network) routing. He knows how ECNs work, when to use them, which is fastest, what type of orders are allowed, the costs of usage, and most importantly which stocks are most liquid on each ECN.

My point is that behind the guise of being nonchalant about being a super trader beats the heart of one totally committed to his or her craft, a true student of the market. As you get into trading, you become amazed how large and complex a subject it really is. You cannot grasp, at first, all the facets you must master.

As an individual trader, you must first be a financial analyst and become totally involved in analyzing the macroeconomic and microeconomic trends. Then you must select the stocks to trade and plan your trades. Next you get to execute the trades by running your very own order desk and entering your orders directly into the market. This means you must master order routing to ensure you get good fills fast. To do this you must know the type of orders to use and the system to place them on. It also help to have a solid grasp of trading software platforms, modems, Internet providers, the World Wide Web, and transmission lines and be able to troubleshoot when necessary. A basic knowledge of security rules and regulation also helps. You also are responsible for tracking, checking, and evaluating your trading and your securities account, all of which are online. Nowadays, it is common for an individual trader to replace several levels of administration previously done by securities industry professionals.

This is not the pursuit in which slothful people would be expected to succeed—and they do not. But the hard work can pay off in greater confidence, allowing you to take advantage of opportunities that appear out of nowhere. You find yourself making better, faster, and more profitable decisions. Trades can go off in microseconds using current technology. The only way to be prepared is by doing plain, old-fashioned hard work.

SELF-KNOWLEDGE = SUCCESS

So far, I have discussed the cardinal sins as they impact trading on the surface of your life. This is just the tip of the iceberg, the part you see above the water line. Beneath the surface of your mind lies the other two-thirds of the iceberg that can present a real threat to shipping and your ability to succeed as a trader. I can only spend a little time in this book helping you realize that understanding your own personality is the single, most important factor (other than sheer luck) in determining whether you will become a market wizard or a market clown.

To begin with, there are literally hundreds of methods and theories used by psychologists and psychiatrists to analyze the human mind. I will just present one that has been kicking around the world for centuries. I am speaking of the enneagram. The enneagram is actually two things that are closely related. First it is a geometric figure described as a circle with a nine-pointed starlike figure within. As a symbol, its use has been traced back to Pythagoras, the Greek mathematician whose theory we all memorized in high school. The enneagram also surfaces in the mysteries of Buddhism and the concept of Nirvana. The symbolic enneagram proposes to assist faithful Buddhists to reach a level of inner peace and unity with nature.

Now, before you begin to think I am way out in left field, the value to you of the enneagram is its modern interpretation and use. It found its way into western culture around the turn of the twentieth century. The psychologists George Gurdjieff, Oscar Ichazo, Claudio Naranjo, Don Riso, Russ Hudson, and many others used it as a personality system to identify nine core personality types. All of us fall into one of these classifications. By knowing which one you are, you obtain an enormous amount of self-knowledge. You can identify your strengths and weaknesses. You gain insights into features of your personality that are generally hidden from you. We all tend to function out of habit. This gets us through our normal routines of work and play. The big problem occurs when we are bombarded with stress. At times of high stress, our habitual way of dealing with problems often becomes dysfunctional. Our normal way of coping no longer works. Therefore our ability to make rational decisions is greatly handicapped. It is common for people to break down when faced with the death of a child, with divorce, or with bankruptcy. The same happens to a somewhat lesser degree when we get in a job overloaded with work or are promoted into a position in which we have little competency. The stress spills over into our life outside work and can be ruinous to family life.

Guess what? You are seriously thinking about taking a very high-stress position in which you have little or no experience. Over the years I have seen hundreds of ordinary people decide to become full- or part-time traders. Most of them had no idea what they were getting into. They did not know what an order desk did in the securities or futures markets. Nor did they know much about selecting which stocks or futures to trade or how to analyze them. Their idea of trading was to buy a stock on a tip and sell it when it went up. If it didn't run up right away, all too often they then held it until it did or until they gave up on it and sold at a loss. That is not trading.

The world of trading, particularly very active trading, is as similar to investing as weekend hacking on the golf course is to playing in a PGA tournament. The pros have swing coaches, physical fitness trainers, mentors, and, most importantly at their level, sports psychologists. To become a trader, you must learn the mechanics of trading, i.e., how the markets work; order routing; operating trading platforms; selecting stocks, futures, options, etc. A good trading school gets you this far. Unfortunately, this is where most end.

It is at the next step, when you are sitting in front of a computer screen actually trading your own money, that the biggest problem arises. I am referring to split-second decision making under extreme stress in an environment in which you are not yet comfortable. All too many new traders are simply overwhelmed by the speed and chaos of the Nasdaq or the Chicago Board of Trade. These markets are not rational. They change direction in the time it takes you to get a cup of coffee. By the time you get back to your seat, your position is down 2 bucks and you must do something immediately.

It is times like these that your normal way of coping with problems fails. It is all too human under these circumstances to act negatively. Anger and fear replace rationality and wisdom. We lash out and hurt ourselves. By having a better understanding of yourself—self-knowledge—you will know what your dark side is and how it will react. Knowing this, you can prevent self-destruction. Knowing how you would negatively react to a stressful situation provides the knowledge you need to act positively. Some instruction and coaching in self-realization could mean an elephantine difference in how well you trade.

I have personally seen trader after trader who absolutely knew mechanically how to trade, yet they were net losers, or at best they broke even. Why? It was not lack of knowledge of their craft. In my opinion it had more to do with their self-image and lack of self-knowledge. As we will see, some personality types are more prone to being fearful. Others don't think they are worthy of being winners. Still others are perfectionists and die on the vine from paralysis by analysis. If these traders knew what lurked beneath their psyche, they would be able to deal with it.

I hope I have not gone too far by insinuating that self-knowledge will guarantee trading success, when it is really the opposite. Self-knowledge makes success easier and less stressful. It provides the self-confidence a trader needs to be successful long term—to be able to weather bull and bear swings, the unexpected and the unfair, all of which you must expect from the market. Alas, nothing guarantees success.

What are the nine personality types? I'll provide a brief description of each and what the trading fault of each could be. Remember, this is by no means a detailed discussion that you can use to diagnose yourself. It is simply introduction to the subject of discovering self-knowledge using one of the many techniques available. My hope is that it will illustrate the value of knowing what makes you tick before you become an active and aggressive trader.

Type One

This type of person is the perfectionist. Everything must be in place before he or she is comfortable to act. Type one traders have a propensity for technical analysis because it is so neat and rational. Ones also don't take kindly to criticism, and technical analysis can be seen as black and white; thus you cannot criticize them for following the signals. They like the hard and fast rules. The danger of course is that you can analyze until the cows come home and never put a trade on. Psychologically, the danger of repressing anger is common among ones. All too often they do not realize this, and it causes them to become totally distracted since they have no way of dissipating this negative emotion.

Other trading peculiarities I have noticed is that ones will often try to scale into a scalping trade. By the time they get all their full positions on, the move is over and they are taking losses as they try to exit. This is from lack of self-confidence. It is my contention that a one could become a better trader knowing that his or her personality is predisposed to this behavior.

Some of the adjectives used to describe ones are perfectionist, controlled, idealistic, righteous, orderly, efficient, opinionated, workaholic, inflexible, and compulsive.

Type Two

This type is the mother hen of the trading floor. It seems just about every floor has one. These people really care about others and have strong interpersonal skills. They want to be liked and have a strong desire to help others. They make excellent mentors, if they can control themselves. They need to be aware that the love they show for their students must help the student to become his or her own trader. Most times, however, they do not realize this and attempt to make the students dependent on them. As traders, they must curb their feelings of trying to help everyone on the floor, especially during trading hours. If they don't, they will be distracted from their own trading by giving away valuable trading time. Trading is basically a selfish profession; it is you against the world. Twos often have trouble with this due to the altruism built into their nature. Twos also must guard against becoming domineering and possessive of the other traders they attempt to befriend.

Some of the adjectives that describe twos are caring, generous, give to get, unselfish, gushy, self-important, domineering, coercive, saintly, overbearing, and patronizing.

Type Three

This type tends to be one of the most aggressive traders on any trading floor. Type threes are extremely success-oriented and push themselves to the limit. Threes ride the bubble. They are on the brink whenever possible. As traders, they are often competing against everyone else on the floor. Trading profits measure success; the devil takes the hindmost. If this behavior gets out of whack, they become arrogant exhibitionists. They face the danger of overtrading because they have to prove they are the best. In the worst case, they become narcissistic and worry only about their image. This causes them to trade to perpetuate the image they think is real. Unfortunately, there is nothing behind the image they have of themselves. So they must constantly feed it to make it real for themselves. If they realize what is driving them, then they can adjust. They must learn to trade for only themselves, rather than worrying about what others think of them, by taking what the market is giving on any given day. Instead they often become overly aggressive, trading to feed the myth. This usually results in the threes blowing out of the market completely.

Adjectives describing threes include pragmatic, driving, vapid, image-conscious, status seeking, calculating, exploitative, arrogant, pretentious, and narcissistic.

Type Four

Type fours usually consider themselves the victim of the trading floor. They are self-absorbed and can be somewhat withdrawn. Fours have a propensity to self-knowledge and feel they must understand themselves before they can express themselves. If you trespass onto their territory, you will know about it. As traders, they are at their best when they do have self-knowledge. This gives them an intuition that is invaluable in trading. Some of the best traders in the business come from musical or artistic backgrounds. The repetitious themes found in music and the patterns found in art seem to give some of the fours insights into price movement. Fours will come up with creative trading strategies and imaginative spreads. They will see relationships between indexes and underlying entities no one else will spot. The danger they face is becoming too depressed to the point where they become emotionally paralyzed. This leads to moodiness, hopelessness, and eventual self-destruction.

Adjectives to describe fours are sensitive, temperamental, dramatic, artistic, creative, moody, melancholy, morbid, despairing, hopeless, and decadent.

Type Five

This type is the intellectual of the trading floors of the world. Fives are always studying. It is important to them to understand the market and how it works psychologically and mathematically. You will hear them theorizing about each day's price activity. They will be the ones you will go to if you can't make sense out of the market. After they have been trading a while, they will have a pet theory to explain the market's movement. Fives must guard against becoming too wound up in their research and speculation. It can take them to the point that the market becomes an obsession. Their theories become so involved and convoluted, they lose touch with reality. Knowing this, the fives can guard against reading too much into their analysis and just take advantage of their fine minds and analysis.

Adjectives that describe fives are intense, cerebral, innovative, secretive, visionary, genius, extremist, paranoid, schizophrenic, radical, and intellectual.

Type Six

This type of trader will often appear as a puzzle. At one time sixes will seem self-confident and open. Next they are suspicious and paranoid. Sixes are full of contradictions, to say the least. Much of this is due to an inferiority complex that they sometimes give into, and at other times they act extremely self-confidently in an effort to overcompensate for it. This plays out in their trading. One day they trade with the best on the floor. Their confidence is reacting to their fear, anxiety, and feelings of inferiority. The next day they lose big time because they don't think they are deserving of winning and their inferiority complex is in control. By understanding the dichotomy in their psyche, they have the option to make adjustments—even if it is only walking away from the trading floor when Mr. Loser shows up, and stepping up to the plate when Mr. Conquer the World is home. Not knowing who is at bat leads to confusion, dependency, and trading losses.

Words to describe sixes are loyal, responsible, engaging, troubleshooter, anxious, suspicious, masochistic, dutiful, ambivalent, and trustworthy.

Type Seven

This type can be seen as either the party person or the scatterbrain of the floor. At their best, sevens are achievers with an array of talents. Sevens want the best of everything, and trading is a way for them to get it and have the time to enjoy it. This can be both their motivation and their downfall. Being a connoisseur can be expensive—driving the finest cars, drinking the oldest wine, wearing the latest fashions, etc. Trading simply to fulfill a lifestyle seldom works. Passion for trading is important. Sheer materialism rarely motivates a trader to do the intense work required to be successful. Self-knowledge can put a check on the negative aspects of being a seven to the point that he or she can become a connoisseur of the market.

Some terms that describe sevens are enthusiastic, vivacious, lively, fun-loving, versatile, acquisitive, addictive, compulsive, hyperactive, and dilettante.

Type Eight

Type eights are the wheeler-dealers of the floor. Eights come across as self-assured, risk takers, and highly confident, overcompensating for an extremely fragile sense of self. They are usually the floor leaders because of their forceful and aggressive behavior. If they express the bully side of their personality, they can become little tyrants and ruin a good floor experience. They see themselves as natural leaders. If contained, they can be excellent traders, but they need to be attuned to the fact that they can develop delusions of grandeur. This will lead to overaggressive and reckless trading.

Adjectives used to describe them are powerful, self-willed, confrontational, authoritative, combative, belligerent, megalomaniacal, and overconfident.

Type Nine

This type is the easiest-going person on the floor. Nines want to make friends with everyone and avoid confrontation at all costs. They want to preserve peace on the floor at all costs. At their best, they are emotionally stable, which is a great characteristic for a trader. More importantly they want to get along with the market. They often are trend followers and do very well just taking what is offered, rather than fighting trends. The danger for them is not confronting trading problems they may experience. This leaves them disoriented and dissociated with the market. Understanding their best and worst characteristic leads to profitable trading.

Adjectives to describe nines are easygoing, agreeable, complacent, unself-conscious, unreflective, unresponsive, passive, disengaged, and fatalistic.

WHERE DO YOU FIT INTO THE ENNEAGRAM?

Unfortunately, you cannot make a self-analysis from the brief, thumbnail sketches above. These are strictly to give you an insight into how self-knowledge can be obtained. Your next step should be to do some serious reading and spend some time on the World Wide Web. You will find some titles and web sites in Appendix C. On the WWW, you can get additional background, descriptions of seminars, and a list of instructors and coaches. There are even tests available that claim they will be able to tell what type you are. I would caution you to wait before testing until you have done sufficient reading. The reason is that in most cases you may not have enough of an understanding of the subject and of yourself to answer the questions accurately.

The next step would be to test your newfound self-knowledge. For example, there are two key questions you should be able to answer. The first question is what inside you allows you to want to become a trader? Then once you begin trading, ask yourself what inside you allows you to put on each trade? The answer is not some technical analytic signals or some fundamental data about the entity being traded. The answer must come from inside you. What is driving you to trade in general and put on a specific trade in particular? Is your motivation sound, and have you faced your demons?

Take type ones as an example. They tend to have a problem with self-confidence and are sticklers for details. Have those issues been satisfied? Is the motivation that is driving them in line with their personality traits? Or twos might have to work on minding their own business and focusing on trading. Threes have to worry about not getting into a mode where they are trading only to show off. Fours must avoid becoming depressed when experiencing a losing streak. Remember, losing is like foul weather—it will blow over. Fives should try to keep their trading simple and not overthink each trade. Sixes must keep an eye on their inferiority complex so it does not get in the way. Materialism, as their sole motivation, will not sustain sevens. Eights can easily be crushed when they sustain a substantial loss, so they must be ready to compensate. If the market becomes confrontational and irrational, nines can be thrown into total panic.

If you do not take the time to find out who you are before you begin to trade, you will certainly be made aware of your limitations soon after you begin trading. My grandfather used to say, "Marry in haste, regret in leisure." Another way of saying this is, you can only be as successful as you allow yourself to be. I never really understood this cliché until I spent some time working on uncovering who I am. If you don't do this, you find yourself caught in a maze of emotions when under the stress of trading. These mixed emotional messages short-circuit your ability to make sound trading decisions. Just when you must be totally focused on a trade, you are worrying about your image or some other psychological trash. This is what happens when you know you should do something, like open a position, but you hesitate. Or you know it is time to cut a loser, yet you hold on. Your best trading instincts are being slapped around like a punch-drunk fighter.

You think you want to be a successful trader, but the emotional baggage you are dragging around holds you back. When this happens, you will see traders searching for a new technical analysis system, a faster trading platform, or a different brokerage firm. Lack of success is everybody's fault but the trader's. In reality, it is simply lack of self-knowledge.

Frankly, I believe that self-knowledge can make more difference than anything else when it comes to trading. My reason for saying this is that I have seen hundreds of students dutifully attend trading schools. They learned the basic mechanics of trading. They were warned about how difficult it is and how everything changes when they first begin to trade their own money. But that is where the training ends. What is missing is how to avoid releasing the most negative characteristics within you, i.e., anger, fear, hope, helplessness, lack of confidence, etc., when the stress of loss rears its ugly head.

In any venture, the most important thing you can do in the very beginning is to determine the key principle on which success or failure depends. In my opinion, the key principle of trading is self-knowledge. Know who you are and what motivates you to become a trader before you open a trading account and you will be ahead of 90 percent of those who enter the profession. More importantly, you will have a much greater chance of succeeding.

A

TYPES OF ORDERS

As a direct access trader, one of the key roles you assume is that of order desk clerk. That function requires that you learn how orders are routed and what type of orders to use. Additionally, you must verify that each order has been entered properly and you must track fills. Then you must offset your filled orders when the time comes, which is an inventory function. You cannot expect the brokers at the clearing or brokerage firm to follow your trading as you would a broker at a full-service brokerage firm. Nevertheless, the brokers at a discount or direct access firm will be helpful and will have access to the details of your account. Call them when necessary, but delays slow down the timeliness of trading.

Routing the order is more involved than most traders realize. Besides knowing and having access to a variety of ECNs and exchanges, you must know which ones have the liquidity in the stocks you are trading. Fast fills depend on knowledge of liquidity. There is also the problem of knowing what type of orders will be accepted or rejected. Some ECNs, for example, will not accept market orders. If you enter an order in error when you must be out of a trade, you will delay the process, which could turn out to be very expensive. Since the order placement rules change from time to time, I recommend you visit the web sites of any exchange or ECN you plan to use and get the most updated information. If you

plan to trade Nasdaq-listed issues, visit Nasdaq's web site to learn where
the liquidity is for the stocks you want to trade.

You must also be well trained in the use of the software platform you
will execute your order through. Some have many sophisticated order
entry functions, such as reserve orders and hidden stop orders, that take
time to learn and use effectively.

There are two basic classes of orders you can use in your trading—
conditional and unconditional. Conditional orders put time, price, or quantity stipulations on your orders. Unconditional orders have no restrictions.
Using the right order at the right time can often mean the difference in
profit or loss. Also keep in mind that many of these orders are not accepted by various electronic trading systems.

Here are some terms you should know:

all or none order—This requires your order to be filled completely
or not at all.

cancel-former-order (CFO)—An instruction to cancel the current
order and replace it with the new order, usually resulting from a
change of one element of the order such as the price or quantity.

day orders—These orders are good only for the "day" or trading
session in which they are entered.

discretionary order—An order where you give trading authority to
someone else, often your broker. This could be full discretion, in
which case the broker makes all the trading decisions. Or it
could be limited discretion, in which case you decide on the security, whether to buy or sell, and the quantity. The broker has
discretion on time (when to execute the trade) or on price (at
what price to execute the trade).

fill or kill order (FOK)—Your order must be filled completely and
immediately or it is canceled.

good till—You set the time or date the order is canceled.

good till canceled (GTC)—Your order is in the market until it is
filled.

limit order—You set a limit on the price you will accept. You must
be filled at that price or better.

market if touched (MIT)—The security must reach a specific price.
When it does, your order becomes a market order and is immediately filled.

market-on-close—Your orders should be filled during the closing period of a trading session.

market-on-open—Your orders should be filled during the opening period of a trading session.

market order—This type of order tells the exchange you want to be filled immediately, no matter the price.

stop-limit orders—You place a "stop" price. When that price is hit, your order becomes a limit order.

stop orders—You place a "stop" price. When that price is hit, your order becomes a market order.

Note: ECNs do not accept all types of orders. For example, Island does not accept market orders. You need to learn the types of orders each ECN will accept. Most computerized trading platforms can execute a wide variety of orders, but be sure to check which order types are allowable on the trading platform you plan to use.

B

KNOW THE MARKET MAKERS ON LEVEL 2

As a direct access trader, you will spend considerable time watching the Nasdaq Level 2 screen. It shows you which of the market makers are buying (bidding) or selling (offering) the stock you are trading. Each is represented by a symbol. You will also see symbols for ECNs on the Level 2 screen, for example Archipelago is ARCH and Island is ISDN. In time you will memorize the key players in your favorite stocks.

Aegis Capital Corp.	AGIS	Carlin Equities Corp.	CLYN
Alex Brown & Sons	ABSB	CJLawrence/Deutsche	CJDB
Bear Stearns & Co.	BEST	Coastal Securities LTD.	COST
Bernard Madoff	MADF	Cowen & Co.	COWN
BT Securities Corp.	BTSC	CS First Boston	FBCO
Cantor Fitzgerald & Co.	CANT	Dain Bosworth Inc.	DAIN

Domestic Securities Inc.	DOMS	Piper Jaffray Inc.	PIPR
Donaldson, Lufkin, Jenrette	DLJP	Prudential Securities Inc.	PRUS
ExponentialCapital Markets	EXPO	Punk Ziegel & Knoell Inc.	PUNK
Fahnestock & Co.	FAHN	Ragen McKenzie Inc.	RAGN
First Albany Corp.	FACT	RauscherPierce Refsnes Inc.	RPSC
Fox-Pitt, Kelton Inc.	FPKI	Robertson Stephens & Co.	RSSF
Furman Selz Inc.	SELZ	S.G. Warburg & Co. Inc.	WARB
Goldman Sachs & Co.	GSCO	Salomon Brothers	SALB
Gruntal & Co.	GRUN	Sands Brothers Inc.	SBNY
GVR Co.	GVRC	Sherwood Securities Corp.	SHWD
Hambrecht & Quist Inc.	HMQT	Smith Barney Shearson	SBSH
Herzog, Heine, Geduld	HRZG	SoundviewFinancial Group	SNDV
J.P. Morgan Securities Inc.	JPMS	Southwest Securities Inc.	SWST
Jeffries Co. Inc.	JEFF	Teevan & Co.	TVAN
Kemper Securities Inc.	KEMP	Troster Singer	TSCO
Lehman Brothers	LEHM	Tucker Anthony Inc.	TUCK
M.H. Meyerson & Co.	MHMY	UBS Securities Inc.	UBSS
Mayer Schweitzer Inc.	MASH	Volpe Welty	VOLP
Merrill Lynch & Co.	MLCO	Wallstreet Equities Inc.	WSEI
Midwest Stock Exchange	MWSE	WedbushMorgan Securities	WEDB
Montgomery Securities	MONT	Weeden & Co. LP	WEED
Morgan Stanley	MSCO	Wertheim Shroder & Co.	WERT
Nash Weiss	NAWE	WeselsArnold& Henderson	WSLS
Needham & Co.	NEED	Wheat First Securities Inc.	WEAT
NomuraSecuritiesInt'l., Inc.	NMRA	William Blair & Co.	WBLR
Olde Discount Corp.	OLDE		
Oppenheimer & Co.	OPCO		
Paine Webber	PWJC		
Pershing Trading Company	PERT		

APPENDIX C

SOURCES FOR
MORE
INFORMATION

BOOKS AND PUBLICATIONS

Babcock, Bruce, Jr., *The Business One Irwin Guide to Trading Systems*, Business One Irwin, Homewood, IL, 1989.

Bookstaber, Richard M., *Option Pricing and Investment Strategies*, 3rd ed., Probus Publishing, Chicago, 1991.

Chicago Board of Trade Commodity Trading Manual, Board of Trade of the City of Chicago. (Updated and revised approximately every other year. Check for the latest edition.)

The Encyclopedia of Historical Charts, Commodity Perspective, Chicago.

Fontanills, George A., *Trade Options Online*, John Wiley & Sons, New York, 2000.

Futures Almanac. Harfield has two excellent products of use by futures traders. The first is an annual almanac, calendar, encyclopedia, and yearbook all wrapped into one. It has charts, ratios, fundamentals, technicals, reminders for all key reports, outlook prognostications, and long-term charts—you'll refer to it daily. Keep one handy wherever you do research and scale selections. The second is "The Hightower Report," a newsletter that updates the

Commodity Reference Guide. These two tools will keep you on top of the markets you scale-trade.

Futures and Options Fact Book (annual), Futures Industry Institute, Washington, DC.

Futures Magazine and Annual Sourcebook (250 South Wacker Drive, Suite 1150, Chicago, IL 60606; phone: 312-977-0999; fax: 312-977-1042.) You will find this resource very valuable in helping you keep track of the futures markets. It is filled with news on the exchanges and self-help stories on trading and analysis.

Gann, William D., *How to Make Profits in Commodities,* Lambert-Gann, Pomeroy, WA, 1951.

Gann, William D., *Truth of the Stock Tape*, Financial Guardian, New York. 1932.

Hafer, Bob, *The CRB Commodity Yearbook* (annual), Bridge Commodity Research Bureau, New York.

Jiler, William L., *How Charts Can Help You in the Stock Market*, Standard & Poor's Corporation, New York, 1962.

McCafferty, Thomas A., *All about Commodities*, Probus Publishing, Chicago, 1992.

McCafferty, Thomas A., *All about Futures*, Probus Publishing, Chicago, 1992.

McCafferty, Thomas A., *All about Options*, 2nd ed., McGraw-Hill, New York, 1998.

McCafferty, Thomas A., *Understanding Hedged Scale Trading*, McGraw-Hill, New York, 2001.

McCafferty, Thomas A., *Winning with Managed Futures*, Probus Publishing, Chicago, 1994.

Mehrabian, Albert, *Your Inner Path to Investment Success: Insights into the Psychology of Investing*, Probus Publishing, Chicago, 1991.

Nassar, David, *Rules of the Trade*, McGraw-Hill, New York, 2001.

Natenberg, Sheldon, *Option Volatility and Pricing Strategies: Advanced Trading Techniques for Professionals*, Probus Publishing, Chicago, 1988.

Palmer, Helen, *The Enneagram Advantage*, Harmony Books, New York, 1998.

Riso, Don Richard, *Personality Types*, Houghton Mifflin, Boston, 1987.

Roche, Julian, *Forecasting Commodity Markets: Using Technical, Fundamental and Econometric Analysis*, Probus Publishing, Chicago, 1996.

Samuelson, Paul A., and William D. Nordhaus, *Economics*, McGraw-Hill, New York, 1998.

Schwager, Jack D., *A Complete Guide to the Futures Markets: Fundamental Analysis, Technical Analysis, Trading, Spreads, and Options*, John Wiley & Sons, New York, 1984.

Schwager, Jack D., *Market Wizards: Interviews with Top Traders*, Simon&Schuster, New York, 1989.

Schwager, Jack D., *The New Market Wizards: Conversations with America's Top Traders*, HarperBusiness, New York, 1992.

Teweles, Richard J., Charles V. Harlow, and Herbert L. Stone, *The Commodity Futures Game: Who Wins? Who Loses? Why?* McGraw-Hill, New York, 1974.

NEWSLETTERS AND MAGAZINES

Active Trader, www.activetradermag.com.
"Cycles," Foundation for the Study of Cycles, 2600 Michelson Drive, Suite 1570, Irvine, CA 92715.
"Opportunities in Options Newsletter," P.O. Box 2126, Malibu, CA 90265.
Technical Analysis of Stocks and Commodities, 9131 California Avenue SW, Seattle, WA 98136.

REGULATORY AGENCIES

Commodity Futures Trading Commission
2033 K Street NW
Washington, DC 20581
202-254-6387

National Association of Securities Dealers
1735 K Street, NW
Washington, DC 20006
202-728-8044

National Futures Association
200 W. Madison, Suite 1600
Chicago, IL 60606
Toll-free: 800-621-3570

North American Securities Administration Association
2930 SW Wanamaker Drive
Suite 5
Topeka, KS 66614
913-273-2600

The Options Industry Council
440 S. LaSalle Street
Suite 2400
Chicago, IL 60605

Securities and Exchange Commission
450 Fifth Street, NW
Washington, DC 20006
202-728-8233

INFORMATION SOURCES ON THE WWW

U.S. Department of Agriculture, www.usda.gov

This is the premiere site for information on agricultural commodities. You will find over 300 releases, including crops and livestock reports from the National Agricultural Statistics Service, outlook and situations reports from the Economic Research Service, world trade circulars from the Foreign Agricultural Services, and supply-demand and crop weather reports from the World Agriculture Outlook Board.

You will also find a month-by-month calendar of all reports and release dates. The Department of Agriculture will email you alerts and notices. It is the one-stop ag info center. Check it out.

Option Web Sites (WWW)

Aiqsystems.com
Option-all.com
Optionscentral.com (Options Industry Association)
Option-max.com
Optionvue.com
Optionwizard.com
Pmpublishing.com
ZeroDelta.com

Technical Analysis Web Sites

Barchart.com
BigCharts.com
Futures.tradingcharts.com
Tfc-charts.w2d.com

General Webzines/Financial News Sites

ABC News	www.abcnews.com
Barron's	www.barrons.com
Bloomberg	www.bloomberg.com
Business Week	www.businessweek.com
CNBC	www.cnbc.com

CNNfn	www.cnnfn.com
Dow Jones	www.dowjones.com
Economist	www.economist.com
Financial Newsletter Network	www.financialnewsletter.com
Financial Times	www.ft.com
Fortune	www.fortune.com
Fox Market Wire	www.foxmarketwire.com
Kiplinger Online	www.kiplinger.com
Money.com	www.pathfinder.com/money
Motley Fool	www.fool.com
News Alert	www.newsalert.com
Reuters	www.reuters.com
Thomson Investors Network	www.thomsoninvest.net
USA Today Money	www.usatoday.com/money
Wall Street Journal	www.interactive.wsj.com
Worth	www.worth.com
Yahoo! Finance	www.yahoocom/finance
Zacks Investment Research	www.zacks.com

FUTURES EXCHANGES

Each has a public information department and will send information on request.

Chicago Board of Trade
141 W. Jackson Boulevard
Chicago, IL 60604-2994
www.cbot.com
Phone: 312-435-3500
Fax: 312-341-3306

Chicago Mercantile Exchange
30 S. Wacker Drive
Chicago, IL 60606
Phone: 312-930-1000
Fax: 312-930-3439

Kansas City Board of Trade
4800 Main Street
Suite 303
Kansas City, MO 64112
Phone: 816-753-7500
Fax: 816-753-3944

MidAmerica Commodity Exchange
444 W. Jackson Boulevard
Chicago, IL 60606
www.midam.com
Phone: 312-341-3000
Fax: 312-341-3027

Minneapolis Grain Exchange
150 Grain Exchange Building
Minneapolis, MN 55415
www.mgex.com
Email: info@mgex.com
Phone: (612) 321-7101
Fax: (612) 339-1155

New York Board of Trade
23-10 43rd Avenue
Long Island City, NY 11101
www.nybot.com
Email: webmaster@nybot.com
Phone: 212-742-6000
Fax: 212-748-4321
   Coffee, Sugar & Cocoa Division
   (CSCE)
   New York Commodity Division
   (NYCE)
   New York Futures Division
   (NYFE)
   Cantor Division
   Finex Division

New York Mercantile Exchange
One North End Avenue
World Financial Center
New York, NY 10282-1101
www.nymex.com
Email: exchangeinfo@nymex.com

Phone: 212-299-2000
Fax: 212-301-4700
  COMEX Division

Philadelphia Board of Trade
Philadelphia Stock Exchange
  Building
1900 Market Street
Philadelphia, PA 19105
www.phix.com
Email: info@phix.com
Phone: 215-496-5000
Fax: 215-496-5460

STOCK AND OPTION EXCHANGES:

Chicago Board Options Exchange	www.cboe.com
Chicago Board of Trade	www.cbot.com
Chicago Mercantile Exchange	www.cme.com
Chicago Stock Exchange	www.chicagostockex.com
Nasdaq Exchange	www.nasdaq-amex.com
New York Stock Exchange	www.nyse.com
New York Mercantile Exchange	www.nymex.com
Philadelphia Stock Exchange	www.phlx.com
Pacific Stock Exchange	www.pacificex.com

GLOSSARY

abandon—The act of an option holder to let his or her option expire worthless, neither offsetting nor exercising.

actual—The physical or cash commodity, as distinguished from a commodity futures contract.

administrative law judge (ALJ)—A CFTC official authorized to conduct a proceeding and render a decision in a formal complaint procedure.

American depository receipt (ADR)—A negotiable receipt for a given number of shares of a foreign corporation. Traded on U.S. exchanges just like shares of stock.

ADX—A mathematical formula that measures trend strength in either direction. ADX will use +DI or −DI (directional indicators) to determine directional bias. This information is available through Bloomberg.

advance/decline line—Represents the total of differences between advances and declines of security prices. Considered the best indicator of market movement as a whole.

aggregation—The policy under which all futures positions owned or controlled by one trader or a group of traders are combined to determine reporting status and speculative limit compliance.

allowances—Discounts for grade or location of a commodity due to not meeting contract specifications.

arbitrage—The simultaneous purchase of one commodity against the sale of another in order to profit from distortions from usual price relationships. See also *spread*.

arbitration—A forum for the fair and impartial settlement of disputes that the parties involved are unable to resolve between themselves. The National Futures Association's arbitration program provides a forum for resolving futures-related disputes.

Asian option—An option whose payoff depends on the average price of the underlying asset during some portion of the life of the option.

associated person (AP)—An individual who solicits orders, customers, or customer funds on behalf of a futures commission merchant, an introducing broker, a commodity trading adviser, or a commodity pool operator and who is registered with the Commodity Futures Trading Commission via the National Futures Association.

at-the-market—See *market order*.

at-the-money—An option whose strike price is equal—or approximately equal—to the current market price of the underlying futures contract.

audit trail—The trail of an order, with appropriate time stamps, for inception through execution.

award—See *reparations award*.

back months—Future delivery months furthest in the future.

backwardation—A market condition in which futures prices are progressively lower in the more distant delivery months. The opposite of *contango*.

basis—The difference between the cash or spot price and the price of the nearby futures contract.

basis grade—The standard grade of a commodity for delivery.

basis point—The measurement of change in the yield of a debt security. One basis point equals 1/100 of 1 percent.

basis quote—The offer to sell a cash commodity based on the difference above or below the futures price.

bear market (bear, bearish)—A market in which prices are declining. A market participant who believes prices will move lower is called a *bear*. A news item is considered *bearish* if it is expected to produce lower prices.

bear spread—The simultaneous purchase and sale of two futures contracts in the same or related commodities with the intention of profiting from the decline in price, while limiting the loss potential if the profit does not materalize.

beta coefficient—The measurement of the variability of the rate of return or value of a stock or portfolio of stocks compared with the overall market.

bid—An offer to buy a specific quantity of a commodity at a stated price.

Black-Scholes model—A popular options pricing model developed by Black and Scholes. Initially developed for stock options and later revised for options on futures.

block trade—A trade of 10,000 shares or more.

blue chips—The issues of normally strong, well-established companies that have demonstrated their ability to pay dividends in good and bad times.

board of trade—Any exchange or association of persons who are engaged in the business of buying or selling any commodity or receiving the same for sale on consignment. Usually means an exchange where commodity futures and/or options are traded. See also *contract market* and *exchange*.

booking the basis—A forward contract that locks in the current basis until some time in the future for a buyer or seller.

box transaction—An option position in which the holder establishes a long call and a short put at one strike price and a short call and a long put at another price, all of which are in the same contract month and commodity.

break—A rapid and sharp price decline.

broad tape—A term commonly applied to newswires carrying price and background information on securities and commodities markets, in contrast to an exchange's own price transmission wires, which use a narrow ticker tape.

broker—A person paid a fee or commission for acting as an agent in making contracts or sales; a floor broker in commodities futures trading is the person who actually executes orders on the trading floor of an exchange; an account executive (associated person)—the person who deals with customers and their orders in commission house offices. Also known as a *registered commodity representative*.

brokerage—A fee charged by a broker for execution of a transaction; the fee is charged as an amount per transaction or as a percentage of the total value of the transaction; usually referred to as a *commission fee*.

bucket, bucketing—The illegal practice of accepting orders to buy or sell without executing such orders; the illegal use of the customer's margin deposit without disclosing the fact of such use.

bucket shop—A brokerage establishment that books customers' orders, meaning taking the opposite side of a trade but without actually executing the orders on an exchange.

bull market (bull, bullish)—A market in which prices are rising. A participant in futures who believes prices will move higher is called a *bull*. A news item is considered *bullish* if it is expected to bring on higher prices.

bullion—Bars or ingots of precious metals, normally in a standard size.

bull spread—The simultaneous purchase and sale of two futures contracts in the same futures with the expectation of controlling risk while profiting.

buy or sell on close or opening—To buy or sell at the end or the beginning of the trading session.

buying hedge (long hedge)—Buying futures contracts to protect against the possible increased cost of commodities that will be needed in the future. See *hedging*.

call (option)—The buyer of a call option acquires the right, but not the obligation, to purchase a particular futures contract at a stated price on or before a particular date. Buyers of call options generally hope to profit from an increase in the futures price of the underlying commodity.

called—See *exercise*.

C&F—Cost and freight to move a commodity from location of storage to exchange licensed delivery port.

CCC—Commodity Credit Corporation was organized by Congress for the purpose of stabilizing commodity prices.

car(s)—This is a colloquialism for futures contract(s). It came into common use when a railroad car or hopper of corn, wheat, etc., equaled the amount of a commodity in a futures contract. See *contract*.

carrying broker—A member of a commodity exchange, usually a clearinghouse member, through whom another broker or customer chooses to clear all or some trades.

carrying charges—Costs incurred in warehousing the physical commodity, generally including interest, insurance, and storage.

carryover—That part of the current supply of a commodity consisting of stocks from previous production or marketing seasons.

cash commodity—Actual stocks of a commodity, as distinguished from futures contracts; goods available for immediate delivery or delivery within a specified period following a sale; or a commodity bought or sold with an agreement for delivery at a specified future date. See *actual* and *forward contracting*.

cash forward sale—See *forward contracting*.

certificated stock—Stock of a commodity that has been inspected and found to be of a quality deliverable against futures contracts, stored at the delivery points designated as regular or acceptable for delivery by the commodity exchange.

CFTC Regulations—The regulations adopted and enforced by the federal overseer of futures markets, the Commodity Futures Trading Commission, in order to administer the Commodity Exchange Act.

changer—A clearing member of both the Mid-American Commodity Exchange (MCE) and another futures exchange who, for a fee, will assume the opposite side of a transaction on the MCE by taking a spread position between the MCE and the other exchange which trades an identical, but larger, contract. Through the service, the changer provides liquidity for the MCE and an economical mechanism for arbitrage between the two markets.

charting—The use of graphs and charts in the technical analysis of futures markets to plot trends of price movements, average movements of price volume, and open interest. See *technical analysis*.

churning—Excessive trading of the customer's account by a broker, who has control over the trading decisions for that account, to make more commissions while disregarding the best interests of the customer.

circuit breakers—A system of trading halts to provide a cooling-off period when markets overheat.

clearing—The procedure through which trades are checked for accuracy, after which the clearinghouse or association becomes the buyer to each seller of a futures contract and becomes the seller to each buyer.

clearinghouse—An agency connected with commodity exchanges through which all futures contracts are made, offset, or fulfilled by delivery of the actual commodity and through which financial settlement is made; often the clearinghouse is a fully chartered separate corporation, rather than a division of the exchange proper.

clearing member—A member of the clearinghouse or association. All trades of a non-clearing member must be registered and eventually settled through a clearing member.

clearing price—See *settlement price.*

close—The period at the end of the trading session, officially designated by the exchange, during which all transactions are considered made "at the close."

closing range—A range of closely related prices at which transactions took place at the closing of the market; buy and sell orders at the closing might have been filled at any point within such a range.

commercial grain stocks—Domestic grain stored in public or private elevators at key markets and grain afloat in lakes and seaports.

commission—(1) A fee charged by a broker to a customer for performance of a specific duty, such as the buying or selling of futures contracts. (2) Sometimes used to refer to the Commodity Futures Trading Commission (CFTC).

commission merchant—One who makes a trade, either for another member of the exchange or for a nonmember client, but who makes the trade in his or her own name and becomes liable as principal to the other party to the transaction.

commodity—An entity of trade or commerce, services, or rights in which contracts for future delivery may be traded. Some of the contracts currently traded are wheat, corn, cotton, livestock, copper, gold, silver, oil, propane, plywood, currencies, and Treasury bills, bonds, and notes.

Commodity Exchange Act—The federal act that provides for federal regulation of futures trading.

Commodity Futures Trading Commission (CFTC)—A commission set up by Congress to administer the Commodity Exchange Act, which regulates trading on commodity exchanges.

commodity pool—An enterprise in which funds contributed by a number of persons are combined for the purpose of trading futures contracts and/or options on futures. Not the same as a joint account.

commodity pool operator (CPO)—An individual or organization that operates or solicits funds for a commodity pool. Generally required to be registered with the Commodity Futures Trading Commission.

commodity trading advisers (CTAs)—Individuals or firms that, for a fee, issue analyses or reports concerning commodities and advise others on the value or the advisability of trading in commodity futures, options, or leverage contracts.

complainant—The individual who files a complaint seeking a reparations award against another individual or firm.

confirmation statement—A statement sent by a commission house to a customer when a futures or options position has been initiated. The statement shows the number of contracts bought or sold and the prices at which the contracts were bought or sold. Sometimes combined with a purchase-and-sale statement.

congestion—A period during trading when prices have difficulty advancing or declining.

consolidation—A pause in trading activity in which price moves sideways, setting the stage for the next move. Traders evaluate their positions during periods of consolidation.

consumer price index (CPI)—A measure of inflation or deflation based on price changes in consumer goods.

contango—The market situation in which prices of succeeding delivery months are progressively higher than those of the nearest delivery month, usually due to the cost of holding the commodity, i.e., storage, insurance, interest, spoilage, etc.

contract—A term of reference describing a unit of trading for a commodity.

contract grades—Standards or grades of commodities listed in the rules of the exchanges which must be met when delivering cash commodities against futures contracts. Grades are often accompanied by a schedule of discounts and premiums allowable for delivery of commodities of lesser or greater quality than the contract grade.

contract market—A board of trade designated by the Commodity Futures Trading Commission to trade futures or option contracts on a particular commodity. Commonly used to mean any exchange on which futures are traded. See also *board of trade* and *exchange*.

contract month—The month in which delivery is to be made in accordance with a futures contract.

controlled account—See *discretionary account*.

corner—To secure control of a commodity so that its price can be manipulated.

correction—A price reaction against the prevailing trend of the market. Common corrections often amount to 33 percent, 50 percent, or 66 percent of the most recent trend movement. Sometimes referred to as a *retracement*.

cost of recovery—Administrative costs or expenses incurred in obtaining money due a complainant. Included are such costs as administrative fees, hearing room fees, charge for clerical services, travel expenses to attend the hearing, attorney's fees, filing costs, etc.

cover—To offset a previous futures transaction with an equal and opposite transaction. Short covering is a purchase of futures contracts to cover an earlier sale of an equal number of the same delivery month; liquidation is the sale of futures contracts to offset the obligation to take delivery on an equal number of futures contracts of the same delivery month purchased earlier.

Cox-Ross-Rubinstein option pricing model—An option pricing model that can take into account factors not allowable in Black and Scholes, such as early exercise, price supports, etc.

current delivery (month)—The futures contract that will come to maturity and become deliverable during the current month; also called *spot month*.

CUSIP—The unique nine-character serial number of a registered security.

customer segregated funds—See *segregated account*.

day order—An order that if not executed expires automatically at the end of the trading session on the day it was entered.

day traders—Traders, generally members of the exchange active on the trading floor, who take positions in commodities and then liquidate them prior to the close of the trading day.

dealer option—A put or call on a physical commodity, not originating on or subject to the rules of an exchange, written by a firm that deals in the underlying cash commodity.

debit balance—Accounting condition where the trading losses in a customer's account exceed the amount of equity in the account.

deck—All of the unexecuted orders in a floor broker's possession.

default—(1) In the futures market, the failure to perform on a futures contract as required by exchange rules, such as a failure to meet a margin call or to make or take delivery. (2) In reference to the federal farm loan program, the decision on the part of a producer of commodities not to repay the government loan, but instead to surrender his or her crops. This usually floods the market, driving prices lower.

deferred delivery—The distant delivery months in which futures trading is taking place, as distinguished from the nearby futures delivery month.

deliverable grades—See *contract grades*.

delivery—The tender and receipt of an actual commodity or warehouse receipt or other negotiable instrument covering such commodity, in settlement of a futures contract.

delivery month—A calendar month during which a futures contract matures and becomes deliverable.

delivery notice—Notice from the clearinghouse of a seller's intention to deliver the physical commodity against a short futures position; precedes and is distinct from the warehouse receipt or shipping certificate, which is the instrument of transfer of ownership.

delivery points—Those locations designated by commodity exchanges at which stocks of a commodity represented by a futures contract may be delivered in fulfillment of the contract.

delivery price—The official settlement price of the trading session during which the buyer of futures contracts receives through the clearinghouse a notice of the seller's intention to deliver, and the price at which the buyer must pay for the commodities represented by the futures contract.

delivery versus payment (DVP)—A transaction settlement method in which the securities are delivered to the buying institution's bank in exchange for payment of the amount due.

delta—A term used to describe the responsiveness of option premiums to a change in the price of the underlying asset. Deep in-the-money options have a delta near 1; these show the biggest response to price changes. Deep out-of-the-money options have very low deltas.

discount—(1) A downward adjustment in price allowed for delivery of stocks of a commodity of lesser than deliverable grade against a futures contract. (2) Sometimes used to refer to the price difference between futures of different delivery months, as in the phrase "July at a discount to May," indicating that the price of the July futures is lower than that of the May.

discovery—The process that allows one party to obtain information and documents relating to the dispute from the other party(ies) in the dispute.

discretionary account—An arrangement by which the holder of the account gives written power of attorney to another, often a broker, to make buying and selling decisions without notification to the holder; often referred to as a *managed account* or *controlled account*.

elasticity—A characteristic of commodities which describes the interaction of the supply, demand, and price of a commodity. A commodity is said to be elastic in demand when a price change creates an increase or decrease in consumption. The supply of a commodity is said to be elastic when a change in price creates a change in the production of the commodity. Inelasticity of supply or demand exists when either supply or demand is relatively unresponsive to changes in price.

equity—The dollar value of a security or futures trading account if all open positions were offset at the going market price.

exchange—An association of persons engaged in the business of buying and selling commodity futures and/or options. See also *board of trade* and *contract market*.

exercise—If you exercise an option, you elect to accept the underlying futures contract at the option's strike price.

exercise price—The price at which the buyer of a call (put) option may choose to exercise his or her right to purchase (sell) the underlying futures contract. Also called *strike price*.

expiration date—Generally the last date on which an option may be exercised.

feed ratios—The variable relationships of the cost of feeding animals to market weight sales prices, expressed in ratios, such as the hog-corn ratio. These serve as indicators of the profit return or lack of it in feeding animals to market weight.

Fibonacci number or **sequence of numbers**—The sequence of numbers (0,1,1,2,3,5,8,13,21,34,55,89,144,233, . . .) discovered by the Italian mathematician Leonardo de Pise in the thirteenth century. This sequence is the mathematical basis of the Elliott Wave.

fiduciary duty—The responsibility imposed by the operation of law (from congressional policies underlying the Commodity Exchange Act) which requires that the broker act with special care in the handling of a customer's account.

first notice day—The first day on which notices of intention to deliver cash commodities against futures contracts can be presented by sellers and received by buyers through the exchange clearinghouse.

floor broker—An individual who executes orders on the trading floor of an exchange for another person.

floor traders—Members of an exchange who are personally present on the trading floors of exchanges to make trades for themselves and their customers. Sometimes called *scalpers* or *locals*.

forward contracting—A cash transaction common in many industries, including commodities, in which the buyer and seller agree upon delivery of a specified quality and quantity of goods at a specified future date. A specific price may be agreed upon in advance, or there may be agreements that the price will be determined at the time of delivery on the basis of either the prevailing local cash price or a futures price.

fourth market—The trading of securities directly between institutional investors without the services of a broker, primarily through the use of InstiNet.

Free on Board (F.O.B)—Indicates that all delivery, inspection, and elevation or loading costs involved in putting commodities on board a carrier have been paid.

free supply—Stocks of a commodity which are available for commercial sale, as distinguished from government-owned or -controlled stocks.

fully disclosed—An account carried by a futures commission merchant in the name of an individual customer; opposite of an omnibus account.

fundamental analysis—An approach to analysis of futures markets and commodity futures price trends which examines the underlying factors that will affect the supply and demand of the commodity being traded in futures. See also *technical analysis*.

futures commission merchant (FCM)—An individual or organization that solicits or accepts orders to buy or sell futures contracts or commodity options and accepts money or other assets from customers in connection with such orders. Must be registered with the Commodity Futures Trading Commission.

futures contract—A standardized binding agreement to buy or sell a specified quantity or grade of a commodity at a later date, i.e., during a specified month. Futures contracts are freely transferable and can be traded only by public auction on designated exchanges.

Futures Industry Association (FIA)—The national trade association for the futures industry.

gap—A trading day during which the daily price range is completely above or below the previous day's range, causing a gap between them to be formed. Some traders then look for a retracement to "fill the gap."

grantor—A person who sells an option and assumes the obligation, but not the right, to sell (in the case of a call) or buy (in the case of a put) the underlying futures contract or commodity at the exercise price. Also known as *writer*.

gross processing margin (GPM)—Refers to the difference between the cost of soybeans and the combined sales income of the soybean oil and meal which results from processing soybeans.

guided account—An account that is part of a program directed by a commodity trading adviser (CTA) or futures commission merchant (FCM). The CTA or FCM plans the trading strategies. The customer is advised to enter and/or liquidate specific trading positions. However, approval to enter the order must be given by the customer. These programs usually require a minimum initial investment and may include a trading strategy that will utilize only a part of the investment at any given time.

hedging—The sale of futures contracts in anticipation of future sales of cash commodities as a protection against possible price declines, or the purchase of futures contracts in anticipation of future purchases of cash commodities as a protection against increasing costs. See also *buying hedge* and *selling hedge*.

inelasticity—A characteristic that describes the interdependence of the supply, demand, and price of a commodity. A commodity is inelastic when a price change does not create an increase or decrease in consumption; inelasticity exists when supply and demand are relatively unresponsive to changes in price. See also *elasticity*.

initial margin—A customer's funds required at the time a futures position is established, or an option is sold, to assure performance of the customer's obligations. Margin in commodities is not a down payment, as it is in securities. See also *margin*.

in-the-money—An option having intrinsic value. A call is in-the-money if its strike price is below the current price of the underlying futures contract. A put is in-the-money if its strike price is above the current price of the underlying futures contract.

intrinsic value—The absolute value of the in-the-money amount; that is, the amount that would be realized if an in-the-money option were exercised.

introducing broker (IB)—A firm or individual that solicits and accepts commodity futures orders from customers but does not accept money, securities, or property from the customer. An IB must be registered with the Commodity Futures Trading Commission and must carry all of its accounts through an FCM on a fully disclosed basis.

inverted market—A futures market in which the nearer months are selling at premiums over the more distant months; characteristically, a market in which supplies are currently in shortage.

invisible supply—Uncounted stocks of a commodity in the hands of wholesalers, manufacturers, and producers which cannot be identified accurately; stocks outside commercial channels but theoretically available to the market.

last trading day—The day on which trading ceases for the maturing (current) delivery month.

leverage—Essentially allows an investor to establish a position in the marketplace by depositing funds that are less than the value of the contract.

leverage contract—A standardized agreement calling for the delivery of a commodity with payments against the total cost spread out over a period of time. Principal characteristics include standard units and quality of a commodity and of terms and conditions of the contract; payment and maintenance of margin; closeout by offset or delivery (after payment in full); and no right to or interest in a specific lot of the commodity. Leverage contracts are not traded on exchanges.

leverage transaction merchant (LTM)—The firm or individual through whom leverage contracts are entered. LTMs must be registered with the Commodity Futures Trading Commission.

life of the contract—The period between the beginning of trading in a particular future and the expiration of trading in the delivery month.

limit—See *position limit, price limit, reporting limit,* and *variable limit.*

limit move—A price that has advanced or declined the limit permitted during one trading session as fixed by the rules of a contract market.

limit order—An order in which the customer sets a limit on either price or time of execution, or both, as contrasted with a market order, which implies that the order should be filled at the most favorable price as soon as possible.

liquidation—Usually the sale of futures contracts to offset the obligation to take delivery of an equal number of futures contracts of the same delivery month purchased earlier. Sometimes refers to the purchase of futures contracts to offset a previous sale.

liquidity—A broadly traded market where buying and selling can be accomplished with small price changes and bid and offer price spreads are narrow.

liquid market—A market where selling and buying can be accomplished easily due to the presence of many interested buyers and sellers.

loan program—Primary means of government agricultural price-support operations in which the government lends money to farmers at announced rates, with crops used as collateral. Default on these loans is the primary method by which the government acquires stocks of agricultural commodities.

Long—One who has bought a cash commodity or a commodity futures contract, in contrast to a short, who has sold a cash commodity or futures contract.

long hedge—Buying futures contracts to protect against possible increased prices of commodities. See also *hedging*.

maintenance margin—The amount of money that must be maintained on deposit while a futures position is open. If the equity in a customer's account drops under the maintenance margin level, the broker must issue a call for money that will restore the customer's equity in the account to the required initial levels. See also *margin*.

margin—In the futures industry, it is an amount of money deposited by both buyers and sellers of futures contracts to ensure performance against the contract. It is not a down payment.

margin call—A call from a brokerage firm to a customer to bring margin deposits back up to minimum levels required by exchange regulations; similarly, a request by the clearinghouse to a clearing member firm to make additional deposits to bring clearing margins back up to minimum levels required by clearinghouse rules.

market order—An order to buy or sell futures contracts which is to be filled at the best possible price and as soon as possible. In contrast to a limit order, which may specify requirements for price or time of execution. See also *limit order*.

maturity—The period within which a futures contract can be settled by delivery of the actual commodity; the period between the first notice day and the last trading day of a commodity futures contract.

maximum price fluctuation—See *limit move*.

minimum price fluctuation—See *point*.

misrepresentation—An untrue or misleading statement concerning a material fact relied upon by a customer when making a decision about an investment.

momentum indicator—A line that is plotted to represent the difference between today's price and the price a fixed number of days ago. Momentum can be measured as the difference between today's price and the current value of a moving average. Often referred to as a *momentum oscillator*.

moving average—A mathematical procedure to smooth or eliminate the fluctuations in data. Moving averages emphasize the direction of a trend, confirm trend reversals, and smooth out price and volume fluctuations or "noise" that can confuse interpretation of the market.

National Association of Futures Trading Advisors (NAFTA)—The national trade association of commodity pool operators (CPOs), commodity trading advisers (CTAs), and related industry participants.

National Futures Association (NFA)—The national self-regulatory organization of the futures industry.

nearby delivery (month)—The futures contract closest to maturity.

nearbys—The nearest delivery months of a futures contract.

net performance—An increase or decrease in net asset value exclusive of additions, withdrawals, and redemptions.

net position—The difference between the open long (buy) contracts and the open short (sell) contracts held by any one person in any one futures contract month or in all months combined.

new asset value—The value of each unit of a commodity pool. Basically, a calculation of assets minus liabilities plus or minus the value of open positions (marked-to-the-market) divided by the number of units.

NFA Rules—The standards and requirements to which participants who are required to be members of the National Futures Association must subscribe and conform.

nominal price—The declared price for a futures month sometimes used in place of a closing price when no recent trading has taken place in that particular delivery month; usually an average of the bid and ask prices.

nondisclosure—Failure to disclose a material fact needed by the customer to make a decision regarding an investment.

normalizing—An adjustment to data, such as a price series, to put the data within a normal or more standard range. A technique used to develop a trading system.

notice day—See *first notice day*.

notice of delivery—See *delivery notice*.

offer—An indication of willingness to sell at a given price; opposite of bid.

offset—The liquidation of a purchase of futures through the sale of an equal number of contracts of the same delivery months, or the covering of a short sale of futures contracts through the purchase of an equal number of contracts of the same delivery month. Either action transfers the obligation to make or take delivery of the actual commodity to someone else.

omnibus account—An account carried by one futures commission merchant with another in which the transactions of two or more persons are combined, rather than designated separately, and the identity of the individual accounts is not disclosed.

open—The period at the beginning of the trading session officially designated by the exchange during which all transactions are considered made "at the open."

opening range—A range of closely related prices at which transactions took place at the opening of the market; buying and selling orders at the opening might be filled at any point within such a range.

open interest—The total number of futures contracts of a given commodity which have not yet been offset by opposite futures transactions nor fulfilled by delivery of the actual commodity; the total number of open transactions, with each transaction having a buyer and a seller.

open outcry—A method of public auction for making bids and offers in the trading pits or rings of commodity exchanges.

open trade equity—The unrealized gain or loss on open positions.

option contract—A unilateral contract that gives the buyer the right, but not the obligation, to buy or sell a specified quantity of a commodity or a futures contract at a specific price within a specified period of time, regardless of the market price of that commodity or futures contract. The seller of the option has the obligation to sell the commodity or futures contract or buy it from the option buyer at the exercise price if the option is exercised. See also *call (option)* and *put (option)*.

option premium—The money, securities, or property the buyer pays to the writer(grantor) for granting an option contract.

option seller—See *grantor*.

order execution—Handling of a customer order by a broker—includes receiving the order verbally or in writing from the customer, transmitting it to the trading floor of the exchange where the transaction takes place, and returning confirmation (fill price) of the completed order to the customer.

orders—See *market order* and *stop order*.

original margin—A term applied to the initial deposit of margin money required of clearing member firms by clearinghouse rules; parallels the initial margin deposit required of customers.

out-of-the-money—A call option with a strike price higher or a put option with a strike price lower than the current market value of the underlying asset.

overbought—A technical opinion that the market price has risen too steeply and too fast in relation to underlying fundamental factors.

oversold—A technical opinion that the market price has declined too steeply and too fast in relation to underlying fundamental factors.

P&S statement—See *purchase-and-sale statement*.

par—A particular price, 100 percent of the principal value.

parity—A theoretically equal relationship between farm product prices and all other prices. In farm program legislation, parity is defined in such a manner that the purchasing power of a unit of an agricultural commodity is maintained at its level during an earlier historical base period.

pit—A specially constructed arena on the trading floor of some exchanges where trading in a futures or options contract is conducted by open outcry. On other exchanges, the term *ring* designates the trading area for a futures or options contract.

point—The minimum fluctuation in futures prices or options premiums.

point balance—A statement prepared by futures commission merchants to show profit or loss on all open contracts by computing them to an official closing or settlement price.

pool—See *commodity pool*.

position—A market commitment. For example, a buyer of futures contracts is said to have a long position and, conversely, a seller of futures contracts is said to have a short position.

position limit—The maximum number of futures contracts in certain regulated commodities that one can hold, according to the provisions of the CFTC.

position trader—A commodity trader who either buys or sells contracts and holds them for an extended period of time, as distinguished from the day trader, who will normally initiate and liquidate a futures position within a single trading session.

premium—(1) The additional payment allowed by exchange regulations for delivery of higher-than-required standards or grades of a commodity against a futures contract. In speaking of price relationships between different delivery months of a given commodity, one is said to be trading at a premium over another when its price is greater than that of the other. (2) Also can mean the amount paid to a grantor or writer of an option by a trader.

price limit—The maximum price advance or decline from the previous day's settlement price permitted for a commodity in one trading session by the rules of the exchange.

primary market—The principal market for the purchase and sale of a cash commodity.

principal—Refers to a person who is a principal of a particular entity. (1) Any person including, but not limited to, a sole proprietor, general partner, officer or director, or person occupying a similar status or performing similar functions, having the power, directly or indirectly, through agreement or otherwise, to exercise a controlling influence over the activities of the entity. (2) Any holder or any beneficial owner of 10 percent or more of the outstanding shares of any class of stock of the entity. (3) Any person who has contributed 10 percent or more of the capital of the entity.

private wires—Wires leased by various firms and news agencies for the transmission of information to branch offices and subscriber clients.

proceeding clerk—The member of the CFTC's staff in the Office of Proceedings who maintains the commission's reparations docket, assigns reparation cases to an appropriate CFTC official, and acts as custodian of the records of proceedings.

producer—A person or entity that produces (grows, mines, etc.) a commodity.

public elevators—Grain storage facilities, licensed and regulated by state and federal agencies, in which space is rented out to whoever is willing to pay for it; some are also approved by the commodity exchanges for delivery of commodities against futures contracts.

purchase-and-sale statement (P&S)—A statement sent by a commission house to a customer when a futures or options position has been liquidated or offset. The statement shows the number of contracts bought or sold, the gross profit or loss, the commission charges, and the net profit or loss on the transaction. Sometimes combined with a confirmation statement.

purchase price—The total actual cost paid by a person for entering into a commodity option transaction, including premium, commission, and any other direct or indirect charges.

put (option)—An option that gives the option buyer the right, but not the obligation, to sell the underlying futures contract at a particular price on or before a particular date.

pyramiding—The use of profits on existing futures positions as margins to increase the size of the position, normally in successively smaller increments; for example, the use of profits on the purchase of five futures contracts as margin to purchase an additional four contracts, whose profits will in turn be used to margin an additional three contracts.

quotation—The actual price or the bid or ask price of either cash commodities or futures or options contracts at a particular time. Often called a *quote*.

rally—An upward movement of prices. See also *recovery*.

rally top—The point where a rally stalls. A bull move will usually make several rally tops over its life.

range—The difference between the high and low price of a commodity during a given period, usually a single trading session.

reaction—A short-term countertrend movement of prices.

receivership—A situation in which a receiver has been appointed. A receiver is a person appointed by a court to take custody and control of and to manage the property or funds of another, pending judicial action concerning them.

recovery—An upward movement of prices following a decline.

registered commodity representative (RCR)—See *broker* and *associated person*.

reparations—Compensation payable to a wronged party in a futures or options transaction. The term is used in conjunction with the Commodity Futures Trading Commission's customer claims procedure to recover civil damages.

reparations award—The amount of monetary damages a respondent may be ordered to pay to a complainant.

reporting limit—Size of positions, set by the exchange and/or by the CFTC, at or above which commodity traders must make daily reports to the exchange and/or the CFTC about the size of the position by commodity, by delivery month, and according to the purpose of trading, i.e., speculative or hedging.

resistance—The price level where a trend stalls. Opposite of a support level. Prices must build momentum to move through resistance.

respondents—The individuals or firms against which a complaint is filed and from which a reparations award is sought.

retender—The right of holders of futures contracts who have been tendered a delivery notice through the clearinghouse to offer the notice for sale on the open market, liquidating their obligation to take delivery under the contract; applicable only to certain commodities and only within a specified period of time.

retracements—Price movements in the opposite direction of the prevailing trend. See *correction*.

ring—A circular area on the trading floor of an exchange where traders and brokers stand while executing futures or options trades. Some exchanges use pits rather than rings.

round lot—A quantity of a commodity equal in size to the corresponding futures contract for the commodity, as distinguished from a job lot, which may be larger or smaller than the contract.

round turn—The combination of an initiating purchase or sale of a futures contract and an offsetting sale or purchase of an equal number of futures contracts in the same delivery month. Commission fees for commodity transactions cover the round turn.

sample grade—In commodities, usually the lowest quality acceptable for delivery in satisfaction of futures contracts. See *contract grades.*

scalper—A speculator on the trading floor of an exchange who buys and sells rapidly, with small profits or losses, holding positions for only a short time during a trading session. Typically, a scalper will stand ready to buy at a fraction below the last transaction price and to sell at a fraction above, thus creating market liquidity.

security deposit—See *margin.*

segregated account—A special account used to hold and separate customer's assets from those of the broker or firm.

selling hedge—Selling futures contracts to protect against possible decreased prices of commodities which will be sold in the future. See *hedging* and/or *short hedge.*

settlement price—The closing price, or a price within the range of closing prices, which is used as the official price in determining net gains or losses at the close of each trading session.

short—One who has sold a cash commodity or a commodity futures contract, in contrast to a long, who has bought a cash commodity or futures contract.

short hedge—Selling futures to protect against possible decreasing prices of commodities. See also *hedging.*

speculator—One who attempts to anticipate commodity price changes and make profits through the sale and/or purchase of commodity futures contracts. A speculator with a forecast of advancing prices hopes to profit by buying futures contracts and then liquidating the obligation to take delivery with a later sale of an equal number of futures of the same delivery month at a higher price. A speculator with a forecast of declining prices hopes to profit by selling commodity futures contracts and then covering the obligation to deliver with a later purchase of futures at a lower price.

spot—The market for the immediate delivery of the product and immediate payment. May also refer to the nearest delivery month of a futures contract.

spot commodity—See *cash commodity*.

spread (straddle)—The purchase of one futures delivery month against the sale of another futures delivery month of the same commodity, the purchase of one delivery month of one commodity against the sale of the same delivery month of a different commodity, or the purchase of one commodity in one market against the sale of that commodity in another market, to take advantage of and profit from the distortions from the normal price relationships that sometimes occur. The term is also used to refer to the difference between the price of one futures month and the price of another month of the same commodity. See also *arbitrage*.

stop loss—A risk management technique used to close out a losing position at a given point. See *stop order*.

stop order—An order that becomes a market order when a particular price level is reached. A sell stop is placed below the market; a buy stop is placed above the market. Sometimes referred to as a *stop-loss order*.

strike price—See *exercise price*.

support—A price level at which a declining market has stopped falling. Opposite of a resistance price range. Once this level is reached, the market trades sideways for a period of time.

switch—Liquidation of a position in one delivery month of a commodity and simultaneous initiation of a similar position in another delivery month of the same commodity. When used by hedgers, this tactic is referred to as *rolling forward* the hedge.

technical analysis—An approach to an analysis of futures markets and anticipated future trends of commodity prices. It examines the technical factors of market activity. Technicians normally examine patterns of price range, rates of change, and changes in volume of trading and open interest. The data are often charted to show trends and formations that serve as indicators of likely future price movements.

tender—The act on the part of the seller of futures contracts of giving notice to the clearinghouse that he or she intends to deliver the physical commodity in satisfaction of the futures contract.

The clearinghouse in turn passes along the notice to the oldest buyer of record in that delivery month of the commodity. See also *retender*.

tick—Refers to a change in price up or down. See also *point*.

ticker tape—A continuous paper tape transmission of commodity or security prices, volume, and other trading and market information which operates on private or lease wires by the exchanges, available to their member firms and other interested parties on a subscription basis.

time value—Any amount by which an option premium exceeds the option's intrinsic value.

to-arrive contract—A type of deferred shipment in which the price is based on delivery at the destination point and the seller pays the freight in shipping it to that point.

traders—(1) People who trade for their own account. (2) Employees of dealers or institutions who trade for their employer's account.

trading range—An established set of price boundaries with a high price and a low price within which a market will spend a marked period of time.

transferable notice—See *retender*.

trendline—A line drawn that connects either a series of highs or a series of lows in a trend. The trendline can represent either support, as in an uptrend line, or resistance, as in a downtrend line. Consolidations are marked by horizontal trendlines.

unauthorized trading—The purchase or sale of commodity futures or options for a customer's account without the customer's permission.

underlying futures contract—The specific futures contract that the option conveys the right to buy (in the case of a call) or sell (in the case of a put).

variable limit—A price system that, under certain conditions, permits larger than normally allowed price movements. In periods of extreme volatility, some exchanges permit trading and price levels to exceed regular daily limits. At such times, margins may be automatically increased.

variation margin call—A mid-season call by the clearinghouse on a clearing member, requiring the deposit of additional funds to bring clearing margin monies up to minimum levels in relation to changing prices and the clearing member's net position.

volatility—A measure of a commodity's tendency to move up and down in price, based on its daily price history over a period of time.

volume of trade—The number of contracts traded during a specified period of time.

warehouse receipt—A document guaranteeing the existence and availability of a given quantity and quality of a commodity in storage; commonly used as the instrument of transfer of ownership in both cash and futures transactions.

wirehouse—See *futures commission merchant.*

writer—See *grantor.*

Note: This glossary is included to assist the reader. It is neither a set of legal definitions nor a guide to interpreting any securities act or any other legal instrument. For all legal assistance, please contact your personal attorney.

Index

Abandoning positions (*see* Selling)
Account size requirements, 8
Advice, 71–73, 83, 150–151
Analyst reports, 134–135
Anger, 172–173
Anticipation, 138–139
Aquinas, Thomas, xi
ARCHEX, xii, 110
Average maximum retracement (AMR), 160
Average size of losing trade, 148–149, 153–154
Averaging positions, 131

Back office, 121
Backing away, 89
Backlogged orders, 105
Bandwidth, 113, 121
Bar charts, 42
Barclay CTA Index, 155
Barton, Mark O., 172
Base-building phase, 53–54, 96
Bearish phase, 53, 54, 56
Beginning Net Asset Value (BNAV), 155, 156
Beta, 136
Blame, 70–71
Blue-chip stocks, 5–6
Boone, Daniel, 164–167, 170–171
Boredom, trading out of, 47
Breakout, 54, 95–96
Broker-dealers:
    back office of, 121
    clearing firm, 160–161
    reports of, 11–12, 119, 130, 161–162
Bubbles, 105, 179
Buck fever, 114
Budget, 18–20, 75–77
Buffett, Warren, 123
Bull flags, 86
Bullish phase, 53, 54, 55, 56, 63–64

Candlestick charts, 42–43
Capitalization, 51
Cardinal sins of trading, 167–175
Caring, 178–179
Cash accounts, 4–5, 8–9

Cellular telephone, 76, 121
Clearing firms, 160–161
Close, trading, 43, 73, 136–138
Clubs, trading, 122
Commissions, 67, 75–76, 149
Commitment, 17, 64, 122
Commitment of Traders Report (COT), 100–101
Commodities:
    exchanges for trading, 57
    futures contracts versus, 57
    hedging, 100–101
    markets for, 50–51
    reports, 58, 59, 73, 100–101
    sectors of, 50, 57–59, 90–91
    trading strategies, 83–84
    (*See also* Futures contracts)
Commodity Futures Trading Commission (CFTC), 90, 100, 155–156
Commodity Research Bureau (CRB), 155
Commodity trading advisers (CTAs), 83–84, 154, 155–156
Competitiveness, 179
Confidence, 20, 165–166, 170–171, 180–181
Confidential information, 119
Confusion, 32
Congestion phase, 37, 53, 55
Contrarians, 56
CRB (Commodity Research Bureau), 155
Creativity, 173, 180
Curb rules, 6

Daily reports, 11–12, 161
Daily trader's log, 18, 140–141
Day trading, 7
    defined, 8, 39
    margin account minimums, 8
Decimalization, 7, 89
Demand (*see* Supply-demand model)
Direct access trading, 109–114
    bandwidth, 113
    basic information tools, 111
    decision-making tools, 111–112
    described, 109–110
    hardware, 112–113

Direct access trading (*Continued*)
    from home, 120–122
    order execution, 112
    RealTick, 94, 97, 110–112
    simulators, 33, 113–114
    transparency in, 110–111
Discipline, 5, 23, 32, 44, 67–68, 86–87,
        121–122, 123–141, 166
    anticipation, 138–139
    assessment of market, 129–130
    averaging positions, 131
    avoiding tips, 21–22, 73–74, 132–133
    close and, 43, 73, 136–138
    daily trader's log, 18, 140–141
    developing, 124
    fear and, 12–13, 128
    focus in, 139–141, 173–174
    humility and, 2, 24, 125, 128–129, 169–
        171
    loss-taking, 124–126, 131–132
    mechanical systems, 135–136
    net winning and, 130
    open and, 68, 73, 136–138
    rules of trading, 124–126
    selling into strength, 55–56, 133–134
    short selling, 126–128
    stop orders, 2–3, 126
    timing and, 129
    using analyst information, 134–135
    (*See also* Trading plan; Trading strat-
        egy)
Divine law, xi
Donchian, Richard, 45
Downtrending phase, 96, 100
Drawdowns, 4, 149, 153–154
Drudge Report, 95
Due diligence, 83–84

Easy-going people, 182
echarts.com, 35
ECNs (electronic communications net-
        works), xii, 5–6, 76–77, 175
Econometric models, 43–44
Edge on the markets, 29–30, 101, 108
Efficiency ratio, 159
Elastic demand, 50–51
Emotions, 1–2, 12–13, 18, 65, 169

Ending Net Asset Value (ENAV), 155,
        156
Energy complex, 59, 90
Enneagrams, 176–184
    personality types on, 178–182
    self-analysis with, 182–184
Envy, 171–172
Eternal law, xi
Exit strategy, 137–138
Experience, 44
Exponential moving averages, 46

Fear of market, 12–13, 128
50-day moving averages, 54, 55, 56
Filters, 92–94
Financial analyst reports, 134–135
Financial analysts, 134–135
Financial complex, 91
5-month charts, 96
Float, 16, 40, 51, 83
Floor-based exchanges, 5–6
Floor traders, 6
Focus, 139–141, 173–174
Following the ax, 88–89
Food and fiber complex, 50, 58–59, 90
45-day charts, 95–96
Free equity, 5, 8, 9
Front running, 132–133
Fundamental analysis:
    avoiding paralysis by analysis, 94–95
    supply-demand model and, 35, 49
    technical analysis versus, 31–36, 59
    in trading, 39, 59
Futures contracts:
    commodity versus financial, 6
    lack of insider information, 34, 58, 74
    lock limits, 44
    margin rules, 10
    moving averages, 45, 46
    physical commodities versus, 57
    supply-demand model for, 57–59

Gain-to-retracement ratios, 159–160
Gaming, 29, 106–109
Gaps, 70, 98–99, 137
Generosity, 171
Gluttony, 173–174

Google.com, 92, 94
Grain complex, 50, 57–58, 90, 91
Great Grain Robbery, 57–58
Greater fool theory, 87
Greed, 169, 171
Gurdjierff, George, 176

Hard stops, 138
Hedge fund managers (HFMs), 38, 105,
    154
Hedging, 100–101
Holding power, 46–47
Honesty, 23
Hot issues, 104–105
Hours of trading, 39, 97
Hubris, 170
Hudson, Russ, 176
Human law, xi
Humility, 2, 24, 125, 128–129, 169–171

Ichazo, Oscar, 176
Ideal trader, 163–184
    confidence of, 165–166
    discipline of, 166
    passion of, 164–165
    self-knowledge of, 167–184
    seven cardinal sins of trading, 167–175
In-the-money contracts, 6–7, 10
Inelastic demand, 50–51
Inferiority complex, 180–181
Initial margin:
    futures, 6
    stock, 5
Initial public offerings (IPOs), 40, 103–
    106
Insider information, 34, 58, 74, 88, 100
Instincts, 23–25, 44, 135, 180
Intellectuals, 180
Interest:
    on day trades, 4
    (See also Margin accounts; Margin
    calls)
Internet, 3
Interpersonal skills, 178–179
Intraday trading:
    defined, 7
    margin calls, 9–10

Intuition, 23–25, 44, 135, 180
Investing:
    saucer (rounded) bottoms in, 54
    trading versus, 3–4, 31–32, 38–43, 54,
    130
Investor's Business Daily, 91

Japanese candlestick charts, 42–43
Jones, Deane Sterling, 157–158
Jones, Paul Tutor, 151–152

Learning to trade:
    components of, 27–47
    constant nature of, 24, 79, 167
    costs of, 18–20, 75–77
    trading school in, 19, 44–47, 77–79, 87,
    114–116
    (*See also* Mentor; Trading plan)
Lemming reflex, 87
Leveraging, 4, 5
Limit orders, 9, 98
Line charts, 41
Liquidity, 82
Long options, 10
Losing streaks, 150–151
Loss-taking, 2–7, 18, 32–33, 91–92, 124–
    126, 131–132, 148–149, 153–154
Lust, 173

Maintenance margin, 4–5
Maintenance margin calls, 10
Manias, 105
MAR Qualified Universe Indices, 155–
    156
Margin accounts, 4, 5
    calculating margin amount, 9
    of day traders, 4, 8
    minimum requirements, 8
Margin calls, 4, 5, 8–10, 130
Market-maker trading system, 72–73, 89
Market wizards, xiv, 16–17, 84, 106, 151–
    152, 170, 174–175
Mean, 145–147
Meat complex, 58–59, 90
Mentor, 116–112
    advice from, 71–73, 83, 150–151
    attitude of other traders toward, 119–120

Mentor (*Continued*)
  caring, 178–179
  finding, 118–122
  importance of, 16, 30, 71–73, 89, 117
  loss-taking and, 32–33
  paying for services of, 120
  review of trading plan, 64–65, 70
  trust and, 71, 150–151
Metals complex, 59, 90, 91
MIC (market impact costs), 78
Microsoft Excel, 147–148, 160
Midterm trading, 20–21
Mistakes, 174
Momentum trading, 13, 20–21, 98, 135
MOMs (managers of managers), 160
Money management, 18–20, 67, 74–79
Mood of market, 36–37
Morningstar, 155
Moving averages, 45–47, 97–98
  in base-building phase, 53–54
  50-day, 54, 55, 56
  200-day, 46–47, 54, 55
  in uptrending phase, 54–55
Multipreferencing, 9–10
Mutual fund managers, 38, 54, 154–155, 156

Naranjo, Claudio, 176
NASD (National Association of Securities Dealers), 8, 116
Nasdaq, 5–6, 71–73
National Futures Association (NFA), 90, 155
Natural law, xi, xiii
New issues, 40, 103–106
New York Stock Exchange, 72, 83, 134
News:
  breaking, 73–74, 87–88, 100
  in supply-demand model, 51–52
Norwood Index, 155

Online trading, 8, 109–110, 137
Open, trading, 68, 73, 136–138
Options, 6–7, 106–108
  in-the-money, 6–7, 10
  margin rules, 10
  out-of-the-money, 6–7

Order execution, 78, 112
Order routing, 3, 78, 87, 175
Order types, 185–187
OTC (over-the-counter) (*see* Nasdaq)
Out-of-the-money contracts, 6–7
Overmanagement, 153
Overnight (Reg T) margin calls, 5, 8–9, 10, 130
Overtrading, 22, 109, 179
Oz, Tony, 94

Pacing, 22
Paper trading, 33
Partial fills, 9
Party person, 181
Passion for the market, 16–21, 24–25, 164–165, 171–172
Penny moves, 7
Percentage charts, 41
Perfectionism, 178
Personality type, 68–70
  cardinal sins of trading and, 167–175
  enneagrams and, 176–184
  trading strategy and, 21–22, 24–25
Phases of markets:
  bearish, 53, 54, 56
  bullish, 53, 54, 55, 56, 63–64
  congestion, 37, 53, 55
Pits, 52
Planning (*see* Trading plan)
Price, 169–171
Price charts, 34
  mood of market and, 36–37
  observations of, 37–43
  types of, 41–43
Price-earnings ratios, 50
Profit and loss report, 11–12, 119, 130, 162
Pythagoras, 176

Raschke, Linda Bradford, 86
Rate of return, 154–162
  commodity trading advisers (CTAs), 154, 155–156
  mutual fund managers and, 154–155, 156
  volatility of, 153, 157, 158

RealTick, 94, 97, 110–112
Recovery plans, 151
Reg T margin calls, 5, 8–9, 10, 130
Reports:
    analyst, 134–135
    commodities, 58, 59, 73, 100–101
    daily, 11–12, 161
    profit and loss, 11–12, 119, 130, 162
Resistance, 93, 96, 106
Respect for market, 12–13
Risk-reward ratio, 3, 10–11, 93, 98–100,
    107–108
Riso, Don, 176

Safekeeping of securities, 63
Saucer (rounded) bottom, 54
Scalping, 7, 11, 178
Scatterbrain, 181
Schwager, Jack, xiv, 16–17, 84, 86, 151–
    152, 170
Screen-based exchanges, 6
Seasonality, 91
Seat fees, 76, 116, 117
Secondary market, 40, 51
Sectors:
    commodity, 50, 57–59, 90–91
    filters and, 93
    futures, 90–91
Securities and Exchange Commission
    (SEC), 100, 104
Self-absorption, 179–180
Self-knowledge, 3, 21–22, 67–71
    cardinal sins of trading and, 167–175
    enneagrams and, 182–184
    success and, 175–184
    trading plan and, 3, 21–22, 67–71
Selling:
    abandoning positions, 39
    exit strategy, 137–138
    loss-taking, 2–7, 18, 32–33, 91–92,
        124–126, 131–132, 148–149, 153–
        154
    short selling, 31, 56, 101, 126–128
    into strength, 55–56, 133–134
Sentiment of market, 36–37
Setups, 86, 95, 96, 138
Seven cardinal sins of trading, 167–175

Shannon, Brian, 88, 89–90, 95–97, 98,
    101, 135
Sharp ratio, 159
Short options, 10
Short selling, 31, 56, 101, 126–128
Short squeeze, 101, 127, 137
Signals, 35
Simulators, 33, 113–114
SIPs (small incremental profits), 7, 110
60-minute chart, 97–98
Sloth, 174–175
SOES (Small Order Execution System),
    88–89
Software (see Trading software platform)
Specialist trading system, 5–6, 72, 83,
    134
Specialization strategy, 83–85, 86–87
Spread, 110
SROs (self-regulatory organizations), 76, 77
Standard deviation, 143–149, 153–154,
    157
Sterling ratio, 157–158
Sticks, 23–24
Stock ahead, 127
Stock filters, 92–94
Stock option plans, 40
Stock splits, 51, 74, 138–139
Stocks:
    margin rules, 4, 5, 8–10
    new issues, 40, 103–106
    secondary market, 40, 51
    volatility of, 5–6
Stop-limit orders, 3, 126
Stop-loss orders, 2–3, 23, 33, 40, 66–67,
    91–92, 98, 136, 153
Stop orders, 2–3, 126
Strategy (see Trading strategy)
Street name, 50, 63
Supply-demand model, 40, 49–59
    basic rules of, 50
    elasticity and inelasticity in, 50–51
    fundamental analysis and, 35, 49
    for futures contracts, 57–59
    news in, 51–52
    selling into strength, 55–56, 133–134
    trends in, 52–55
    volume in, 99–100

Support, 96, 98
Swing trading, 11, 20–21, 39, 95–96, 135–136
Systemic momentum, 159
Systemic risk, 159

Technical analysis:
    abnormal swings and, 87–88
    analyst characteristics, 44
    criticisms of, 40–41, 47
    fundamental analysis versus, 31–36, 59
    futures trading and, 91
    moving averages, 45–47
    outcomes for any trade, 148
    price charts in, 36–43
Terrorist attacks (September 11, 2001), 38, 136
Thinly traded securities, 71–72, 82–83
Time horizon, 4, 46–47, 52
Tips, 21–22, 73–74, 132–133
Tony Oz.com, 94
Topping phase, 56, 88, 129
Trade analysis, 161–162
Trade distribution, 152–153
Trader's journal, 18, 140–141
Trading clubs, 122
Trading floors, public, 19, 83, 113, 114–122
    caveats, 109, 133
    daily routine, 117–118
    market commentary, 117–118
    seat fees, 76, 116, 117
Trading hours, 39, 97
Trading plan, 61–80
    developing, 61–63
    discipline and, 67–68
    education in, 77–79
    finding weaknesses in, 65–66, 168–169
    goals in, 66–79
    guidelines for, 80
    money management and, 18–20, 67, 74–79, 116–117
    review by others, 64–65, 70
    self-knowledge and, 67–71
    specifications in, 71–74
    visualization and, 65, 137–138
    (See also Trading strategy)

Trading schools, 19, 44–47, 77–79, 87, 114–116
    mentors and, 116–122
    outline of programs, 78–79, 114–115
Trading software platform:
    characteristics of, 111–113
    costs of, 19, 76, 116
    free equity calculation, 9
    short selling and, 127
    simulators, 33, 113–114
Trading strategy, 7, 81–122
    of Brian Shannon, 88, 89–90, 95–97, 98, 101, 135
    avoiding paralysis by analysis, 94–95
    close in, 43, 73, 136–138
    commodity, 83–84
    day trading, 7, 8, 39
    developing, 16, 20–21, 83–122
    direct access trading in, 109–114
    filters in, 92–94
    following, 22–23, 135–136
    following the ax, 88–89
    initial public offerings (IPOs), 40, 103–106
    objectives in, 101–102
    open in, 68, 73, 136–138
    options, 106–108
    personality type and, 21–22, 24–25
    public trading floors in, 19, 76, 83, 109, 113, 114–122
    risk-reward ratio in, 98–100
    selection criteria, 89–91
    self-knowledge and, 3, 21–22
    7P's in, 95–100
    specialization, 83–85, 86–87
    swing trading, 11, 20–21, 39, 95–96, 135–136
    variety of approaches, 85–88
    volume in, 99–100
    watch lists in, 89–91, 92, 95–96
    (See also Discipline; Trading plan)
Trailing stops, 66, 174
Transparency, 110–111
Treasury stock, 40, 51
Trending, 16, 37, 52–55, 87, 153 (See also Technical analysis)

Trendlines, 33
200-day moving averages, 46–47, 54,
    55

U.S. Department of Agriculture (USDA),
    58, 59
Uptick rule, 56, 127
Uptrending phase, 54–55, 96, 99–100

Vacation from trading, 174
Value Line, 155
VAMI, 155–156
Visualization, 65, 137–138
Volatility, 2, 5–6
    margin rules, 10
    measuring, 143–148
    as opportunity, 34
    profits and, 153
    rate of return and, 153, 157, 158

of shallow markets, 82
standard deviation and, 143–149, 153–
    154, 157
in stock filters, 93
Volume, 45, 88
    in base-building phase, 53–54
    in stock filters, 92–93
    thinly traded securities, 71–72, 82–83
    in trading strategy, 99–100

Watch lists, 89–91, 92, 95–96
Weather, commodities and, 58–59
Weighted moving averages, 46
Wheeler-dealers, 181–182
Willing suspension of disbelief, 38
Win-loss period ratios, 159–160
Window analysis, 160, 161–162

Zero-uptick rule, 127

About the Author

Thomas McCafferty has been involved in the cash commodity, futures, options, and securities business since the early seventies. He has studied, traded, brokered, and, most importantly, observed traders plying their profession. He gathered a considerable amount of information about trading and traders when preparing to write *Winning with Managed Futures: How to Select a Top Performing Commodity Trading Advisor.* Additionally, he has been part of the Market Wise Trading School and author of books on stock and futures options and hedged scale trading of commodities. Mr. McCafferty has been an avid student of trading and has experienced the transition from the heyday of broker-assisted trading to the revolution of electronic direct access trading. Some of his other titles include *All about Commodities, All about Futures, All about Options,* and *Understanding Hedged Scale Trading.*